Innovations in Psychosoc
Interventions for Psycho

Despite the steady acceptance of psychological interventions for people with psychosis in routine practice, many patients continue to experience problems in their recovery. The need to develop new approaches, particularly for those who are more difficult to engage and have significant co-morbidities is therefore important. *Innovations in Psychosocial Interventions for Psychosis* positions psychological formulation as a key organising principle for the delivery of care within multidisciplinary teams. The interventions described all have the common theme of supporting recovery and achieving goals that are of primary importance to the service user which targets interventions on broader obstacles to recovery.

Along with their experienced contributors, Alan Meaden and Andrew Fox introduce new developments in psychological interventions for people affected by psychosis who are hard to reach, working in a variety of settings with people at various stages of recovery. The book is divided into three parts. In Part I brief interventions and approaches aimed at promoting engagement are described as interventions in their own right. Part II is focussed on longer term interventions with individuals. Some of these highlight new developments in the evidence base whilst others draw on work applied less frequently to psychosis drawing from the broader psychological therapy practice-based evidence field. In Part III attention is given to innovations in group settings and those aimed at promoting greater multidisciplinary working in settings where a whole team approach is needed.

Each chapter describes the theory underpinning a different approach, its development, key strategies, principles and stages, and contains case examples that illustrate the use of the approach in a clinical setting. *Innovations in Psychosocial Interventions for Psychosis* will be an invaluable resource for professionals working with this client group, including clinical and counselling psychologists, psychiatrists and other allied health professionals.

Alan Meaden is a consultant clinical psychologist at the Birmingham and Solihull Mental Health NHS Foundation Trust and is the lead for the trust's Assertive Outreach and Non-Acute Inpatient Services.

Andrew Fox is a senior clinical psychologist at Birmingham and Solihull Mental Health NHS Foundation Trust.

Innovations in Psychosocial Interventions for Psychosis

Working with the hard to reach

Edited by Alan Meaden
and Andrew Fox

Routledge
Taylor & Francis Group

LONDON AND NEW YORK

First published 2015
by Routledge
27 Church Road, Hove, East Sussex, BN3 2FA

and by Routledge
711 Third Avenue, New York, NY 10017

Routledge is an imprint of the Taylor & Francis Group, an informa business

British Library Cataloguing in Publication Data
A catalogue record for this book is available from the British Library

Library of Congress Cataloging in Publication Data
Innovations in psychosocial interventions for psychosis : working with the hard to reach / Alan Meaden and Andrew Fox (Eds).—First Edition.
    pages cm
Includes index.
1. Psychoses—Patients—Services for. 2. Psychoses—Patients—Rehabilitation.
3. Psychoses—Alternative treatment. I. Meaden, Alan, 1961– editor.
II. Fox, Andrew (Clinical psychologist) editor,
RC512.I44 2015
362.2'6—dc23   2014035572

ISBN: 978-0-415-71070-1 (hbk)
ISBN: 978-0-415-71073-2 (pbk)
ISBN: 978-1-315-72845-2 (ebk)

Typeset in Times New Roman
by Keystroke, Station Road, Codsall, Wolverhampton

Printed and bound in Great Britain by
TJ International Ltd, Padstow, Cornwall

I would like to dedicate this book to my wife Ann whose support is always there and to Mark Swain for reminding me that there are no problems, only solutions waiting to be found.

Alan Meaden

I would like to dedicate this to Amy, for her patience, and to Glynn Farmer for showing me that the owls are never what they seem.

Andrew Fox

Contents

Figures

Tables

List of abbreviations

AOT	Assertive Outreach Team
CARM	Cognitive Approach to Risk Management
CBT	Cognitive Behavioural Therapy
CTO	Compulsory Treatment Order
EWS-P	Early Warning Signs of Psychosis
EWS-R	Early Warning Signs of Risk
HDU	High Dependency Unit
MDT	Multidisciplinary Team
PLF	Personal Level Shared Formulation
PICU	Psychiatric Intensive Care Unit
REBT	Rational Emotive Behaviour Therapy
SAFE	Shared Assessment, Formulation and Education

Contributors

Deborah Allen, Clinical Psychologist, Derbyshire Healthcare NHS Foundation Trust. Deborah Allen is a clinical psychologist working within a RAID model liaison team in Derbyshire. Her work includes supporting people who are admitted to hospital for physical health problems and who may experience an onset of mental health difficulties or have pre-existing mental health problems. Her work also includes supporting people who attend at the emergency department having undertaken an act of deliberate self-harm.

Catherine Amphlett, Principal Clinical Psychologist, Birmingham and Solihull Mental Health NHS Foundation Trust. Catherine Amphlett is a clinical psychologist for the recovery and rehabilitation inpatient services at Birmingham and Solihull Mental Health NHS Foundation Trust. She also trained as an existential psychotherapist at the New School of Psychotherapy and Counselling and uses an existential approach as a basis for therapeutic integration in her clinical work.

Richard Barker, Consultant Clinical & Forensic Psychologist, Oxford Health NHS Foundation Trust. Richard Barker is a consultant clinical and forensic psychologist working with mentally disordered offenders for Oxford Health NHS Foundation Trust. He was part of the Centre for Mental Health's working group on recovery in forensic settings and believes passionately that recovery principles can be applied in forensic settings. He also teaches on the University of Birmingham Forensic Psychology Doctorate and Clinical Psychology Doctorate courses as well as at Oxford Brookes University.

Richard Bennett, Principal Clinical Psychologist, Birmingham and Solihull Mental Health NHS Foundation Trust. Richard Bennett is a clinical psychologist and cognitive behavioural psychotherapist working with offenders in a low secure rehabilitation service. He also works in higher education, training a range of professionals in cognitive behavioural therapies. He has a particular interest in transdiagnostic models of emotional distress.

Mark Bernard, Clinical Psychologist, Birmingham and Solihull Mental Health NHS Foundation Trust. Mark Bernard is a senior clinical psychologist in early intervention in Birmingham and Solihull Mental Health NHS Foundation Trust. His current interests include the contribution of attachment, shame and difficulties in emotional regulation to emotional dysfunction (e.g. depression, anxiety, trauma) following psychosis and the development of CBT-based approaches for emotional dysfunction following psychosis.

Max Birchwood, Research Director, YouthSpace and Professor of Youth Mental Health, University of Warwick. Max Birchwood is Professor in Youth Mental Health at Warwick University. Max worked for many years as Clinical Director of Youth Mental Health Services and Director of Research and Innovation in Birmingham and Solihull Mental Health Foundation Trust. He pioneered the concept and practice of early intervention in psychosis in the UK and has been instrumental in the development and dissemination of cognitive behavioural therapy for psychosis. His current interests include prevention and early intervention in youth mental health problems, emotional dysregulation in psychosis, and developing and testing the cognitive model of voices.

Andrew Fox, Clinical Psychologist, Birmingham and Solihull Mental Health NHS Foundation Trust. Andrew Fox is a clinical psychologist for the recovery and rehabilitation inpatient units at Birmingham and Solihull Mental Health NHS Foundation Trust. Much of his current work involves developing an understanding of social-psychological factors important in complex mental health difficulties, and trying to work out what to do about them to improve people's well-being.

Morna Gillespie, Clinical Psychologist, Birmingham Community Healthcare NHS Trust. Morna Gillespie is a clinical psychologist currently working for Birmingham Community Healthcare NHS Trust in a community team for people with learning disabilities who have committed offences. Prior to that she worked for more than ten years in assertive outreach in Birmingham and Solihull NHS Foundation Trust. This post involved working with people with complex mental health difficulties who were hard to engage.

David Hacker, Consultant Clinical Neuropsychologist and Lead for Acute Traumatic Brain Injury, Queen Elizabeth Hospital Birmingham Major Trauma Centre. David Hacker is a consultant clinical neuropsychologist working for Birmingham and Solihull Mental Health NHS Foundation Trust at the Queen Elizabeth Hospital Birmingham. His previous area of work was in mental health, particularly with people with psychosis and problem behaviours, where he co-developed the SAFE approach with Alan Meaden. He now specialises in acquired brain injury and, in particular, traumatic brain injury in both statutory and medico-legal settings but maintains a research interest in psychosis and its treatments.

Chris Harrop, Principal Clinical Psychologist, West London Mental Health NHS Trust. Chris Harrop is Principal Clinical Psychologist in the Hounslow

Early Intervention Service in West London Mental Health NHS Trust, and also in the Crisis Resolution Team. His research is mainly around interventions for young people with psychosis.

Helen Hewson, Counselling Psychologist, Birmingham and Solihull Mental Health NHS Foundation Trust. Helen Hewson is a counselling psychologist working within an assertive outreach service at Birmingham and Solihull Mental Health NHS Foundation Trust. Her current work is focussed on the development of specialist psychological interventions for clients who present with complex and enduring mental health difficulties. Her interests include critical psychology, social constructionism and narrative psychology.

Chris Jackson, Consultant Clinical Psychologist, Birmingham and Solihull Mental Health NHS Foundation Trust. Chris Jackson is a consultant clinical psychologist in early intervention in Birmingham and Solihull Mental Health NHS Foundation Trust. Chris has been involved in the development of psychological therapies for first episode psychosis including cognitive behavioural approaches for the treatment of trauma following psychosis. His current interests include suicide prevention and emotional dysfunction following psychosis, and refining the delivery of early intervention services.

Sophie L. Mayhew, Chartered Consultant Clinical Psychologist, Plymouth Community Healthcare CiC. Sophie Mayhew is a chartered consultant clinical psychologist and is lead for the specialist adult mental health psychology services (acute inpatient, recovery and psychosis services) and Compassion Focussed Therapy lead in the psychotherapy service. She is a founder member and associate of the Compassionate Mind Foundation and specialises in the provision of CFT and the training and supervision of CFT practitioners. Her specialist area of interest is psychosis and difficult to reach service users.

Alan Meaden, Consultant Lead Psychologist, Birmingham and Solihull Mental Health NHS Foundation Trust. Alan Meaden is a consultant clinical psychologist working for Birmingham and Solihull Mental Health NHS Foundation Trust. His area of work for nearly 20 years has been with hard to reach groups who have complex mental health and behavioural needs. He has worked extensively as part of the leading research team for more than a decade on the development of theory and practice for the treatment of command hallucinations. His main interest is in working with teams, promoting and enabling multidisciplinary approaches to care.

Louise Pearson, Principal Clinical Psychologist, Birmingham and Solihull Mental Health NHS Foundation Trust. Louise Pearson is a clinical psychologist working with male offenders in medium secure care who have complex mental health problems. She has a special interest in helping people recover from trauma and in reducing distress related to paranoia.

Gert van Rensburg, Clinical Psychologist, Independent Practice. Gert Janse van Rensburg held a post as a clinical psychologist for the recovery and rehabilitation inpatient units at Birmingham and Solihull Mental Health NHS Foundation Trust for a number of years during which time he encountered and applied the approach described in his chapter. Currently he is working as a clinical psychologist in independent practice in South Africa with an interest in adapting the Open Dialogue approach in different cultures.

Chapter 1

The need for innovation when providing services for the difficult to engage

Alan Meaden and Andrew Fox

In contemporary mental health, recovery and social inclusion are key concepts that underpin the delivery of services (e.g. No Health Without Mental Health, Department of Health, 2011). However, complex mental health needs and engagement difficulties can act as a barrier to recovery and social inclusion (Meaden & Hacker, 2010). In this text we have drawn together descriptions of various psychosocial approaches that are currently being used with people who have complex mental health needs (such as those associated with diagnoses such as schizophrenia and other psychoses), but who can be difficult to engage in services. We describe psychosocial interventions as referring to a broad range of psychological treatments which aim to address the way in which psychological and social factors interact in the emergence and course of psychotic symptoms and experiences. We would also include the way in which individuals respond to biological factors in this description.

Early texts such as that by Birchwood and Tarrier (1992) led to a significant increase in the range of psychosocial interventions offered to people with psychosis. Indeed, relapse prevention, behavioural family therapy and, not least, Cognitive Behavioural Therapy (CBT), have all now been adopted as part of routine practice. However, not all individuals report benefit (Yung, 2012). Indeed there remains a group of people who are persistently hard to reach and resistant to these treatments. In this book we attempt to further the range of interventions offered by drawing on the work of a broad range of authors working in diverse settings. In many cases we have been fortunate to have worked alongside them and shared the emergence of their ideas and therapeutic endeavours.

It has also on a personal level been part of our on-going efforts to enable and support a group of service users all too often neglected in the rush to endorse NICE-compliant treatments (sometimes to the exclusion of other approaches) in their recovery. The approaches detailed in this book offer various ways through which people – who may, at best, be ambivalent about their involvement in services – can be supported to progress in their recovery. We believe these approaches can be labelled as 'innovative' in that they represent novel modifications, adaptations and syntheses of existing psychosocial approaches tailored to meet the needs of a disengaged population of people with complex mental health difficulties. These innovations have been developed through clinical work in a variety of inpatient and community settings, including acute inpatient wards, assertive outreach teams and inpatient rehabilitation services. In this way, we believe that this text represents 'practice-based evidence' (Green, 2008), acting both as a guide for intervention and as a catalyst for the development of research that evaluates the effectiveness of these approaches in practice. There is clear evidence across all chapters of a shared commitment to using innovative clinical practice to enhance recovery and social inclusion for those who are experiencing complex mental health difficulties. We would echo the sentiments that 'you need hope to cope' (Perkins, 2006: 112) and believe that this collection offers some direction and optimism to clinicians who wish to use psychosocial interventions to support those with the most complex mental health and behavioural needs.

References

Birchwood, M. & Tarrier, N. (1992). *Innovations in the psychological management of schizophrenia: Assessment, treatment and services.* Chichester, Sussex: John Wiley & Sons.

Department of Health (2011). *No health without mental health: A cross-government mental health outcomes strategy for people of all ages.* London: Department of Health.

Green, L. W. (2008). Making research relevant: If it is an evidence-based practice, where's the practice-based evidence? *Family Practice, 25*(Suppl. 1), i20–i24.

Meaden, A. & Hacker, D. (2010). *Problematic and risk behaviours in psychosis: A shared formulation approach.* Hove, E. Sussex: Brunner-Routledge.

Perkins, R. (2006). First person: 'You need hope to cope'. In G. Roberts, S. Davenport, F. Holloway & T. Tattan (eds), *Enabling recovery: The principles and practice of rehabilitation psychiatry* (pp. 112–124). London: Gaskell.

Yung, A. R. (2012). Early intervention in psychosis: Evidence gaps, criticism, and confusion. *Australian and New Zealand Journal of Psychiatry, 46,* 7–9.

Part I

Innovations in engagement and brief therapies

Chapter 2

The Adapted Open Dialogue approach

Gert van Rensburg

Introduction

Open Dialogue (OD) is an approach to working with people experiencing complex mental health difficulties that in many ways departs from 'traditional' Western psychiatric approaches. It involves a re-conceptualisation of the way mental health teams work with people with psychosis (and their families) and the roles of these people in treatment. Following a workshop facilitated by the originators of the approach, Jaakko Seikkula and Tom Andersen, this was considered for implementation within an inpatient rehabilitation setting. It was proposed that critical elements of the OD approach could enhance therapeutic work with people who are difficult to engage. The current chapter aims to provide a brief overview of the background to the development of the original ideas and theoretical constructs of OD, followed by a detailed description of how these have been applied in a low-secure environment within an inpatient rehabilitation service for people with complex mental health needs in the UK.

Theoretical background and development: Need Adapted Treatment

It is not possible to understand OD without reviewing the Need Adapted Treatment (NAT) orientation from which it developed. NAT originated from what Alanen (1997) describes as the "Turku Schizophrenia Project" initiated in 1968 in Turku, Finland. Through both research and therapeutic interventions, the project set out to construct the best possible treatment for psychosis associated with schizophrenia. The project ran uninterrupted but with much development along the way through into the 1990s, by which stage the approach was known as Need Adapted Treatment.

Alanen describes the original developmental goal as follows: 'To develop the treatment of Schizophrenia-group patients with an integrated but psychotherapeutically oriented approach' (Alanen, 1997: 141). The focus was on developing and fostering a basic psychotherapeutic attitude in the approach employed by staff as well as developing the hospital wards to become psychotherapeutic communities. This included the use of family therapy and activities, a focus on the development of individual therapeutic relationships and pharmacotherapy as treatment supportive of the psychological therapy. An emphasis on team work was supported by supervision and training to equip all staff members to become involved in the therapeutic work. There was a commitment to the systematic evaluation of the approach to monitor the treatment needs of the patients and to ascertain how the development of the approach affected treatment outcomes.

Concept and principles

Alanen (1997) acknowledges that the term NAT has not gone unchallenged. A specific query relates to the concept of 'need'. Alanen argues that needs are not to be defined in terms of philosophical or social psychological constructs but rather as a clinical concept that describes what is required for a specific individual at a given point of treatment. The term NAT therefore reflects the heterogeneity and uniqueness of the therapeutic needs of each person requiring treatment.

NAT involves a hermeneutic approach with the aim being to arrive at a psychological understanding of the difficulties as they present in the context of the individual and their environment. This includes not only difficulties caused by symptoms but also the significance the symptoms have for the individual. This psychological understanding then becomes the bedrock guiding all therapeutic interventions. Aaltonen and Räkköläinen (1994) propose the concept of 'shared mental representation' to be employed to steer the treatment process. This is similar to the concept of 'shared formulation' (Meaden & Hacker, 2010), with the same intended aim of integrated treatment guided by an evidence-based psychological understanding of the difficulties.

NAT emphasises the importance of sharing the psychological understanding amongst the treatment team, the service user and members of their immediate social network. Further emphasis is placed on treatment as a process rather than an episode or event where needs are real and changing (hence 'need adapted'). Alanen (1997) also argues that not only do service users often not receive the treatment they need, but many also receive treatment they do not need, such as unduly long hospital admissions and excessive neuroleptic treatment. Thus NAT aims to provide the required treatment as determined by the psychological understanding and to prevent unnecessary interventions (Alanen, 1997).

Alanen summarised NAT in terms of four general principles (Alanen et al., 1991; Alanen, 1997):

- All therapeutic activities are planned and carried out flexibly and individually as each case demands.
- Assessment and treatment are underpinned and guided by a 'psychotherapeutic attitude'. This requires clinicians to develop an understanding of past and present events for the service user as well as the people in their social network and how these can be utilised in the overall approach. It further requires observation of the clinician's own emotional responses when in dialogue with the service users.

- Different therapeutic approaches should supplement each other rather than constitute an 'either/or' approach.
- Treatment should be characterised by a continuous process rather than a series of interventions.

The development and implementation of the Open Dialogue approach

Jaakko Seikkula and his colleagues in Western Lapland, Finland, implemented the NAT in the city of Keropodus. Whilst adhering to the general principles of NAT, they developed a further innovation they termed Open Dialogue (OD; Seikkula *et al.*, 2001). The basic premise of OD is to arrange treatment (psychological and other) for all patients within their own social support system. This required the development of a family-centred and network-centred psychiatric treatment model. The model is underpinned by a number of ideas that have emerged developmentally and through research since the intervention's inception in the 1980s. Seikkula *et al.* (2006) summarise this as:

- An immediate (within 24 hours) response to the presentation;
- The participation from the outset of the patient's family and other key members of their social network;
- Inpatient treatment is postponed whenever feasible. This is achieved by arranging home visits (often daily) in an attempt to limit admissions to people who cannot be stabilised/contained outside hospital;
- The use of what is termed Treatment Meetings wherein a dialogical approach is applied.

All psychiatric presentations irrespective of the diagnosis are dealt with using the same intervention principles. Where a person first presents at hospital in crisis the crisis clinic in the hospital arranges an admission meeting, either before the decision to admit for voluntary admissions, or during the first day of inpatient treatment for compulsory admissions.

At the first meeting a case-specific team is nominated. This multi-agency multi-professional team is tailor made for each case. This team takes charge of the entire treatment sequence, regardless of site of delivery (at home or in hospital) or duration of treatment. Flexibility is achieved by the team consisting of both inpatient and outpatient staff and the same team continuing the work throughout.

Outcomes of the OD approach are promising and have remained consistently so in a number of studies spanning more than a decade. Seikkula *et al.* (2011) found that among a population of people experiencing their first episode of psychosis, more than 80 per cent had no residual psychotic symptoms up to five years following treatment using OD. A similar percentage of individuals had returned to work or resumed studies while less than 30 per cent were maintained on neuroleptics – suggesting that the approach can minimise the need for medication (Seikkula *et al.*, 2011). The duration of untreated psychosis had declined and a significant amount of individuals had participated in the Treatment Meetings, which may have played a role in preventing first episodes from developing into long-term illness and disability (Seikkula *et al.*, 2011).

Aims, stages, strategies and techniques

The main forum for therapeutic interaction is a 'Treatment Meeting' (Seikkula *et al.*, 2006). This was adopted from NAT where the value of joint meetings was noted. Here the people affected by the problem – the patient, their family, members of their social network and other authorities – gather to discuss all the issues associated with the reported problem. All interventions and decisions – including assessment, formulation and care planning – are made with everyone present. There are no other treatment planning discussions among the staff. The principal aim of the conversation in the Treatment Meeting is to construct a new language for the difficult experiences of the patient and those nearest him or her, which are connected with (affected by) the disturbing (often psychotic) behaviour.

Psychotic speech is viewed as a way of handling difficult and often terrifying experiences in the life of the patient. It is postulated that due to the terrifying nature of such experiences people find it often difficult to communicate in a manner that others understand other than through the language of the hallucination or delusion. The person is robbed of the ability to formulate a rational spoken narrative, and it could be said that these experiences 'do not yet have words' (Seikkula *et al.*, 2001). Holma and Aaltonen (1997) defined this as the pre-narrative quality of psychotic experience.

A large part of the therapeutic task is to construct new meanings to describe the psychotic experiences. In the safety of the Treatment Meetings, through dialogue, shared understanding and construction of new meaning, what initially presented as terrifying and confusing becomes less so. This aim can be achieved only with the collaboration of all the people present in the Treatment Meeting and in the process the understanding of the problem and the context it occurs in is improved.

Treatment Meetings

The Treatment Meeting has three important functions (Alanen, 1997; Seikkula *et al.*, 2006). The first is information gathering, which is done in a manner that facilitates or creates a joint experience about the family's life and the events that led to the crisis. All members of the case-specific team participate in the process. The second function is constructing a treatment plan from the decisions made by all the participants based on the diagnosis and the needs identified. The process includes comments regarding the observations the team members make in the meeting concerning the presentation, the family, the team (e.g. different opinions about treatment) and the relationships between the family and the team. Team members discuss such observations openly with each other and in the presence of the patient and family. The third aim is to establish and generate psychotherapeutic dialogue. Part of the dialogue will include reflecting on the different emerging ideas and sometimes difficult emotions the problem may trigger in team members. By discussing different ideas arising during the conversation the team makes dangerous or threatening issues less so for all present (Seikkula & Sutela, 1990). Alanen *et al.* (1991) refer to a process where regressive behaviour is curtailed (preventing further decline in elements of functioning, such as self-neglect and social withdrawal) by supporting and strengthening the 'adult side' of the patient and normalising the situation.

Andersen (1995) sees the reflective process as a transition between listening and talking. He states that when talking to a listener one is in outer dialogue; while listening to someone talking one is in inner dialogue with that person. Anderson views the reflective process as: 'interrelated, active, mutual. I define listening as attending to, interacting with, responding to and trying to learn about a client's story and its perceived importance' (Anderson, 1997: 152).

It is by implementing these ideas that the Treatment Meeting becomes the treatment – it is both vehicle for and propellant of treatment. The departure point in the Treatment Meeting is the language of each individual family unadulterated as they present in their own words the patient's problem and the difficulties it causes them. The treatment team adopts this language and adapts its own contributions in a manner that fits with the specific needs of each family. The difficulties they encounter and the problems they present with are seen as social constructs formulated and reformulated in every conversation as the process develops (Seikkula, 2002). Great care is taken not to overwhelm the family with terms and language that will often be foreign or threatening to them.

Using an 'open dialogue'

A particular important requirement of the process is an open dialogue. Seikkula (2002) stresses the importance of this without the presence of pre-planned themes to enable the construction of the new shared language and the development of a formulation specific to the needs of the person and the family. In the initial presentation and first phase of treatment (whilst the person and/or family are in crisis) the psychotic speech is not to be challenged but the reality for the person is to be respected. Such utterances are to be given a voice with equal opportunity to be expressed and heard. This does not mean, however, that psychotic speech is accepted as 'real' by all and it is not ignored. Seikkula *et al.* (2006) quote Mikhael Bakhtin when he states: 'For the word (and, consequently, for a human being) there is nothing more terrible than a lack of response' (Bakhtin, 1986: 127). He suggests asking questions such as: "I do not understand how it is possible that you could hear that?", "How is it possible you could control others thoughts?", "I have not been able to hear that or been able to control others thoughts – can you explain this to us?" Team members in turn can be asked what they make or understand of what is said or claimed. Allowing different and even contradicting voices (including the voice of psychosis) to be freely expressed is argued to be an important step in the establishment of an open dialogue characterised by a deliberating atmosphere. In doing so an important process is established and allowed to evolve. Seikkula (2002) refers to the work of Stern *et al.* (1999) in this regard. They mention that in allowing this process the possibility is created for alternative narratives to ultimately be arrived at, referring to such alternatives as narratives of restitution and/or reparation.

The role of clinicians

Seikkula (2002) describes the role of clinicians in the Treatment Meetings as one of introducing and fostering dialogical discourse. In allowing the patient's social network to guide content and introduce their particular language and then to respond in a dialogical way, understanding and the development of new meaning are promoted. Through the ensuing dialogue between members this new meaning starts to develop as a social shared phenomenon. Seikkula (2002) points out that when thinking about psychotic utterances of the patient one has to bear in mind they have no other words apart from the language of hallucinations and delusions. By allowing their words to be expressed in the Treatment Meeting, their reality is 'opened up', it becomes shared and various possibilities can be considered.

Seikkula refers to Bakhtin (1984, 1986) again when he states that one has to understand dialogue as the vehicle whereby ideas are arrived at. Meaning develops in the exchanges between people, not within either person's mind alone, but rather in the interpersonal space. Dialogue thus has two characteristics – it is both the aim of the Treatment Meeting as well as 'the way of being in language' in the Treatment Meeting. It requires the team to reflect more on how to respond to the utterances of all parties and dictates a different way of being present in the conversation. Clinicians have the responsibility to 'draw out the voices of every participant' (Seikkula & Arnkil, 2006: 109) present. Meaning is constantly generated and transformed and in this process allows alternative and new resources to become available to the person with psychosis. What is first discussed in the social context of the Treatment Meeting (in outer dialogue) then has the possibility to become part of the internal dialogue of the person. The joint activity of the Treatment Meeting helps create new understanding and meaning.

Reflective discussion

Reflective discussion among team members has proven to be an effective response when employed in the Treatment Meetings (Seikkula *et al.*, 2001). Team members might suggest to the family that they share observations amongst themselves whilst the family remains in the room and observes this process. Such reflective discussions not only convey the team's observations but serve an important therapeutic function, serving to construct and distil treatment plans *in vivo*. In this transparent process alternative as well as divergent options can be discussed and shared with all members.

Seikkula (2006) emphasises the difference between Systemic Family Therapy's use of this process and the motivation underlying OD. In the former the idea is to provide a so-called impulse of fresh logic to change the fixed logic of a family (Boscolo & Bertrando, 1998, quoted by Seikkula, 2002). In OD the basic premise is to create a 'new language' (logic) where new meanings are being co-constructed in the shared experience of the Treatment Meetings.

Both OD and Narrative Therapy (Seikkula *et al.*, 2006) view reality as a social construct. However, the Narrative approach proposes a process of re-authoring the problem-saturated story whilst OD, through the process of deliberating dialogues, creates a new narrative that is co-authored in the shared experience of the Treatment Meetings. In OD the family is neither viewed as the cause of the psychosis nor as the primary object for treatment; rather, they are afforded the status of partners in the recovery process.

Main principles of Open Dialogue

The OD approach has seven key principles (Seikkula *et al.*, 2006). These principles were arrived at through treatment and process evaluations conducted over a number of years.

- Immediate help
- Social network perspective
- Flexibility and mobility
- Responsibility
- Psychological continuity
- Tolerance of uncertainty
- Dialogism.

Immediate help

Seikkula (2002) advocates commencement of treatment as soon as possible after a crisis is identified. The case-specific team convened at time of referral/ admission arranges the first meeting preferably within 24 hours of first contact. The source or pathway of contact is not important.

Social network perspective

Inviting key members of the patient's social network acts as a powerful generator to mobilise support to both patient and the family. A wide range of members may be invited to a first meeting including extended family, neighbours, friends, colleagues or outside authorities to support vocational rehabilitation. Attendance is generally determined by the person who initiates contact. This is achieved by asking them who they think may be concerned by the presentation and/or whose presence might be beneficial at that early stage. Future attendance of any of these parties are then discussed and collaboratively decided at the first meeting.

Flexibility and mobility

The elements of flexibility and mobility involve adapting the whole of the treatment response to the specific and changing needs of each case, the person, family and network and the manner they experience the crisis. Determining factors in deciding which therapies best fit each case include aspects such as the language they employ, their lifestyle and the collective ability to utilise the available treatment options. Time (duration of interventions) and timing are further crucial factors to be considered (Seikkula *et al.*, 2006).

Responsibility

Whoever is involved in the first contact assumes responsibility for arranging the first multi-attendant, multi-professional meeting. Decisions about further treatment are made in this first meeting and responsibility to implement these is carried by the case-specific team who assumes responsibility of the entire treatment process from beginning to end.

Psychological continuity

The case-specific team assumes responsibility throughout the duration of the treatment. This multi-agency team contributes to continuity by being able to access a variety of treatment options and settings irrespective of the modality or whether the case requires outpatient or inpatient treatment. Continuity is further enhanced by inviting members of the social network to attend Treatment Meetings throughout the process as determined by the identified needs (Seikkula, 2002; Seikkula *et al.*, 2006).

Tolerance of uncertainty

Uncertainty in this context refers in part to the distress experienced by both patient and family members caused by the 'abnormality' or inexplicable nature of the crisis. 'Uncertainty' is a useful way of capturing a major part of the experience of the phenomena and strange presentation of the family member. A major contribution in the effectiveness of the Treatment Meeting seems the ability of the case-specific team (including the family and the individual affected) to tolerate the uncertainty accompanying a crisis. The relationships built in the Treatment Meetings contribute to creating sufficient safety to allow exploration of uncertainties for which answers still do not exist and to support mobilisation of the resources inherent in the members (Seikkula *et al.*, 2006).

Seikkula *et al.* (2006) suggest daily Treatment Meetings at least for the first 10–12 days of the period closest to the onset of the crisis. This appears to create the safety required to tolerate the uncertainty characterising the onset of a crisis. Cultivating a tolerance of uncertainty is partly achieved by focussing on the process instead of focussing solely on diagnosis and symptomology. This not only enhances tolerance of uncertainty but (almost paradoxically) increases the possibility of certainty. This requires the avoidance of immature conclusions and treatment decisions – for example, neuroleptic medication is not started in the first meeting, but, instead, is suggested that it should be discussed in at least three meetings before being prescribed.

Dialogism

The possibility of discussing the difficulties, uncertainties and fears increases the sense of agency for all involved. This is enhanced when the context of the Treatment Meeting is defined as safe, accepting and tolerant (Holma & Aaltonen, 1997). The focus is primarily on promoting dialogue, and secondarily on promoting change in the patient or network. Dialogue assists in constructing new understanding and is the primary agent in constructing a joint language for the difficult to describe phenomena. Instead of a specific interviewing procedure, the aim is to follow the themes and the way of speaking as introduced by the client, family and the social network.

Case illustration: Dwayne[1]

Dwayne is 40 years old and lives in a low-secure residential rehabilitation service for people with complex mental health needs. On Unit, Dwayne is very guarded and suspicious of most attempts to engage him. The content of discussion remains largely limited to external factors such as leave involving visiting family or other excursions. Attempts to engage Dwayne in discussions of symptoms, experience of psychosis, or contact with mental health services leads to disengagement. Dwayne will participate in various social groups and activities on Unit, however he remains largely aloof, displaying behaviours that keep people at a distance. Such behaviours include 'spinning' round and round whilst walking (at times bumping into others), minimal conversation and taking his meals at the same table on the same chair – at times physically removing fellow residents from what he indicated to be his place.

Dwayne's first contact with Mental Health Services occurred at the age of 19. Reports reflect that Dwayne began to show obsessional behaviour from age 14 followed by social withdrawal, antisocial behaviour and a decline in academic performance. He was admitted under section when he presented with what were described as 'florid first rank symptoms' and diagnosed as suffering from schizophrenia. This was followed by numerous admissions whenever independent living was no longer deemed a safe viable option for him. Dwayne has now been in various types of residential treatment for 11 years.

Initial intervention

A concerted effort was made to engage Dwayne in a more therapeutic manner. This was prompted by the MDT's belief that Dwayne could potentially move from his current level of care to a less restrictive environment associated with a higher level of independence. However, the historical risk profile and persistent unwillingness to engage therapeutically presented barriers to such plans. Dwayne was offered regular 1:1 sessions with an Assistant Psychologist (at the same time and same place, regardless of whether he attended) and despite initial suspicion he cautiously started to engage with these regular, open slots. The sessions attempted to introduce Dwayne to regular contact with the Psychology team in an attempt to foster engagement and break the isolation he maintained on the Unit.

This gradual engagement was interrupted when Dwayne unexpectedly and without clear triggers destroyed Unit property. In total three incidents occurred where he removed framed pictures from the wall and dropped them onto the floor, shattering the glass and frames. All attempts at inquiry were met with: "I don't want to talk about it". In the light of the unexpectedness and subsequent unsuccessful attempts to understand the motivation, the multidisciplinary team expressed frustration that they were at an 'impasse'. It was suggested that adopting OD principles might offer a solution.

Open Dialogue principles

Two principles of OD were the main focus of this case: tolerance of uncertainty and dialogism. It was felt that these two principles were essential elements of the approach, as tolerance of uncertainty and dialogism are present throughout the OD approach and none of the other principles is applied without consideration given to these. Other principles were considered and attempted but various factors influenced the degree to which they were successfully implemented within the inpatient residential setting.

Initial implementation of Open Dialogue

In a presentation and a series of discussions the MDT was exposed to the background of NAT, OD and the possible implementation of this approach (Adapted Open Dialogue; AOD). Once it was agreed as a potentially useful way of working, Dwayne was approached and invited to a joint meeting with his Named Nurse and Clinical Psychologist. It was decided to limit the amount of people present given the caution and distrust generally displayed by Dwayne. Dwayne was cautious and demanded to know the purpose and content of the meetings. In explaining the purpose of the meetings the two facilitators (with Dwayne present) discussed their reflections on the recent incidents including the impact such events had on fellow residents, but Dwayne was not directly questioned on the incidents that he had caused. Dwayne, being aware of other similar incidents (not involving him), could relate to this without having to discuss his own actions directly at the time. The two facilitators opted to discuss this in the presence of Dwayne reflecting on the general impact of incidents on the Unit as a whole, how various individuals could respond differently and how the MDT reacted to such incidents. Had this been a direct 1:1 discussion with Dwayne he would not have had the opportunity to listen to a dialogue exposing different views and he possibly would have felt compelled to contribute, increasing the chances of him feeling defensive and disengaging. However, Dwayne appeared very interested in the discussion between the facilitators and seemed to pay close attention to the discussion, even taking notes and choosing not to leave.

Immediate help

Perhaps the most obvious OD principle that could not be implemented was that of applying OD at the immediate point of contact. Dwayne had been in contact with mental health services for a total of 21 years of which 11 years had been compulsory detention in residential services.

Social network

Dwayne's social network was limited to staff and fellow patients on the Unit, the latter of whom he had minimal interactions with. He had limited contact with any members of his family as they lived at great distance from the Unit. In addition to the geographical distance his limited leave allowance had precluded frequent visits for many years. He had no exposure to off-Unit vocational activities and therefore no social network linked to these.

Flexibility

Flexibility in the OD approach requires adapting interventions to the unique and changing needs of the client and the family. Seikkula *et al.* (2006) mention specifically adapting to the language and way of living of the person. In the case of the latter, particular attention was given to the fact that Dwayne had been resident in the same low-secure residential Unit for 8 years. Such Units by nature are at times characterised by volatility and periods where one or more residents experience distress affecting the wellbeing of residents (Wilkinson, 2008). It is in this context that Dwayne's needs manifested and had to be accommodated in the best way possible. This is illustrated by the choice of room for the proposed AOD sessions. Dwayne was asked where he would like to meet to talk, and he opted for a small lounge despite the fact that the door to the room contained an observation window, and that fellow residents could potentially enter. In discussion he explained that this was his temporary home where he felt most comfortable. It is possible that he felt less of a 'patient' in a lounge than he would have been in an office or designated meeting room. It later transpired that this room had additional meaning for him in that he could get up and leave (which indeed happened a few times), whenever he needed. He later explained that he viewed it as less rude to leave your own lounge than it is to leave another person's office.

Concerning the OD guidance of adapting to the language of the service user, Dwayne's long-term exposure to services caused him to be familiar with the language of mental health services. However, this did not equate to acceptance and much discussion was centred on the meaning of words and concepts held for him personally.

Responsibility

The Unit had in operation a case-specific team approach whereby each patient was assigned a Named Nurse and Health Care Assistant responsible for overseeing the implementation of care plans and day to day management. It was decided to delegate the responsibility for AOD to the Psychologist and the Named Nurse. They were joined at times by a combination of various MDT members including the RMO, Unit Manager, Occupational Therapists, HCAs and medical student. In each case a clear need and motivation was established in dialogue with Dwayne before any of the staff mentioned joined.

Psychological continuity

The principle of psychological continuity was difficult to implement. Dwayne was originally from out of the area and wanted to return there. As the process of OD developed, a number of joint meetings were successfully scheduled with members of the referring team and current treatment team visiting each other to plan care and reflect on progress. Dwayne was in attendance at these meetings.

Tolerating uncertainty and dialogism

Seikkula *et al.* (2006) equate tolerating uncertainty with creating safety, initially in the presenting crisis situation. This is mentioned as a primary task of the Clinicians in OD to conduct meetings in such a manner that it becomes 'a place of safety' where attendants can speak without fear of being silenced or having their contributions marginalised. Various elements are important in achieving this. It includes an acknowledgment on the part of the professionals that they might not necessarily have all the answers. Taking the lead from Bakhtin (1984) the position of the therapists changes from being 'interventionists' to participants in a mutual process. It further requires allowance of different points of view and acceptance that all contributions are valuable including those made in psychotic speech (Seikkula *et al.*, 2001).

The initial meetings were characterised by more dialogue between the Clinicians than dialogue between all three attendants. The Clinicians followed Andersen's (1995) suggestion that a useful way to respond is to initiate reflective conversation. As an example, from the outset it was suggested to Dwayne that there was to be 'a freedom of speech' and that no topic was to be barred nor enforced. It was further clarified that understanding each other might not always be easy; however, understanding was not to be automatically assumed, but rather strived toward through dialogue. These discussions happened mostly between the two facilitators with Dwayne listening. Inviting him to share his views was initially met with little or no response.

Throughout the initial sessions Dwayne took notes, and this had been observed during previous MDT meetings. Dwayne would take out some crumpled and folded paper and the refill of a pen and would write things during the session. Dwayne would not answer when asked about this, but the Clinicians commented on it and shared some of their ideas with each other that it could perhaps be a sign of his interest in the meetings or that he would maybe reflect on the ideas in between sessions and maybe comment in subsequent meetings. Being able to listen to this seemed to intrigue him and he would smile or increase his note-taking.

As sessions progressed the note-taking decreased and was replaced by more attentive listening. This proved to be an intermediate stage, as the attentive listening eventually gave way to active participation in dialogue. Dwayne's first dialogical contributions were in the form of questions. Initially these were tentative and 'directed outward' – his questions offered very little of himself but were directed at the Clinicians. Some of the questions he asked were general whilst others (later) were more directed; for example, he asked whether the facilitators had ever experienced any mental illness, and whether they believed medication could be helpful. The dialogue in the meeting then centred on whether Dwayne might be wondering whether he could trust the Clinicians to answer questions and whether they were comfortable acknowledging when no concise answer were to be found. Throughout the process observations and ideas regarding Dwayne's behaviour and his contributions were shared openly in the meeting to indicate that the focus of the meetings was to increase understanding of Dwayne and his context. Explicitly inviting Dwayne to help formulate answers when they were difficult to find and even when they were appeared to be more easily at hand drew him more into the dialogue.

Elements featured in the dialogue

Two major themes emerged in the dialogues with Dwayne: that of hearing voices and that regarding the concept of 'illness'.

Voice hearing

Over many years it had been noted that Dwayne appeared to experience auditory hallucinations. However, he had chosen not to discuss this despite being asked about such phenomena on numerous occasions over many years by different people from different services, professions and skill levels. It seemed however that at times Dwayne would listen to something other than the discussion in the room, and so, in dialogue, the Clinicians commented on this by reflecting how he seemed to be absent, as if engaging with his own thoughts, or perhaps hearing a voice. Although Dwayne initially had a tendency to deny the experience of voice-hearing, he eventually became less inclined to deny this. Dwayne asked the Clinicians why they could not hear it when it was very obvious to him. This led to a dialogue with Dwayne about the phenomenology of hearing the voices. Many meetings occurred where this dialogue developed and evolved.

Gradually, an understanding was constructed between Dwayne and the Clinicians about his experience of hearing voices over the years:

- There had been limited interest shown by various Clinicians in understanding the experiences that frightened and bewildered him;
- This had been followed by attempts to convince him that the experience was not real;
- He had noted that engaging in discussions about voices typically led to increased restrictions so he had acted to conceal and deny this experience.

This on-going dialogue led to a clearer understanding of the risks associated with Dwayne, which then allowed a reduction in the use of restrictive management practices (e.g. leave entitlement).

Confronting the illness concept

Through the developing dialogue sessions, Dwayne explained that he had never been convinced by the explanations and definitions given him over the years as to what constitutes a diagnosis of schizophrenia. He believed that such a diagnosis would render him 'at the mercy' of mental health services for the rest of his life. He also believed that his only way out of the system was 'not to be ill', and there were only two ways of achieving this status: either by being cured or not having been ill in the first instance. In the past, such claims from him had been taken as examples of his lack of insight; however, Dwayne had developed his own understanding of what he considered to be the problem. Dwayne selected a paragraph for discussion from a report in his file:

> "Dwayne is a 40 year old male residing at The Unit for the past 8 years. He has a diagnosis of Paranoid Schizophrenia characterised by auditory hallucinations that he often responds to."

Dwayne used the dialogue sessions to rewrite this paragraph to reflect his own understanding of his experiences:

> "Dwayne is a 40 year old male residing at The Unit for the past 8 years. He is affected by what he believes to be a parasite-like illness that feeds off his

brain, causing him to hear things, mostly voices, that others cannot hear but remains very real to him. Sometimes he finds it necessary to engage in conversation or respond to these voices."

Adapted Open Dialogue outside Treatment Meetings

It was initially difficult to not discuss the sessions in between Treatment Meetings and not to have pre-planned topics or strategies. However, the spirit of the OD approach was introduced in the MDT meetings as far as it concerned Dwayne. In this regard the MDT was particularly supportive and participated in the implementation. Dwayne would be alerted that a MDT meeting was scheduled and he was invited to attend. No discussion was initiated before he joined the meeting and when he chose not to the discussion was postponed. During the meetings he was invited to give comment on the sessions or would be asked for his consent for one of the facilitators to do so.

Dwayne made good progress and was eventually discharged to a supported living placement with the goal being to move towards more independent living.

Conclusions and implications

Although it has been necessary to adapt the OD approach to fit within the systems within a traditional inpatient rehabilitation setting, it appears that there are gains to be made from this approach. Particularly when working with people who are reluctant to engage in traditional mental health services, it appears that significant gains in engagement can be achieved by adopting the principles of OD. Anderson (2002) discusses how to translate OD principles to other services that might be quite different from the setting where it was developed. She argues that by focussing on its relevance, proven efficacy and underlying philosophy it becomes possible to implement an 'Adapted Open Dialogue' approach (Anderson, 2002). However, specific research is required to establish which elements appear to contribute to better therapeutic outcomes to ensure that the critical components of the approach can be retained.

What OD advocates is a particular way of 'being in language' as well as relationship with others. In this dialogical process engagement fosters deeper understanding of the meaning individuals attach to things and events. Seikkula referred to deliberating dialogues as a particular feature of the Treatment Meetings – the safe space where such dialogues occur. This respectful way of engagement becomes the virtual seeding place for not only the sowing of individual ideas but the cultivation of mutually constructed meanings and understanding. What is then first uttered in outer dialogue in the shared space between participants has the potential to become part of the inner dialogue of the individual.

There are of course difficulties in applying OD in more traditional mental health settings, some of which have been articulated in the case study. In particular, the original OD approach focussed on first episode psychosis, and it remains to be seen to what extent the approach can be successfully implemented in teams and systems that are involved in working with people with complex and enduring mental health needs who perhaps have been in treatment for much longer and with symptoms more entrenched. However, it appears that, despite the various difficulties in implementation, there appears to be merit in using this approach to increase engagement and improve outcomes for people with these complex needs.

Note

1 Special thanks to Paul and John Blick for support with co-facilitating Open Dialogue sessions.

References

Aaltonen, J. & Räkköläinen, V. (1994). The shared image guiding the treatment process. A precondition for integration of the treatment of schizophrenia. *British Journal of Psychiatry, 164* (23 Suppl.), 97–102.

Alanen, Y. O. (1997). *Schizophrenia: Its origins and Need-Adapted Treatment.* London: Karnac Books.

Alanen, Y. O., Lehtinen, K., Räkköläinen, V. & Aaltonen, J. (1991). Need-adapted treatment of new schizophrenic patients: Experiences and results of the Turku Project. *Acta Psychiatrica Scandinavica, 83,* 363–372.

Andersen, T. (1995). Reflecting processes; acts of informing and forming: You can borrow my eyes but you must not take them away from me! In S. Friedman (ed.), *The reflective team in action: Collaborative practice in family therapy* (pp. 11–37). New York: Guilford Press.

Anderson, H. (1997). *Conversation, language and possibilities: A postmodern approach to therapy.* New York: Basic Books.

Anderson, H. (2002). In the space between people: Seikkula's Open Dialogue Approach. *Journal of Marital and Family Therapy, 28*(3), 279–281.

Bakhtin, M. (1984). *Problems of Dostoevsky's poetics.* Minneapolis, MN: University of Minnesota Press.

Bakhtin, M. (1986). *Speech genres and other late essays.* Austin, TX: University of Texas Press.

Boscolo, L. & Bertrando, P. (1998). *Genom tidens lins.* Stockholm: Mareld.

Holma, J. & Aaltonen, J. (1997). The sense of agency and the search for a narrative in acute psychosis. *Contemporary Family Therapy, 19*(4), 463–477.

Meaden, A. & Hacker, D. (2010). *Problematic and risk behaviours in psychosis: A shared formulation approach.* Hove, E. Sussex: Routledge.

Seikkula, J. (2002). Open Dialogues with good and poor outcomes for families with psychotic crisis: Examples from families with violence. *Journal of Marital and Family Therapy, 28*(3), 263–274.

Seikkula, J. & Arnkil, T. E. (2006). *Dialogical meetings in social networks.* London: Karnac Books.

Seikkula, J. & Sutela, M. (1990). Coevolution of the family and the hospital: The system of boundary. *Journal of Strategic and Systemic Therapies, 9,* 34–42.

Seikkula, J., Aaltonen, J., Alakare, B., Haarakangas, K., Keränen, J. & Lehtinen, K. (2006). Five-year experience of first-episode nonaffective psychosis in open-dialogue approach: Treatment principles, follow-up outcomes, and two case studies. *Psychotherapy Research*, *16*(2), 214–228.

Seikkula, J., Alakare, B. & Aaltonen, J. (2001). Open Dialogue in psychosis I: An introduction and case illustration. *Journal of Constructivist Psychology*, *14*, 247–266.

Seikkula, J., Alakare, B. & Aaltonen, J. (2011). The comprehensive open-dialogue approach in Western Lapland: II. Long-term stability of acute psychosis outcomes in advanced community care. *Psychosis*, *3*(3), 192–204.

Stern, S., Doolan, M., Staples, E., Szmukler, G. I. & Eisler, I. (1999). Disruption and reconstruction: Narrative insights into the experience of family members caring for a relative diagnosed with serious mental illness. *Family Process*, *38*, 353–369.

Wilkinson, C. E. (2008). *An exploration of service users' experiences of a low secure forensic mental health service*, DClinPsy manuscript, University of Leeds, UK, http://etheses.whiterose.ac.uk/id/eprint/428.

Chapter 3

Using Pre-Therapy in forensic settings

Richard Barker

Introduction

This chapter focuses on the use of Pre-Therapy (Prouty, 1976, 2001) within a forensic setting as an engagement tool for use with clients with whom psychological contact is difficult to build or maintain because of their psychosis or withdrawal. Pre-Therapy offers a strategy for working with contact-impaired clients who are not yet at the point where contact with others is sufficient to be used as a basis for collaboration and recovery.

Although this book is focussing on 'new developments' in working with psychosis, Pre-Therapy has been in existence since the early 1980s and 1990s, yet mainstream awareness and use appear poor, at least in the UK, despite a body of research and anecdotal evidence supporting its utility. This chapter draws on Pre-Therapy, but also considers it in the context of current developments in person-centred therapy, phenomenological perspectives on psychosis and from a wider recovery-oriented perspective.

Theoretical background and development of Pre-Therapy

At its heart, Pre-Therapy is a grounding process, one that literally 'points to the concrete' (Prouty, 2003, citing Buber, 1964: 547); so too is this chapter grounded by the case study described later. Pre-Therapy describes a strategy by which human contact – at its most basic elemental level – can be forged with the most distant of clients. Whilst this chapter focuses exclusively upon the use of Pre-Therapy with clients experiencing psychosis, it has also been used with clients with dementia, (Dodds, 2008), catatonia (Prouty & Kubiak, 1988) and severe learning disabilities (Pörtner, 1990). As well as professionals, the approach has also been adopted by carers to develop and maintain relationships with service users (Clarke, 2006).

This chapter draws from the author's experiences working in forensic services, in which clients usually present with the twin difficulties of mental health problems and risk behaviours. They typically have complex histories, in which trauma, abuse and exposure to violence are not uncommon. However, many clients are not as difficult to reach as the one described in the case study – at least not because of their psychosis. Often of far more relevance when building a therapeutic relationship in such settings is the difficulty that exists because of the nature of forensic services, both in terms of the population from which we draw our clients, but also because of the restrictive nature of the environments. In situations where clients are detained against their will and often have challenging attitudes towards authority, building any kind of psychological contact becomes a key outcome for the services in and of itself. Therapeutic relationships in such a culture are not something that can be assumed or taken for granted.

As a result, staff in forensic services often have to strike a difficult balance between building relationships sufficient to assist a person's recovery, and at the same time carefully maintaining clear boundaries to ensure their safety and the safety of the clients. Empathy and compassion are core attributes of staff in such an environment, and nowhere are these more tested than in intensive care settings, where holding the hope for someone who may not be in a position to consider a positive future can be a day-to-day challenge. Building the bridge of communication with clients whose experiences of hallucinations, delusions and fear drive them to withdraw or push others away is a vital first step in both the client's recovery, and the staff's ability to hold hope for them is a challenge that can be helped by a formal engagement intervention like Pre-Therapy.

Pre-Therapy as a bridge

Pre-Therapy was developed by Garry Prouty in the 1970s partially in response to his own personal experience of attempting to communicate with his brother who experienced both schizophrenia and developmental disabilities (Prouty, 2008). It has its theoretical and clinical basis in the development of client-centred psychotherapy (Rogers, 1951) and the phenomenological-experiential movements that founded Gestalt therapy (Perls, 1969). When approaching how he might work with contact-impaired clients he met whilst working in an American psychiatric institution in the 1970s Prouty drew from this training and in particular the core conditions that Rogers had defined as being necessary for client-centred therapy to be effective. Of Rogers's six core conditions, the first of these requires that the therapist and client are in 'psychological contact' with one another.

This simple statement clouds what is actually a complex interactional process that is at the core of all human relationships. Without the ability to share thoughts, ideas, beliefs and feelings, human beings would not have evolved to our present state of sophistication and co-operation. Language and symbolism are at the heart of this process so it is necessary for the individual to have sufficient awareness that others are willing and wish to communicate, along with an underlying understanding that such communication will bring rewards and benefit. For individuals experiencing psychotic symptoms, this process can be further challenged by paranoia and fear, withdrawal and avoidance. Prouty's work focussed on developing a strategy by which an individual lost to their internal experiences can be brought out or anchored (Van Werde, 2007) to a shared reality with the person trying to communicate with them.

In forensic settings, engagement work can take up a large proportion of the time spent with a client in their recovery and becomes an intervention in and of itself. This chapter focuses on the use of Pre-Therapy, both as an individual engagement intervention, but also as a tool for use by all staff.

Aims, stages, strategies and techniques

Pre-Therapy as a method has been described in detail by Prouty (1977, 1994) and others (see Sanders, 2007). Pre-Therapy works on the basis that most individuals experiencing psychosis, or any experience that limits contact with a shared reality, tend to be unaware of the limits of their own psychological contact with others.

It is also important to note, as others have done (Sanders, 2007), that Pre-Therapy is not a complete therapy. It is a method for developing the foundations upon which therapy – by which we mean any psychotherapeutic contact – can develop. Perhaps even more prosaically, Pre-Therapy is about developing human connectedness. It draws the disconnected individual back into contact with the world, acting as a bridge upon which communication may take place, emotional expression may develop and the bonds of a genuine working alliance can be founded.

Practitioner core characteristics

In keeping with its roots in Rogerian approaches, Pre-Therapy does demand some basic tenets of the individual attempting to form contact. Unconditional positive regard, empathy, compassion, listening and valuing the experience of the person are core skills of Pre-Therapy as much as they are in any other therapeutic endeavour. Importantly, Pre-Therapy requires the staff member to recognise and respect that the individual's experiences of psychosis *have meaning for them*. For instance, a client once described to the author the loss of the richness of experience that his psychotic beliefs gave him, and the dullness that came with being 'well'. His experiences had meaning for him, and the Pre-Therapy practitioner's role is to help him reach the point of being able to express the meaning in it.

As in any recovery-oriented interaction, it is essential that Pre-Therapy practitioner recognises the individual's autonomy and agency in their pathway to recovery. The importance of being realistically hopeful, compassionate, non-critical and showing respectful curiosity cannot be emphasised enough as principles upon which to base Pre-Therapy work. Moreover, individuals in helping professions often develop skills at engagement naturally as part of the requirements of their job. Pre-Therapy however, requires the *specific* application of a strategy in an overt and deliberate way. In giving some training to staff, a participant pointed out "but we do that already!" Of course to an extent this is true, but the application of Pre-Therapy requires a consistency of approach that has been shown to demonstrate an improvement over and above business as usual (Dekeyser *et al.*, 2007).

Strategy for practice

Pre-Therapy in action has been described as 'deceptively simple' (Sanders, 2007) because in practical terms it involves a process of reality anchoring, encouraging contact with the self, one's environment and others within that environment. An individual with full access to these mechanisms has contact with *reality* (places, things, people, events), *affect* (own moods, feelings and emotions) and *communicative contacts* (the symbols, language and shared reality required to communicate with others) (Prouty, 1983, 1991). Individuals who lose access to these mechanisms, whatever the causes of that loss, can be helped to regain some contact using Pre-Therapy methods. Crucially, these methods need to be planned, and mindfully enacted, with consistency and care, ideally across a whole care team.

Prouty described an individual with full access to these contact skills as having *expressive functioning* – that is, the ability to have adequate contact with ourselves, the world and others in order to function adaptively in it. Individuals who lack that capacity are described in this model as being *pre-expressive* – contact is impaired for them and they are no longer able to reach out to others, or are unwilling to do so for some reason of their own. Developments in Pre-Therapy led to the proposition of a realm between the expressive and pre-expressive self, an area that Van Werde has coined as *grey-zone functioning* (Van Werde, 2002; see Figure 3.1). The degree of contact a person has with the world may vary across a spectrum, and the grey-zone inhabits a region that varies between the fully expressive individual and pre-expressive. It is perhaps in this area that most

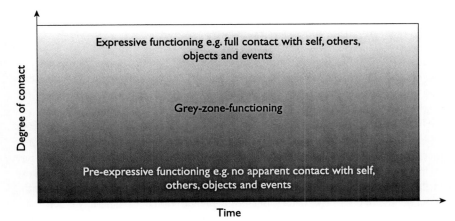

Figure 3.1 Grey-zone functioning
Adapted from Van Werde (2002).

Pre-Therapy takes places, drawing out the client from their exile and isolation using *contact reflections*.

Before going on to explore contact reflections and the process of building contact, an important facet of Pre-Therapy is *contact behaviour*. In the absence of language, behaviour is often a telling mechanism for understanding the inner experience of the individual. In the pre-expressive individual behaviour is often the only mechanism by which they express themselves, and careful observation of an individual's behaviour can be helpful in detecting subtle signs of engagement and contact. Movements, posture, facial expressions, sounds and language are all important aspects of this process. This is described in the chapter's case illustration, and in one example his behaviour (particularly covering his face from contact) is suggestive of an active and possibly protective withdrawal from others. It was also notable that his offensive behaviours stopped as soon as he was sequestered away from others.

The Pre-Therapy trained staff member must be alert for any signs of grey-zone functioning in which the individual may demonstrate any contact with reality. These may be behaviours and utterances that are suggestive of some reality contact. The person may request things, comment on something in their environment or express an emotion, even if it is only in their facial expression. Once identified, it will be important to capitalise upon those behaviours, utilising them as potential opportunities for engagement. Any interaction has the potential to lead to other more positive interactions and staff must be ready to capitalise on such opportunities in a way that is helpful and that increases the degree of contact. In the case study, it was hypothesised that John's withdrawal was driven by fear derived from persecutory beliefs that he had been expressing whilst in the prison and prior to his index offence. If staff were to foster John's engagement, it was vital that their attempts at communication did not support further paranoid interpretations and consequent withdrawal.

Types of contact

Prouty (1976) described psychological contact as having three components or layers, without which the first core condition of person-centred therapy cannot be met. Prouty was influenced by the Gestalt theoretical perspective, particularly the writings of Fritz Perls (Perls, 1969). Gestalt perspectives focus upon *awareness* and the importance of feelings, behaviour and experience as distinct from interpretations or inferences about experiences. Within a Pre-Therapy paradigm, this usefully focuses upon the client's present-moment experience of their psychosis, which may be more accessible than any secondary inferences or interpretations either because of their psychosis, withdrawal or lack of contact. Moreover, focussing upon the concreteness of their experiences means that the individual Pre-Therapy practitioner may establish some common ground upon which to build, because some basic experiences are shared. In contrast, the client's internal beliefs may not be something the client is able to share, or even interpret well enough to communicate.

An individual who has *expressive functioning* is able to communicate their internal world and shared reality, and through this express their sense of self and identity. It is made up of the following components:

Reality contact

This is literally making contact with reality, an awareness of the environment in which one is in, including the people around the client, the objects, the things and events. This also includes contact with time, and the temporal nature of events as they pass by, as well as contact with people, at least in so much as people are also objects that may act upon the environment.

Affective contact

Prouty (2002) describes affective conflict as 'the awareness of moods, feelings and emotions' and being in contact with one's emotions, being able to locate them as belonging to oneself, but also being influenced by others, situations and events. Affective contact also requires individuals to recognise that they are a generator of their own emotions, albeit with an object that may prompt the generation of that emotion. "I am angry with you because you didn't speak to me" – the anger being perceived as belonging to the person, its location being described as being focussed upon another for failing in some way.

Communicative contact

This relates to the importance that language has in helping us construct our identities and connect to others around us. It is the symbolic representation of our reality and affective contact and allows us to link that symbolism to ourselves and others and is at the heart of our shared reality.

There are parallels in Prouty's description of communicative contact with the work of Lysaker on meta-cognition in psychosis. What Lysaker and Lysaker (2006) describe as 'narrative impoverishment' in schizophrenia is the deficit in people's ability to describe their sense of self and their stories (narratives). Without communicative contact, or with only limited communicative contact, the client would be unable to engage effectively in constructing the symbolism required to express their sense of self or narrative about self. They are not able to express the "I" in their story perhaps because they lack access to the necessary higher level symbolism to express the concept. Pre-Therapy works by focussing on what might be termed lower-level symbolism and language: on the concrete and tangible, but offers enough of a grounded contact with the self and others to work towards the expression of high-level symbolism.

The practice of assisting the individual in returning to a level of psychological contact allows them to communicate and be aware of their environmental experience, their feelings and behaviours, and in the act of communicating that to others, their sense of self.

The practice of Pre-Therapy

Sanders (2007) gives a warning to readers examining the principles of Pre-Therapy that it appears 'simple'. This is echoed in the comments from staff undergoing training about how simple Pre-Therapy in practice appears. The warning that Sanders gives is a useful one, because whilst the contact reflections that are described below appear relatively simple, in practice they require considerable skill to use effectively and consistently. Of particular note is that skilled helpers, particularly those with extensive training in psychotherapeutic skills, often find contact reflections *too simple* and will struggle to reduce the intensity of the interaction to that necessary to bring an individual out of grey-zone functioning. The temptation will be to over-estimate the degree of contact the individual is capable of undertaking at that time, and risk further retreat or withdrawal by overwhelming the client or attempting contact at a higher level than they are capable of at that time. An analogy might be found in learning a new language and then being spoken to by someone proficient in that language. So it is with Pre-Therapy – the psychotic individual has to be brought back to a level of unambiguous reality functioning, using Pre-Therapy as the anchoring mechanism.

In order to practise Pre-Therapy effectively practitioners need to exhibit some consistent core values. The first is a commitment to simply *being* with another person, even if that person is not reciprocating and even if those moments are far apart and difficult to reach. The contact-impaired individual is also detached from their world, and this can sometimes lead to professionals being similarly detached because the relationship is at that time absent or difficult to draw upon. This detachment often contributes towards further detachment by staff and may lead to adopting a 'do to' philosophy, rather than the 'do with' approach of a recovery-oriented professional (Slade, 2009). Pre-Therapy allows staff to challenge this detachment in a concrete fashion, and gives them a goal to work towards, in turn providing some focus that may give hope to the future engagement of the client.

Contact reflections

Contact reflections consist of five different types of highly concrete utterances and descriptions of the individual. They are 'plain, meticulously literal reflections which respectfully duplicate, mimic and repeat the client's behaviour ...' (Sanders, 2007: 31). By respectfully reflecting back to the client the concrete observable reality of the individual's environment, or status, the client will hear and start to acknowledge the basic shared reality that is being postulated by the staff member. The communication is therefore at a semantic and phenomenological level that the pre-expressive client can recognise and follow. Some staff express the view that contact reflections seem patronising, akin to talking slowly and loudly when trying to speak to someone who does not speak your own language. Yet, if the client genuinely feels patronised by the simplicity of the interaction, they are probably already functioning at an expressive level, as they will be demonstrating communicative contact by putting voice to their feeling of being patronised. In such an eventuality, it may be wise to consider the formulation of the client's withdrawal as it may not be simply a function of their psychosis (e.g. engagement with psychotic experiences) but may be a deliberate and mindful choice not to communicate.

These reflections aim to help centre the client's concentration and awareness on the shared reality in which they exist with others. It is building 'common ground' upon which the client and therapist may share observations. These reflections direct the client's attention to clear observable phenomena, like the environment they are in, the behaviour they are exhibiting or even the utterances they make. It is crucial that these reflections are devoid of interpretation or the potential for inference. They are statements of observable fact, in and of themselves, and should leave little or no room for hidden meaning. By helping the client to observe or bring into awareness something that can be shared between the two people in the interaction, a bridge of contact can be built.

There are five types of contact reflections. A skilled Pre-Therapist will use all five types of contact, and switch between them to best draw out the individual, focussing on whichever mode is likely to draw out the individual at that point.

Situational reflections (SR)

These are observations about the shared reality of the environment (people, places, objects, events) in which the person is. At a basic level they may reflect the environment in which the client is in, and the client's relationship to that environment. In the case study, situational verbal reflections are offered:

- "You are sitting with your back to us";
- "You are holding your blanket over your head".

They may also be spoken in the third person to reflect the observers' perspective: "John is looking out of the window". As noted above, these utterances appear simple observations of what is occurring in the room, but by doing this they are designed to help centre awareness upon something concrete and something that has the potential to be shared between the client and therapist on a fundamental level.

Facial reflections (FR)

These are observations about the facial expressions used by the client, and can also include reciprocal mimicking of the client's facial expressions. Because our faces are, apart from when using language, the most obvious way of expressing our emotional inner life, facial reflections often focus upon the development of the emotional contact with the client, and can, in the author's experience, be the most powerful mechanism for drawing people out. This was the case with John, when a reflection on his facial expression provided an opportunity for him to express his feelings. When it was reflected to him that he looked scared, John uttered that he was, allowing for a brief moment of contact that formed the basis for further opportunities for John to express the need for safety.

Body reflections (BR)

Occasionally individuals with psychosis may place their bodies into strange positions, or display odd incongruent gestures or movements. The therapist can reflect these body reflections verbally "John is rocking under the blanket" or non-verbally by reflecting the client's body motion. Another client would stand in his room doorway for hours at time in a crouching position and did not engage with staff until they echoed his position by crouching against the wall next to him.

Word-for-word reflections (WWR)

Individuals may also use language in a non-expressive or non-shared fashion when in psychotic states. Word salads, thought disorder and neologisms mean that the use of shared language is a vital part of having the shared reality that will engender genuine therapeutic contact. Word-for-word reflections can be used to provide a feedback loop to the client about their utterances. It is assumed that such utterances have some communicative intent, but may not be understood by the therapist. The task of the therapist is to listen carefully and reflect back to the client the word or utterance in the hope that the client will then expand upon the word or add more detail. This certainly worked with John, who often had a tendency to utter one or two words about his internal world, which when reflected back to him usually drew out a greater response.

Reiterative reflections (RR)

Within the Pre-Therapy model of contact, people will move from being pre-expressive to being fully expressive in fits and starts, existing at different levels of grey-zone functioning over time. Reiterative reflections are used to convey a sense of the temporal reality in which the client exists, reflecting back to the client how their contact may have changed over time. This can be short term and within the session, or longer term, maintaining that contact over time and bringing consistency to the pattern of contact. This can be as simple as repeating a phrase that a client has uttered before and resulted in an increase in contact "You said last time that . . ." or reflecting that there has been some passage of time – "Earlier you look scared, you do not now" by injecting a temporal concept into other reflections. Reiterative reflections tend to be useful (in the author's experience) with clients who have already shown some improvement in psychological contact, introducing some focus on how that contact has changed over time; especially where in between sessions the client has returned to more pre-expressive functioning.

The application of Pre-Therapy to psychosis

Pre-Therapy is concerned with using contact reflections to assist the individual in a journey from their pre-expressive self, back to being in full contact with reality – the expressive self. Prouty theorises that in the pre-expressive state, the individual in a state of psychosis cannot construct the boundaries necessary to form the full sense of self (1977, 1983). Contact reflections assist in grounding the individual in the present moment with definitive statements or observations that relate to something tangible and overt. There are parallels in this process with the ringing of bells or sounds used in mindfulness techniques to bring a person's attention away from the cacophony of internal thoughts to present-moment clarity and awareness (Mace, 2008).

> We see psychosis as pre-expressive behaviour. That means we see such behaviour as a way of expressing meanings that are there, but are not fully in process or available to the person.
>
> (Van Werde, 2002: 79)

Using Pre-Therapy with hallucinations can be challenging because the individual does not experience the hallucination as being something that is within themselves. Rather, the hallucination is experienced as external to them, although experienced by them. Prouty, exploring the phenomenological basis of hallucinations, compares them with dreams, in that dreams are internal, they belong and are experienced as being within the boundaries of the self. Hallucinations, in comparison, are external; they are experienced by the individual as being externally applied, beyond the limits of the self or not of the self. Prouty makes this phenomenological distinction and goes on to observe that the self is divided (Prouty, 2004, citing Laing, 1969). The individual's hallucinations are not part of their experience of the self and the dissonance this causes leads to confusion and a search for meaning or explanation as the person attempts to integrate the hallucinatory experience into their personal narrative. The task of the Pre-Therapist here is to assist in the re-integration of the self. Pre-Therapy provides the building block for this process, by helping the client identify the boundaries of the self and the basic shared reality upon which reintegration of the self can begin.

Case illustration: John

John has come to us from the local prison, where he had been held in health care for several weeks awaiting a bed in a medium secure unit. He had been prescribed medication in prison and had the benefit of oversight from the team that would look after him in hospital. In prison he had been violent towards staff and other inmates, expressing persecutory beliefs, and necessitating him to be restrained and secluded on a number of occasions. More recently he had become uncommunicative and would sit for hours in his cell with his blanket hiding his face.

Upon arrival at our Unit he was initially placed within the Intensive care area, which is a small, highly staffed Unit with only five other clients. He was uncommunicative with staff although some feel that he acknowledges staff through his actions. Within two hours of being admitted he assaulted two clients and a member of staff before he was restrained. He has been placed in seclusion for his safety and the safety of others. It is not clear what prompted the assaults, as they appeared unpredictable and without any apparent provocation.

Seclusion rooms are not necessarily nice places to be, being primarily designed to be safe. Whilst ours has a window to look out of, along with a separate toilet and shower space, the only other part of the room consists of a solid plinth against one wall upon which sits a blue tear-proof rubber mattress, a tear-proof pillow and a blanket. The door is steel, with a smaller door set within the main door at waist height through which staff can communicate and pass food and other items. A viewing panel sits at eye level. John is sat with his back to the door, the blanket covering his head. Any attempt to engage him in conversation is ignored. He shows no interest in staff, although he will come and take food and drink, usually without any comment. Medication is prescribed, but ignored, and the team are considering restraining him to give him medication. He has barely made any comment since arriving on the Unit, nor has he changed his clothes or washed since arriving.

Despite this, there is still a sense of John being present some of the time when attempts are made to engage him. When he is not hiding behind a blanket, his eyes seem to watch what is happening around him. As the Psychologist on the Unit, I am presented with a simple task: How are we going to engage with this man?

Our working formulation is that his withdrawal is due to delusional persecutory paranoia. This was based on the observations by the team of his behaviour when he first came to the Unit, and observations by health-care staff in the prison.

Using contact reflections

Following his placement in seclusion, John was compliant with medication, but did not communicate with anybody in the process, refusing conversation or staring at them. The next day, he had been relatively settled and consideration was being given to allowing him out of seclusion, but concern was raised by the care team because he had not spoken to anyone in any depth. When I went to see him that afternoon he had had removed the blanket from his face, making the possibility of contact perhaps more likely. The seclusion room door was open and had been open for several hours. I was stood on the threshold of the door while

John was sitting on the bed, and was sporadically looking at me and then looking away. The type of reflection used is shown in brackets.

T: (SR)   John you are looking at me then looking away
C: *no verbal response, but looked back toward me from the window*
T: (SR)   You are looking back at me
T: (SR)   John, you are looking me in the eye
T: (SR)   You are pulling a face
T: (FR)   *I pulled the same fear face that John was pulling*
T: (FR)   You look scared
T: (SR)   You are safe here
T: (BR)   *John was curled up on the bed. I hunched down to make myself smaller by the wall opposite him*
C: Not safe
T: (WWR)   Not safe?
C: *John pulled the blanket around him, but did not obscure his face, he looked away*
T: (SR)   You've pulled the blanket around you
T: (SR)   You are looking out the window
T: (RR)   You are safe here
C: *looking back* I don't know you
T: (WWR)   You don't know me. My name is Richard
T: (SR/RR)   You are safe here. You can talk to me
C: *draws knees up to his chest and sighs then looks out the window*
T: (BR)   *sits on floor, draws knees up to chest and sighs*
T: (SR)   I'm sitting like you
No comments for a short while from John
T: (SR)   It's raining outside (*drawing the client's attention to the outside world*)
C: Yes, *continues to look outside*
C: making it rain
T: (WWR)   making it rain?
C: It's my fault
T: What is your fault?

From this point we were able to have a developing conversation about John's persecutory beliefs and ideas of reference. He tolerated my presence for a further thirty minutes before stopping speaking again. Later on that evening after I had gone, a member of nursing staff, using the same techniques engaged him again.

T: (SR)   You are staring at me
T: (SR)   You look puzzled
T: (FR)   *mimics puzzled expression*

C:	made it happen
T: (WWR)	You made it happen?
C:	Yes
C:	*starts rocking, clearly distressed*
T: (SR)	You are rocking John
T: (RR)	You are safe here *using the same reflection we had agreed on early in the day*
T: (SR)	You are sitting on the bed, you look distressed and upset
C:	had to do it
T: (WWR)	had to do it?
C:	Yes
T: (WWR)	Yes?
T: (SR)	You've stopped rocking and are looking at me
C:	I don't want to be here

John started to express some awareness of where he was and how he felt. Over the next few days he started to become more familiar with staff, disclosing more about his persecutory beliefs. Having a few key members of staff who were Pre-Therapy trained meant that they were able to capitalise on these times to draw John out from his experience of psychosis to a more concrete dialogue.

Outcomes

John went on to recover well from his experience of psychosis, although he stated that he recalled little from our early encounters. He did have a key memory of feeling safe enough to start talking when I sat against the wall and mimicked the way he was sitting. Far from feeling patronised by this, he stated that he felt less threatened by it and even reflected that he felt that he could talk to me as a consequence. He also spoke about the times I and other staff were willing to just sit with him and expressed a feeling of safety that he had not felt previously.

When using Pre-Therapy, it is also important to be flexible in its approach. There were times when John's reality contact was better than others as he moved up and down the scale of *grey-zone functioning* described by Van Werde (2002). As a useful rule of thumb, it is helpful to match the response to the contact initiated by the client. Thus, word-for-word utterances are matched by word-for-word reflections, facial expressions by facial reflections and so on. Whilst there is no particular hierarchy that has been observed in the process of building contact reflections, anecdotal experience suggests that word-for-word reflections and facial reflections often prompt greater degrees of contact than bodily or situations reflections, simply because they are more likely to draw out a greater response. Reiterative reflections are also important as they convey the passage of time and consistency over time, but they tend to be of greater value once some level of contact is built, even if it is fluctuating over time.

Conclusions and implications

As noted earlier, Pre-Therapy is not a complete therapy. It is a beginning for those individuals whose experience of psychosis is so all-consuming that they struggle to express their experiences and sense of self to others. The experience of using Pre-Therapy can be a powerful one. It is a privilege to have someone share their experiences and private moments with you, and nowhere is this more keenly experienced as when an individual who has been lost to their experiences re-connects to the world through you.

Pre-Therapy offers a strategy for doing this in a way that is consistent, considered and has a theoretical basis. Whilst it has been in existence for some time as a methodology, its research base remains limited, at least in part due to the numbers of clients upon which it has been used. There has, as yet, been no large-scale assessment of its utility nor randomised control trials. There are however a wide range of single case studies and small-scale studies, and a growing European network of practitioners and advocates (see the Pre-Therapy network) who continue to support its development and an annual Pre-Therapy international network meeting. Surprisingly, though, Pre-Therapy does not appear to be a mainstream practice when working with those who experience psychosis or those whose 'negative symptoms' are such that they appear to be too lost to engage. Yet Pre-Therapy offers the possibility of engagement and recognises that all human connectedness starts with simply being in the presence of another person and acknowledging their existence and experience.

In other settings (e.g. community teams) the opportunities for contact may be less. One option is to utilise any available others (e.g. residential care staff, carers) who could be trained in Pre-Therapy.

Because of the nature of Pre-Therapy it is important that any training includes a large component of experiential techniques, and role playing. The simplicity of Pre-Therapy contact reflections belies the complexity of their application and staff will have to overcome any feelings of inhibition to practise. This is best overcome with humour through role-play, either in small groups or in front of the whole group. Dodds (2007) has observed that part of the difficulty in training staff in using contact reflections is not in their use with individuals who are pre-expressive, but in individuals who are in the grey zone between pre-expressive and fully expressive. It is tempting for those new to Pre-Therapy (especially those trained in other psychosocial interventions) to move towards Socratic questioning, or even a curious enquiry, particularly when individuals begin to respond with greater degrees of verbal contact. Alternatively, staff may apply contact reflections mechanistically – 'doing to', rather than 'doing with'. For this reason, following training, supervision and the development of shared formulations can be used to support Pre-Therapy practice. This may need to be frequent to ensure consistency of practice and facilitate problem solving.

References

Clarke, C. (2006). Pre-Therapy: A carer's perspective of Prouty's contact work. *The Meriden West Midlands Family Programme Newsletter*, 2(11), 5–8.

Dekeyser, M., Prouty, G. & Elliott, R. (2007). Pre-Therapy process and outcome: A review of research instruments and findings. *Person-Centered and Experiential Psychotherapies*, 7, 37–55.

Dodds, L. (2008). Pre-Therapy and dementia care. In G. Prouty (ed.), *Emerging developments in Pre-Therapy: A Pre-Therapy reader* (pp. 49–74). Ross-on-Wye, UK: PCCS Books.

Lysaker, P. H. & Lysaker, J. T. (2006). A typology of narrative impoverishment in schizophrenia: Implications for understanding the process of establishing and sustaining dialogue in individual psychotherapy. *Counselling Psychology Quarterly*, 19(1), 57–68.

Mace, C. (2008). *Mindfulness and mental health: Therapy, theory and science*. London: Routledge.

Perls, F. (1969). The ego as a function of the organism. In *Ego, hunger and aggression*. New York: Vintage Books.

Pörtner, M. (1990). Client-centered psychotherapy with mentally retarded persons: Catherine and Ruth. In G. Leitaer, J. Rombauts & R. Van Balsen (eds), *Client-centered and experiential psychotherapy in the nineties* (pp. 659–670). Leuven: Leuven University Press.

Prouty, G. (1976). Pre-Therapy – a method of treating pre-expressive psychotic and retarded clients. *Psychotherapy: Theory, Research and Practice*, 13, 290–295.

Prouty, G. (1977). Protosymbolic method: A phenomenological treatment of schizophrenic hallucinations. *Journal of Mental Imagery*, 2, 339–342.

Prouty, G. (1983). Hallucinatory contact: A phenomenological treatment of schizophrenics. *Journal of Communication Therapy*, 2, 99–103.

Prouty, G. (2001). The practice of Pre-Therapy. *Journal of Contemporary Psychotherapy*, 31(1), 31–40.

Prouty, G. (2002). Humanistic psychotherapy with schizophrenic persons. In D. Cain & J. Seeman (eds), *Handbook of research and practice in humanistic psychotherapies* (pp. 579–601). Washington, DC: American Psychological Association.

Prouty, G. (2003). Pre-Therapy: A newer development in the psychotherapy of schizophrenia. *Journal of the American Academy of Psychoanalysis and Dynamic Psychiatry*, 31(1), 59–73.

Prouty, G. (ed.) (2008). *Emerging developments in Pre-Therapy: A Pre-Therapy reader.* Ross-on-Wye, UK: PCCS Books.

Prouty, G. & Kubiak. M. (1988). The development of communicative contact with a catatonic schizophrenic. *Journal of Communication Therapy*, 4(1), 13–20.

Prouty, G., Van Werde, D. & Pörtner, M. (2002). *Pre-Therapy: Reaching contact-impaired clients.* Ross-on-Wye, UK: PCCS Books.

Rogers, C. (1951). *Client centred therapy*. London: Constable.

Sanders, P. (ed.). (2007). *The contact work primer*. Ross-on-Wye, UK: PCCS Books.

Slade, M. (2009) *Personal recovery and mental illness: A guide for mental health professionals*. Cambridge: Cambridge University Press.

Van Werde, D. (2002). A contact milieu. In G. Prouty, D. Van Werde & M. Pörtne. (eds), *Pre-Therapy: Reaching contact-impaired clients* (pp. 77–114). Ross-on-Wye, UK: PCCS Books.

Van Werde, D. (2005). Facing psychotic functioning: Person-centred contact work in residential psychiatric care. In S. Joseph & R. Worsley (eds), *Person-centred psychopathology: A positive psychology of mental health* (pp. 158–168). Ross-on-Wye, UK: PCCS Books.

Van Werde, D. (2007). Contact work in a residential psychiatric setting: Bridging person, team and context. In P. Sanders (ed.), *The contact work primer* (pp. 60–71). Ross-on-Wye, UK: PCCS Books.

Chapter 4

Adapting Relapse Prevention strategies for use with difficult to engage populations

Morna Gillespie

Introduction

Psychosis is often associated with relapse and there are now well-developed interventions for identifying the warning signs and implementing strategies to reduce relapse rates (Birchwood *et al.*, 2000). However, much of the research on this area has focussed upon individuals who demonstrate active engagement with services and are therefore likely to self-monitor for signs and take action accordingly (e.g. Gleeson *et al.*, 2009; Lobban *et al.*, 2010). This chapter examines the use of Relapse Prevention strategies and outlines ways of adapting this approach for use with people who are difficult to engage in services.

Theoretical background and development: detecting and preventing relapse

The relapse signature

Psychotic relapse can be defined as the recurrence of clinically significant and sustained positive symptoms that follow a period of remission (Gleeson *et al.*, 2010). Relapse can result in hospitalisation, but can in some instances be managed in the community. It has been known for some time that psychotic relapse is preceded by subtle changes in people's thoughts, feelings and behaviour (Birchwood *et al.*, 2000). These changes can be identified by people with psychosis and those close to them (Herz & Melville, 1980). Identification of these early warning signs can predict psychotic relapse with high levels of sensitivity (50–79 per cent) and specificity (75–81 per cent) (Subotnik & Neuchterlein, 1988; Birchwood *et al.*, 1989; Jorgenson, 1998). Therefore, the identification of these signs and the development of a 'Relapse Prevention Plan' that describes possible coping strategies for each of these signs (typically broken into early, middle and late signs of relapse) can be useful.

Early warning signs and the order in which they occur differ across individuals. Each person's early warning sign pattern is unique to them, representing a 'relapse signature'. Dysphoric symptoms (e.g. depression, sleep problems, withdrawal) usually precede psychotic symptoms (e.g. hearing voices, paranoia) (Docherty *et al.*, 1978). The process of relapse tends to occur over a period of less than four weeks (Birchwood *et al.*, 1989).

Packages to enable people with psychosis to identify their relapse signature, triggers to relapse and appropriate coping strategies have been developed (e.g. Birchwood *et al.*, 2000; Smith, 2003), alongside tools such as the Early Signs Scale (Birchwood *et al.*, 1989) to help people monitor for signs of relapse. Most of the packages are similar in nature and typically cover areas such as those outlined in Smith's (2003) ten-stage model of Relapse Prevention:

1. Attitude to Relapse Scale and Awareness of Early Signs Questionnaire
2. Card sort exercise and timeline
3. Early Signs Scale
4. Stress triggers
5. Coping strategies
6. Self-medication strategy
7. Involvement of others
8. Action plan
9. Taking action/rehearsal/review
10. Attitude to Relapse Scale – evaluation.

People with lived experience of using mental health services have developed a Relapse Prevention tool known as the Wellness Recovery Action Plan (WRAP; Copeland, 1997). The WRAP emphasises 'wellness' rather than focussing on relapse and talks about having a 'wellness toolbox', which includes strategies for maintaining mental health. It also incorporates core concepts that are covered by other packages such as identifying early warning signs, triggers and coping strategies. Additionally it includes crisis planning and post-crisis planning. Recently, a 'WRAP app' has been developed for iPhones and iPads to enable people to add to and refer to their WRAP more easily.

Coping Strategy Enhancement

Coping strategies can be divided into the categories of cognitive, behavioural and physiological (Falloon & Talbot, 1981) and sensory (Tarrier, 1987). It has been found that coping strategies are more effective if the person has a number of strategies they can use, rather than relying on one strategy (Tarrier, 1987). People are more likely to use problem-solving strategies when they are experiencing low levels of stress and are more likely to use emotional coping strategies when experiencing high levels of stress (Perona Garcelán & Galán Rodriguez, 2002). Problem-solving strategies are more likely to be effective during low/moderate levels of stress and acceptance-based strategies more effective when people are experiencing high levels of stress during psychotic relapse (Perona Garcelán & Galán Rodriguez, 2002). People's coping strategies are more likely to work if they can identify antecedents and triggers to relapse (Falloon & Talbot, 1981). In summary, if people are able to identify their triggers and early warning signs to relapse, they can use a range of strategies. If utilised at an early stage they are more likely to be successful in avoiding relapse. This underpins the basis of what is termed Relapse Prevention. Service users are supported to identify their triggers, early warning signs and develop a range of coping strategies.

Coping Strategy Enhancement (CSE) is an approach to exploring and identifying coping strategies currently used and to evaluate their effectiveness (Tarrier *et al.*, 1993). It supports people to look at how they can build on or adapt their current coping strategies to make them more effective and to use them more systematically. It also explores what additional coping strategies could be used, in order to increase people's coping strategy repertoire. CSE has been shown to be effective at reducing positive symptoms in psychosis (Tarrier *et al.*, 1993) and is an important part of Relapse Prevention.

Evidence base

Relapse Prevention, using packs such as those described above, has been found to be effective in reducing the risk of relapse in psychosis, particularly in people with first-episode psychosis (e.g. Hewitt & Birchwood, 2002; Gleeson *et al.*, 2009). The findings with regards to people with more severe and enduring psychosis are mixed. Lobban *et al.* (2010) found that people with psychosis in a community mental health team who received manualised individual Relapse Prevention, compared with treatment as usual, had increased time to relapse and increased functioning over time. However, another study looking at Relapse Prevention delivered in a group setting found an improvement in coping knowledge but no significant difference in relapse rates, as measured by admission days (Foster & Jumnoodoo, 2008). Relapse Prevention has also been found to be effective in increasing medication compliance in people with psychosis (Lee *et al.*, 2010). The use of WRAP has been found to result in increased self-advocacy, greater hopefulness, better environmental quality of life and fewer psychiatric symptoms (Jonikas *et al.*, 2011). Service users report that they value Relapse Prevention as it provides a better understanding of their psychosis and better ways of managing it (Pontin *et al.*, 2009). A qualitative study also found that there were advantages to involving relatives in Relapse Prevention (Peters *et al.*, 2011). These advantages included increasing the relatives' understanding of Relapse Prevention and their ability to monitor for triggers and early warning signs; however, some service users expressed concerns about involving relatives in Relapse Prevention.

There are no published studies looking at the effectiveness of Relapse Prevention specifically with difficult to engage populations. Barriers to implementing other psychosocial (e.g. CBT) interventions with this group include: lack of dedicated time; crisis work; lack of supervision; the difficulty of implementing the structured nature of the intervention and the predominance of the medical model (Williams, 2008; Griffiths & Harris, 2008).

National policy

Despite these mixed findings the importance of service users having a Relapse Prevention Plan including a crisis action plan and outlining of the actions to be taken in the event of a crisis has been well established in the UK (e.g. National Service Framework for Mental Health; DoH, 1999). Consequently, care plans now contain a section for relapse planning which typically includes: early warning signs of relapse; triggers to relapse; coping strategies; and who to contact in an emergency. Relapse Prevention is identified as a psychological intervention that should be available to people with psychosis in order to promote recovery. The National Institute for Health and Care Excellence (NICE) guidelines also advocate the use of Relapse Prevention with people with schizophrenia and bipolar disorder (National Institute for Health and Care Excellence, 2009, 2006).

Aims, stages, strategies and techniques

There are a number of factors which make it harder to carry out Relapse Prevention with difficult to engage populations. Poor engagement could be due to a variety of reasons such as substance use (Hall et al., 2001), negative past experience of services or too much focus on medication (Sainsbury Centre for Mental Health, 1998). Gillespie and Meaden (2010) provide a useful overview of factors which have been found to help or hinder engagement. From the outset, collaboratively developing a relapse plan is likely to be more difficult when people are not well engaged with mental health services. Secondly, some difficult to engage service users may feel that they do not suffer from psychosis. If a person does not agree with their diagnosis, then they are less likely to participate in a process that reduces the risk of relapse. Thirdly, difficult to engage service users will often have experienced a number of episodes of relapse, sometimes spanning decades. The picture of relapse is often a complex one that changes over time and as such it can be hard to get an accurate picture of the person's relapse signature, triggers and coping strategies. Fourthly, this population can often find it difficult to remember details of their relapses. This may be due to cognitive difficulties as a result of their psychosis or a reluctance to remember due to the distress it causes.

Engaging difficult to reach service users in Relapse Prevention

Engaging difficult to reach service users in Relapse Prevention work often takes longer and requires a large amount of time to firstly prepare the service user to start the work. This might involve:

- Taking time to build a collaborative, trusting relationship.
- Addressing any worries or fears they might have about engaging in the work. For example, some might fear that if they start talking about their psychotic

experiences they will become worse or their medication may be increased or, worse still, that they will be hospitalised.

- Providing examples of how Relapse Prevention work can be beneficial. For example, discussing the evidence that it reduces the risk of relapse and hospitalisation, increased self-advocacy, greater hopefulness, better environmental quality of life and fewer psychiatric symptoms.
- It can sometimes be helpful for service users to meet other service users who have been through the process and found it beneficial.
- Emphasising that the person is an expert in their own mental health and that the Relapse Prevention process capitalises on this. This also gives the person more control over their own situation.
- Using terminology that fits with the person's understanding of their mental health. For example, some people may find it more acceptable to talk about ways of recognising that they are feeling 'stressed', rather than talking about signs of 'relapse'. Another way of describing Relapse Prevention is 'a way to support you to recognise when things are getting on top of you and looking at what you can do to stay well and out of hospital'.
- Normalising the principle – "We all have times when we get stressed/things get on top of us. It can be useful to know the things that can cause this to happen and what we can do to cope". It can be useful to give examples, "When people get stressed they may have difficulty sleeping, become irritable and not want to talk to anyone. Some people can become stressed if they take on too much. In order to reduce stress people may talk to others about how they are feeling, do some exercise, or reduce the amount of caffeine to help them sleep better". It can be helpful to discuss examples of famous people who have experienced psychosis.

Assessing suitability for Relapse Prevention

There are a number of tools which can help to identify whether a person is likely to engage in Relapse Prevention directly, or whether an indirect approach, involving staff and carers, is more suitable. A person scoring high on the Early Signs Scale (Birchwood et al., 1989) may find it hard to engage in the process due to the intensity of their psychotic experiences. An example of this might be a person who regularly hears voices and consequently finds it hard to concentrate in order to participate in a Relapse Prevention session. The Recovery Style Questionnaire (Drayton et al., 1998) can be used to assess a person's ability to make sense of their psychotic experiences and their willingness to incorporate them into their view of themselves. A person categorised as having a 'sealing over' recovery style by the scale may find it hard to identify with having psychotic experiences and therefore be less likely to engage in Relapse Prevention. The Insight Scale (Birchwood et al., 1994) is another measure that can be employed to assess a person's understanding of their psychosis. Techniques such as normalising and using more acceptable terminology, as mentioned above, may be helpful with people who 'seal over' or who score low on the Insight Scale. It is important to remember that people need not agree with their psychotic diagnosis, or with the medical model of psychosis, in order to be able to benefit from Relapse Prevention. This is where terminology such as that used in the WRAP can be valuable.

Learning from the past

Difficult to engage service users often come with lengthy histories, involving many relapses which may be difficult to remember. Time given to reading over old files is very beneficial, if laborious, but yields rich information. Exact details of antecedents to hospital admission and early warning signs can often be found and recurring themes identified.

Adapting sessions

When carrying out psychological work with a difficult to engage population, the format of individual sessions benefits from adaptation. This might include:

- Shorter sessions, due to concentration difficulties.
- A less formal approach (e.g. taking the opportunity whilst driving to an appointment to discuss the person's early warning signs). Conversely, some people may benefit from regular, structured sessions where the focus is explicitly on Relapse Prevention. This can help people focus on the session and reduce the likelihood of the person introducing other topics (e.g. help with their benefits).
- Repetition of material to ensure retention.
- Making information accessible. For example, use of DVDs to assist psychoeducation and symbolised Relapse Prevention cards for people with reading and/or cognitive difficulties.
- Engaging carers/relatives/friends in the process, with the consent of the service user.

Involving others

It is often very helpful to include people who know the service user well. This could be relatives, partners, friends or paid carers. The involvement of others usually makes a relapse plan far more detailed and useful. The perspective of those who know the person well is very valuable, especially if a person struggles to remember details of their relapse. People can struggle to remember details of their relapse because they were too unwell at the time or because they are reluctant to discuss details that cause them embarrassment. It can be helpful to involve others in all or some of the sessions. Interesting discussions are often had between the service user and the person who knows them well during card sort exercises (cards used to choose from possible relevant relapse experiences). Relapse Prevention sessions provide a safe, controlled environment for people with psychosis to talk to those close to them about their experiences, often for the first time.

Relapse Prevention manual

Psychologists working at Birmingham and Solihull Mental Health NHS Foundation Trust's Assertive Outreach and Non-Acute Inpatient services developed a Relapse Prevention manual in 2006, entitled "Enhancing Wellbeing". The manual incorporated existing approaches developed locally: "Back in the Saddle" (Birchwood *et al*., 2000) and other packs (Smith, 2003) as well as that developed by the Trust's Manic Depression Service. The resulting manual developed is divided into sections on:

1.   Introduction
2.   Getting started
3.   Early signs
4.   Early signs pattern (including stress triggers)
5.   Coping strategies
6.   Action plans
7.   Monitoring
8.   Advance Directives.

Useful tools which were added that were not included in previous manuals:

- A flowchart outlining the Relapse Prevention process (see Figure 4.1). The flowchart identifies the core components in the process of Relapse Prevention and the tools necessary to support the process.
- "Early Signs: A Guide" – a leaflet that can be given to service users outlining the process and how it can be helpful.
- Guidance on completing Relapse Prevention without service user involvement.
- A troubleshooting guide. This includes commonly reported difficulties and possible solutions.
- Card sorts for stress triggers and coping strategies were developed as an addition to existing card sorts for early signs. These were not included in previous manuals. The 'stress triggers' card sort was based on stressful life events taken from the Holmes and Rahe Stress Scale (Holmes & Rahe, 1967). The 'coping strategy' card sort includes fifty strategies (cognitive, behavioural, physiological and sensory). Card sorts are a useful tool to help prompt service users to think about early signs, coping strategies and stress triggers. Service users who are too embarrassed to mention a specific experience may feel able to talk about it when it is shown to them in a card sort. The card sorts also provide a very concrete way of focussing on the topic of Relapse Prevention. This is especially helpful for people who have the tendency to drift off topic.

Screening (Early Signs Scale should be less than 50) – if not consider completing without the person

Hand out and talk through early signs/Relapse Prevention leaflet

Attitude to Relapse and Awareness of Early Signs Interview(s)/questionnaire(s)

Early signs Interview

Early signs checklist or card sort

Timeline (early, middle, late signs)

Stress triggers card sort

Current coping strategies and new/future coping strategies card sort

Action plan: service user action points and service/team action points for early, middle and late signs

Active signs monitoring

Advance Directive

Figure 4.1 Completing early signs with the person

The very action of moving cards to put them in order of occurrence helps people to feel engaged in the process. The card sorts introduce concepts which then serve as a basis for further more detailed discussion.

• Advance Directives.

In order to support staff to engage this complex service user group in Relapse Prevention, a number of tools were included in each section. For example, to try to elicit a person's early warning signs, a member of staff could use an early signs checklist, card sort, prompt sheets (with examples of each early sign) or interview format. This gives staff a number of options to try. There are also versions that can be used with carers, should the service user struggle to identify their relapse signature.

Monitoring strategies

A variety of monitoring strategies were incorporated into the Relapse Prevention manual for assertive outreach service users. These include strategies for service users to self-monitor such as the Early Signs Scale (Birchwood *et al.*, 1989) and Mood Rating Scale (George, 2001). Graphs were also included where service users can plot their scores from the scales to help visually monitor their mental health over time. This can provide positive feedback in an easily accessible format when a person is doing well (i.e. scores are low). It can also alert the person to early signs that they are starting to become unwell (i.e. scores increase) and prompt them to think about utilising coping strategies. Service users and staff are encouraged to develop an Early Signs Scale that is personalised to the service user. This means constructing a checklist of early signs that are pertinent to the individual and getting them to rate the frequency as they would with the Early Signs Scale. This helps monitoring of early signs that are relevant to the person and increases the chances of picking up on signs of relapse at an early stage. It also encourages the service user to home in on the signs that are relevant to them and to monitor them on a regular basis. If a service user is unable to monitor for signs of relapse, then this can be done by people who have regular contact with them, such as paid carers, family members, partners or friends.

Team debriefs

This is a useful procedure for teams when a service user has experienced a relapse (with or without hospital admission). It involves getting the team together to discuss the service user's relapse. It provides a structure for discussing early signs, triggers and coping strategies. This helps the team to amend and update the person's relapse plan based on team observations. It also provides a forum for discussing other things that might be attempted in the future to help the person cope and minimise the chance of future relapses.

The format for team debriefs covers areas such as:

- Possible triggers – specific changes (e.g. drugs/alcohol use, relationships, social circumstances, medication compliance, support, engagement) in the month prior to signs of relapse noted;
- Nature of hospital admission if admitted (e.g. voluntary, compulsory);
- Coping strategies used by the service user and their effectiveness;

- The mental health team's response to signs of relapse and the effectiveness of the response;
- How the mental health team might respond differently next time;
- Interventions that might help reduce the risk of future relapse;
- Changes to be made to the person's relapse plan.

Care planning meetings

Care planning meetings can be a useful forum to construct a relapse plan. These meetings are attended by the key professionals involved in the person's care; e.g. psychiatrist, care co-ordinator, psychologist, etc. This collective knowledge can provide valuable information when compiling a relapse plan. It can highlight gaps in knowledge and prompt staff to collect this information. Additionally it can identify service users who are likely to collaborate in the process. For those who already have a detailed relapse plan, it is a useful arena to review and update the plan from a team perspective. There is evidence that such team-based interventions can have an impact within assertive outreach teams. A recent audit showed an improvement in the completion and quality of triggers, early signs and coping strategies following the introduction of Relapse Prevention training and a weekly care planning slot (Gillespie & Bansal, 2012).

Group work

CBT for schizophrenia delivered in a group format has shown benefits in terms of reduced feelings of hopelessness and improved self-esteem (Barrowclough *et al.*, 2006). However, in this study there were no improvements on measures of symptoms, functioning or relapse. Other studies have also found no reduction in relapse rates following group CBT for schizophrenia (Bechdolf *et al.*, 2004) and group Relapse Prevention interventions (Foster & Jumnoodoo, 2008).

Despite this, there are many potential benefits to carrying out Relapse Prevention in a group format. It facilitates the sharing of experiences and learning from one another. This is a very powerful intervention that cannot be achieved through 1:1 work. Often many people have never had the opportunity to talk to others about their psychotic experiences. It can be highly beneficial for people to realise that they are not alone (the principle of 'universality'; Yalom & Leszcz, 2005). The author's experience of running Relapse Prevention groups in assertive outreach has been very positive. The groups had the core components of:

- Introduction to the Relapse Prevention/wellness action planning approach;
- Introduction to the cognitive behaviour model;
- Psychoeducation about psychosis and other mental health problems such as anxiety and depression;
- Identification of early signs;
- Identification of triggers;

- Coping Strategy Enhancement including:
  - Problem-solving
  - Stress management
  - Sleep management
  - Information on healthy eating and exercise
  - Information from a psychiatrist on medication and the opportunity to ask questions about medication;

- Compilation of a relapse plan by the service user which was then shared with their care co-ordinator and added to by the care co-ordinator if necessary.

When asked about their views of the group, one person said "*it is good to learn that others have the same symptoms as me. It made me feel normal*". It was helpful for people to hear how other people have coped with their mental health problems. Getting information about mental health and coping strategies was also found to be beneficial; another service user stated that "*Getting detailed information about bipolar disorder was helpful and realising that it is not a hopeless illness. There are ways to manage other than medication.*"

   The group showed improvements in depression, anxiety and stress as measured by the Depression, Anxiety & Stress Scale (Lovibond & Lovibond, 1995), which were maintained at six month follow-up. Scores on the Early Signs Scale (Birchwood *et al.*, 1989) including negativity, anxiety, incipient psychosis and disinhibition showed improvement after attending the group, which was also maintained at six month follow-up. People felt they had more control over their relapse, were less fearful of relapse and catastrophised less about relapse (Gillespie, 2012). Two of the people who attended the group were discharged from assertive outreach due to the progress they made. The other three attendees have remained well and out of hospital over the past eighteen months.

Using Advance Directives

A natural follow-on from Relapse Prevention work is the completion of an Advance Directive. This is a document which outlines how a person would like to be supported if they were to become unwell. It details things such as what has worked for them in the past, what has been unhelpful, who they would like to be informed if they are admitted into hospital, dietary needs, spiritual needs, etc. An Advance Directive is completed by the service user, either on their own or with the support of someone such as a Community Psychiatric Nurse, relative or Psychologist.

Case illustration: David

David is a 38-year-old man with a diagnosis of paranoid schizophrenia. He has been with the Assertive Outreach Team (AOT) for less than a year. Prior to coming to the team he was supported by the local Community Mental Health

Team. Unfortunately, his mental health deteriorated eighteen months ago and he was admitted to hospital. David lives with his girlfriend, who he has been with for four years and who is very supportive of him. David has a history of cannabis use but has been abstinent since his last admission to hospital. In his youth, David associated with local gangs. When David's mental health deteriorates he becomes paranoid, thinking that others are looking at him and wish to harm him. At extreme times David believes that his neighbours are spying on him and planning to kill him; he interprets sounds in his house as neighbours tunnelling under his floor, with the aim of harming him. At these times he also hears auditory hallucinations in the form of a young child's cries and believes that the neighbours are harming the child. When unwell, David is at risk of harming others in a bid to protect himself from perceived danger.

Initial assessment and engagement

Initially when David's Care Co-ordinator broached the idea of Relapse Prevention with him, David was sceptical about its usefulness. Some work was done with David outlining the benefits of Relapse Prevention, highlighting that it would give David more control over his mental health problems. David eventually agreed to give it a try and was motivated by the idea of being able to move onto a less intensive mental health team and eventually out of mental health services completely, if he gained more control and better management of his mental health problems.

David's score on the Recovery Style Questionnaire fell into the sealing-over category, indicating that he was someone who may find it hard to engage with Relapse Prevention. In the first few sessions, David was reluctant to talk in detail about his psychotic experiences. Some work was done to reassure David that it was safe to talk about his experiences without fear of hospitalisation and/or increased medication. David's reluctance to discuss his psychosis was in part protective as it served to protect his view of himself as a capable, well-functioning man.

Relapse planning

When carrying out the Relapse Prevention work it was helpful to talk about "signs that you are starting to get stressed about the neighbours" rather than "early warning signs of psychotic relapse". The use of card sorts helped prompt David to talk about his experiences. During the trigger card sort, David opened up about his previous use of cannabis and how this had affected his thoughts, feelings and behaviour. This paved the way to work on addressing his cannabis use, which included psychoeducation about the effects of cannabis and reasons for its use. Relapse and Relapse Prevention cycles were developed (Graham *et al.*, 2004) which helped David identify ways of minimising the risk of smoking cannabis in the future.

Involving David's girlfriend in some of the sessions was very beneficial. She provided useful information about David's early warning signs and what coping strategies worked and what did not. The work was shared with David's Care Co-ordinator who added their perspective to it. Throughout the process David retained ownership of his Relapse Prevention Plan (see Figure 4.2). This was important as it was an intervention that he was collaborating in rather than being done on him (which he described as his previous experience of mental health services when he had been sectioned and taken to hospital by the police). David's plan was shared with his Consultant Psychiatrist and everyone signed it to say that they agreed with it. The plan was then integrated into David's electronic care plan, so that it was accessible to those involved in his care. David asked that a copy be sent to his mother, who he saw regularly. David's plan is reviewed at his six-monthly Care Programme Approach Reviews where everyone involved in his care has the opportunity to update it. David's Care Co-ordinator goes through his early warning signs with him every couple of weeks as a way of monitoring his mental health. Coping strategies are also discussed and rehearsed. For example, if David was spending increasing amounts of time on his own (an early warning sign), then his Care Co-ordinator would discuss what he found helpful as outlined in his plan (e.g. talking to others about how he is feeling, attending the day centre three times a week, visiting his mother).

The Relapse Prevention work has enabled David to have an open dialogue with the AOT and his partner about his mental health and they now have a better understanding of his triggers, early warning signs and coping strategies. The Relapse Prevention work has helped David to take more control over his mental health. It has also provided him with a positive experience of mental health services which has assisted in building a strong, trusting relationship with the AOT. David has remained well and out of hospital.

Conclusions and implications

There are a number of factors that contribute to the successful implementation of Relapse Prevention with difficult to engage service users. Good quality Relapse Prevention *training* from a clinician experienced in Relapse Prevention (preferably experienced in working with difficult to engage service users), using a structured approach/manual ensures that all team members are able to utilise and support this work. Similarly regular *supervision* is important to maintain skills and solve problems encountered. This can be done on a 1:1 basis or in a group format. The latter allows clinicians to learn from one another, share ideas and encourages a reflective approach to relapse prevention. Joint working with someone experienced in Relapse Prevention, in order to build skills and confidence can also be beneficial. A regular review of plans though the debriefing process will ensure that plans are kept up to date. This approach combined with regular audits has been shown to improve the quality and completion of Relapse Plans in AOTs in Birmingham (Gillespie & Bansal, 2012).

Even this more flexible multi-layered approach is difficult to implement. Factors appear to be continuous symptoms, lack of clear triggers and non-use of

Name: David Smith

Date: February 2014

Pattern	Coping strategies
Early signs • Spending more time on my own in my room • Not wanting to see family and friends • Wanting to mix with acquaintances who smoke cannabis • Feeling tense and uptight – neck and head ache • Lack of money • Irritability • Reversed sleep pattern • Stop attending day centre	**What to do** • Talk to staff/partner/mother about how I am feeling and problem-solve any difficulties I am having • Review work on pros and cons of cannabis use • Avoid people who smoke cannabis • Continue attending day centre • Continue to visit mother weekly • Use sleep strategies • Continue to take medication as prescribed
Middle signs • Thinking that people are looking at me strangely • Increased hostility, lack of warmth • Disengage from services • Hearing scraping sounds at night. Think that neighbours are tunnelling under my floor • Wearing dirty clothes, not shaving	**What to do** • See Community Psychiatric Nurse (CPN) weekly as arranged • Ask for review with Psychiatrist and consider increasing medication • Check out paranoid ideas with others • Use relaxation strategies
Late signs • Hearing the sound of a young child crying. Believe that the neighbours are harming a child • Feeling that others want to harm me and feel the need to protect myself e.g. by carrying a knife	**What to do** • Increased visits from CPN • Consider respite • Ask mother to take any potential weapons e.g. knives • If I or others feel that I am a risk to myself or others consider admission and refer to Advance Directive
Known triggers * Smoking cannabis * Stress caused by arguments with girlfriend or family * Not taking medication * Stress caused by lack of money	
Additional information Current medication: x mg Risperidone twice daily Plan shared with: partner, mother, Dr Brown (GP), Lisa Day (Occupational Therapist), Jackie Jones (Day Centre Manager)	
Contact details Mon – Fri, 9–5, contact your team on xxx Outside these hours please contact Home Treatment on xxx	
Signed Person:_____ Care Co-ordinator:_____ Psychiatrist:_____	

Figure 4.2 Early signs action plan

coping strategies. In such cases it may be about staff and carers monitoring for signs of relapse and implementing risk management strategies as appropriate.

Relapse Prevention is a useful intervention for people with psychosis. With adaptations it can be used successfully with people who are difficult to engage.

Further research needs to be carried out on the effectiveness of Relapse Prevention with this difficult to engage population. It would also be useful to compare the effectiveness of delivering Relapse Prevention in a group setting versus 1:1 format.

References

Barrowclough, C., Haddock, G., Lobban, F., Jones, S., Siddle, R., Roberts, C. & Gregg, L. (2006). Group cognitive-behavioural therapy for schizophrenia: Randomised control trial. *British Journal of Psychiatry, 189*, 527–532.

Bechdolf, A., Knost, B., Kuntermann, C., Schiller, S., Klosterkötter, J., Hambrecht, M. & Pukrop, R. (2004). A randomized comparison of group cognitive-behavioural therapy and group psychoeducation in patients with schizophrenia. *Acta Psychiatrica Scandinavica, 110*, 21–28.

Birchwood, M., Smith, J., Macmillan, F., Hogg, B., Prasad, R., Harvey, C. & Bering, S. (1989). Predicting relapse in schizophrenia: The development and implementation of an early signs monitoring system using patients and families as observers. *Psychological Medicine, 19*, 649–656.

Birchwood, M., Smith, J., Drury, V., Healy, J., Macmillan, F. & Slade, M. (1994). A self-report insight scale for psychosis: Reliability, validity and sensitivity to change. *Acta Psychiatrica Scandinavica, 89*, 62–67.

Birchwood, M., Spencer, E. & McGovern, D. (2000). Schizophrenia: Early warning signs. *Advances in Psychiatric Treatment, 6*, 93–101.

Copeland, M. E. (1997). *Wellness Recovery Action Plan.* Dummerston, VT: Peach Press.

DoH (1999). *A National Service Framework for Mental Health: Modern standards & service models.* London: Department of Health.

Docherty, J. P, Van Kammen, D. P., Siris, S. G. & Marder, S. R. (1978). Stages of onset of schizophrenic psychosis. *American Journal of Psychiatry, 135*, 420–426.

Drayton, M., Birchwood, M. & Trower, P. (1998). Early attachment experience and recovery from psychosis. *British Journal of Clinical Psychology, 37*, 269–284.

Falloon, I. & Talbot, R. (1981). Persistent auditory hallucinations: Coping mechanisms and implications for management. *Psychological Medicine, 11*, 329–339.

Foster, J. H. & Jumnoodoo, R. (2008). Relapse prevention in serious and enduring mental illness: A pilot study. *Journal of Psychiatric and Mental Health Nursing, 15*(2), 552–561.

George, S. (2001). *Mood Rating Scale.* Birmingham: Northern Birmingham Mental Health Trust, Manic Depression Service.

Gillespie, M. & Meaden, A. (2010). Psychological processes in engagement. In C. Cupitt (ed.), *Reaching out: The psychology of assertive outreach* (pp. 15–42). Hove, E. Sussex: Routledge.

Gillespie, M. (2012). *Outcomes from wellbeing group in assertive outreach.* Unpublished manuscript, Birmingham and Solihull Mental Health NHS Foundation Trust, Birmingham.

Gillespie, M. & Bansall, K. (2012). *Audit of relapse plans in assertive outreach.* Unpublished manuscript, Birmingham and Solihull Mental Health NHS Foundation Trust, Birmingham.

Gleeson, J. F. M., Cotton, S. M., Alvarez-Jimenez, M., Wade, D., Gee, D., Crisp, K. . . . McGorry, P. D. (2009). A randomized control trial of relapse prevention therapy for first-episode psychosis patients. *Journal of Clinical Psychiatry, 70*(4), 477–486.

Gleeson, J. F. M., Alvarez-Jimenez, M., Cotton, S. M., Parker, A. E. & Hetrick, S. (2010). A systematic review of relapse measurement in randomized controlled trials of relapse prevention in first-episode psychosis. *Schizophrenia Research, 119*, 79–88.

Graham, H. L., Copello, A., Birchwood, M. J., Mueser, K., Orford, J., McGovern, D. . . . Georgiou, G. (2004). *Cognitive-Behavioural Integrated Treatment (C-BIT): A treatment manual for substance misuse in people with severe mental health problems.* Chichester, Sussex: John Wiley & Sons Ltd.

Griffiths, R. & Harris, N. (2008). The compatibility of psychosocial interventions (PSI) and assertive outreach: A survey of managers and PSI-trained staff in UK assertive outreach teams. *Journal of Psychiatric and Mental Health Nursing, 15*, 479–483.

Hall, M., Meaden, A., Smith, J. & Jones, C. (2001). The development and psychometric properties of an observer-rated measure of engagement with mental health services. *Journal of Mental Health, 10*(4), 457–465.

Herz, M. & Melville, C. (1980). Relapse in schizophrenia. *American Journal of Psychiatry, 137*, 801–812.

Hewitt, L. & Birchwood, M. (2002). Preventing relapse of psychotic illness. *Disease Management & Health Outcomes, 10*(7), 395–407.

Holmes, T. H. & Rahe, R. H. (1967). The Social Readjustment Rating Scale. *Journal of Psychosomatic Research, 11*, 213–218.

Jonikas, J. A., Grey, D. D., Copeland, M. E., Razzano, L. A., Hamilton, M. M., Floyd, C. B. . . . Cook, J. A. (2011). Improving propensity for patient self-advocacy through Wellness Recovery Action Planning: Results of a randomized controlled trial. *Community Mental Health Journal*, doi: 10.1007/s10597-011-9475-9. Retrieved March 10, 2014, from http://www.mentalhealthrecovery.com/wrap/documents/Improving PropensityforPatientSelf-Advocacy.pdf.

Jorgenson, P. (1998). Early signs of psychotic relapse in schizophrenia. *British Journal of Psychiatry, 172*, 327–330.

Lee, S. H., Choi, T. K., Suh, S., Kim, Y. W., Kim, B., Lee, E. & Yook, K. H. (2010). The effectiveness of a psychosocial intervention for relapse prevention in patients with schizophrenia receiving risperidone via long-acting injection. *Psychiatry Research, 175*, 195–199.

Lobban, F., Taylor, L., Chandler, C., Tyler, E., Kinderman, P., Kolamunnage-Dona, R. . . . Morriss, R. K. (2010). Enhanced relapse prevention for bipolar disorder by community mental health teams: cluster feasibility randomised trial. *British Journal of Psychiatry, 196*, 59–63.

Lovibond, P. F. & Lovibond, S. H. (1995). The structure of negative emotional states: Comparison of the Depression Anxiety Stress Scales (DASS) with the Beck Depression and Anxiety Inventories. *Behaviour Research and Therapy, 33*, 335–343.

National Institute for Health and Care Excellence (2006). *The management of bipolar disorder in adults, children and adolescents in primary and secondary care, NICE Clinical Guideline 38.* London: National Institute for Health and Care Excellence.

National Institute for Health and Care Excellence (2009). *Schizophrenia: Core interventions in the treatment and management of schizophrenia in adults in primary and secondary care, NICE Clinical Guideline 82.* London: National Institute for Health and Care Excellence.

Perona Garcelán, S. & Galán Rodriguez, A. (2002). Coping strategies in psychotics: conceptualization and research results. *Psychology in Spain, 6*(1), 26–40.

Peters, S., Pontin, E., Lobban, F. & Morriss, R. (2011). Involving relatives in relapse prevention for bipolar disorder: A multi-perspective qualitative study of value and barriers. *BMC Psychiatry, 11*(1), 172.

Pontin, E., Peters, S., Lobban, F., Rogers, A. & Morriss, R. K. (2009). Enhanced relapse prevention for bipolar disorder: A qualitative investigation of value perceived for service users and care coordinators. *Implementation Science, 4*(4), doi:10.1186/1748-5908-4-4.

Sainsbury Centre for Mental Health (1998). *Keys to engagement: Review of care for people with severe mental illness who are hard to engage with services.* London: Sainsbury Centre for Mental Health.

Smith, J. (2003). *Early warning signs: A self-management training manual for individuals with psychosis.* Worcester, UK: Worcester Community and Mental Health Trust.

Subotnik, K. L. & Neuchterlein, K. H. (1988). Prodromal signs and symptoms of schizophrenic relapse. *Journal of Abnormal Psychology, 97*, 405–412.

Tarrier, N. (1987). An investigation of residual psychotic symptoms in discharged schizophrenic patients. *British Journal of Clinical Psychology, 26*, 141–143.

Tarrier, N., Beckett, R., Harwood, S., Baker, A., Yusupoff, L. & Ugarteburu, I. (1993). A trial of two cognitive-behavioural methods of treating drug-resistant residual psychotic symptoms in schizophrenic patients: I. Outcome. *British Journal of Psychiatry, 162*, 524–532.

Williams, C. H. J. (2008). Cognitive behaviour therapy within assertive outreach teams: Barriers to implementation: A qualitative peer audit. *Journal of Psychiatric and Mental Health Nursing, 15*, 850–856.

Yalom,. I. D. & Leszcz, M. (2005). *The theory and practice of group psychotherapy.* New York: Basic Books.

Chapter 5

Brief interventions and single sessions as stages in a change process for people with psychosis

Deborah Allen

Introduction

> People are generally better persuaded by the reasons which they have themselves discovered, than by those which have come to the mind of others.
>
> (Pascal, 1958: 10)

In this chapter, the therapeutic benefits of single sessions and brief interventions for people with psychosis who are hard to engage are explored. Whilst such brief contact can be valuable for promoting engagement or as preparation for longer term work, it is proposed it can be equally valuable as stand-alone interventions. The philosophical underpinning of brief interventions is firstly reviewed before the strategies and techniques which may be utilised to make limited contact useful are described. This work draws on a number of perspectives and approaches which are drawn together into a clinically useful framework. The emphasis in brief intervention is upon enabling individuals to make informed choices about how and where to get assistance and to feel empowered to manage their own difficulties, without needing further professional support.

Theoretical background and development: brief interventions

An important point to consider when planning any intervention with people experiencing psychosis is the role of trauma. This is especially relevant to consider when advocating for the role of brief interventions. People may struggle to engage in a longer term therapeutic relationship for a variety of reasons. Trauma in particular may mitigate against the person's ability to form and make use of such relationships. A number of authors now attest to how psychotic disorders, particularly schizophrenia, are often borne out of painful and traumatic life experiences (Boyle, 1990; Dillon *et al.*, 2012; Johnstone, 2014; Larkin & Morrison, 2006; Murphy *et al.*, 2013; Turner *et al.*, 2013*)*. Read and Gumley (2008) describe how childhood trauma impacts upon attachment relationships and subsequently affects the way in which people with psychosis regulate their sensory experience and internal mental states; potentially affecting their ability to develop a coherent sense of self. Turner *et al.* (2013) in their review further highlight how trauma often results in feelings of shame. Shame has been described as a social emotion which may prevent individuals seeking help since they anticipate existing negatively in the minds of other people (Gilbert, 2000). This may be further reinforced by the appraisal of powerful voices which exercise their power (including prohibiting therapy and disclosure) by means of threats to reveal bad or shameful aspects of the person to others (Meaden *et al.*, 2012).

In addition to the role trauma may play in the causes of psychosis and personality development Larkin and Morrison (2006) and more recently Turner *et al.* (2013) suggest that acquiring a diagnosis of psychosis can itself be a source of further trauma; recognising the stigmatising impact of receiving such a diagnosis. Coles *et al.* (2009) suggest that the adoption of an 'illness' model may lead to the personalisation of difficulties and blaming the person seeking help if changes are not achieved. This may be experienced by the person as being blamed for an internal emotional experience (Hagan & Smail, 1997b; Masland *et al.*, 2014). Perhaps unsurprisingly people may be less likely to engage in therapeutic interventions, especially given that discussion may be shame-evoking (Gilbert, 2000). They may consequently avoid relationships in an attempt to keep themselves safe and subsequently isolate themselves from help, missing opportunities to gain alternative perspectives or develop alternative understandings about abusive and psychotic experiences (Hagan & Gregory, 2001: 197).

In addition to trauma and shame issues the prospect of engaging in a discussion of experiences may also act as a trigger for intrusive thoughts about a recurrence of psychotic illness (White & Gumley, 2009). Previous experiences of mental health services may itself have been traumatic: admission under section, being restrained and injected. Contacts with services are also likely to feature, where disclosure of psychotic symptoms and experiences may have led to compulsory treatment and detainment (Meaden *et al.*, 2012).

Meaden *et al.* (2012) highlight the role of power in therapeutic relationships and how this mirrors the now well-established power relationships between voice hearers and their voices and other social relationships. Hagan and Smail (1997a) however suggest that talking therapy alone is not able to facilitate change, suggesting that therapy will not release powers from within the individual to make a difference to their circumstances. Instead, they suggest there is a need to address components of power within an individual's life in order to facilitate change and recovery. An increasing body of literature emphasises how people are often taking action that they believe is best for them and has logical foundations; that is, individuals act in ways to gain positive outcomes for themselves (Gilbert, 2010; Hagan & Gregory, 2001; Miller & Rollnick, 1991; Smail, 2005; Talmon, 1990). Kelly's (1955) Personal Construct Theory proposes that human beings are already 'scientists' in their own right and take action to prove or disprove personal hypotheses about how to act in the world. However, as a result of trauma, avoiding being re-traumatised, feeling ashamed or stigmatised people find it difficult to self-heal but for these same reasons are unable to easily engage in helping relationships. As Hagan and Smail (1997a, 1997b) recognise, people who have experienced abuse can place abuse interpretations onto other inter-personal relationships through operant conditioning.

Helpful models for initiating a therapeutic enquiry that is supportive of the brief therapy approach, which takes into account the barriers mentioned above, advocate the practitioner as the 'naïve enquirer' (Barker, 2005; Corrigan *et al.*, 2001; Miller & Rollnick, 1991; Padesky, 1993). The role of 'naïve enquirer' allows the professional to suspend judgements about what the person is saying; to actually listen to the individual and gain an understanding about what is happening for the person; explore what they have already attempted in order to resolve the difficulty and explore where they would prefer to be. There is also an assumption that the person can identify answers and solutions to their own difficulty. It is therefore not the responsibility of the professional to formulate professional answers/solutions. In this sense it is akin to the principle of guided discovery (Padesky, 1993): to explore what solutions the person has available to them to resolve the difficulty.

Often, professionals can adopt a role of trying to 'fix' a problem or having to 'come up with' all the answers. When a professional adopts this role, they can often fall into a trap of trying to generate solutions, meaning they are listening to their own thoughts and not listening to the person. This can act to make the professional feel threatened by the problem and can inadvertently communicate that the problem is frightening or overwhelming, which may impact on the individual's sense of shame or that they are not seen as valuable in the mind of another person (Gilbert, 2000; Turner *et al.*, 2013). Brief approaches are of necessity solution focused. The aim is therefore to enhance the sense of personal power of the individual, to change their circumstances and increase their ability to make the changes necessary to make improvements in their life (Hagan & Smail, 1997a).

In developing a brief model of naive enquiry that promotes engagement and enables the person with psychosis to generate their own solutions, it is important subsequently to develop some type of formulation. Dudley and Kuyken (2014) have proposed a 5Ps formulation model (described below) which can usefully support a brief approach. It is proposed that 'problems' are identified as such due to the arrival of a set of circumstances at a point in time that put a person in a situation of Cognitive Dissonance (Festinger & Carlsmith, 1957). Possible 'solutions' or movement to Cognitive Assonance may have been blocked by the person or, more likely, the solutions have been set with very fine parameters (restricted by complex elements of deprivations of power) that cause difficulties. Thinking about problems in this way begins the process of generating possible solutions. Most 'problems' have an infinite number of solutions, but solutions can be 'blocked' or restricted because some of the solutions are not possible or available at the point in time that the 'problem' arrived. Furthermore, the solutions that are available may not be palatable for the individual and/or society. Thus, people become 'stuck' with their difficulty, which can feel disabling and, over time, people can forget they ever had solutions. Furthermore, when people feel 'stuck' with a problem state, with solutions feeling limited, ideas about suicide can often begin to grow, as suicide appears the ultimate solution to any problem.

Aims, stages, strategies and techniques

It is proposed that creating a space where the individual is enabled to talk without shame or negative judgement about their difficulties is an important first step in improving mental health. Talking with other people without shame and negative judgements allows an opportunity to explore what the person has tried in order to resolve their difficulties. This involves active listening to the person and hearing what the individual has to say, without making judgements about the rightness or wrongness of these decisions (Rogers, 1967).

Aims

The aim of intervention is to become inquisitive about the person and to create an environment where the person feels comfortable to share their experiences and their understanding about themselves, based upon their life experience. Within this environment, the role of the professional is not to generate solutions for the person, but to explore the solutions the person has generated for themselves and to enhance or enable solutions to become unblocked, so the person are instrumental in their own change process. The role of the professional is primarily that of another human being, who is prepared to spend time to listen to someone, hear what they are saying, empathise and validate the person's position and tolerate the distress that the person may be expressing. This will involve asking meaningful questions (Padesky, 1993) that allow the person to gain improved understanding of their own position and 'problem', whilst ensuring the person is not shamed or blamed for their position (Gilbert, 2009; Hagan & Smail, 1997a).

A model of a 'problem' representation

The role of a brief or single session intervention is about exploring the problem area and possible solutions that are available, finding out why they are not amenable and exploring what other solutions are available and 'unblocking' solution blocks; that is, removing the barriers that the individual has placed on their own solutions. In this way, the individual gains the satisfaction and sense of enablement from being the person responsible for their own solution and therefore has greater ability to 'solve' their problems for themselves in the future.

Stages

Getting to know the person

The first stage is getting to know the person. This can be done in a number of ways, without necessarily meeting them. Indeed the person may not be willing to engage with professionals at this stage. Meeting with professionals who know the person with the mental health difficulty and applying a 5Ps shared formulation (Dudley & Kuyken, 2014) at this stage can give insight into what the 'problem' may be, which may not be perceived as a difficulty for the person with the mental health problem. Details of approaches that can be applied to get to know the person can be found in the 'Strategies and techniques' section. Once more is known about the person, it is then possible to bring together an understanding of the 'problem' and what may have been tried to resolve it already. After this is done, it can then be possible to explore if solutions have been blocked and explore if they can be unblocked. Alternatively, it can be possible to generate solutions that the person or care team had not thought of applying to the problem. The approach can help to generate an understanding of the difficulties and an exploration of what the person and/or agencies have tried to manage the difficulties. In the application of this model of brief therapy, changes can be suggested in order to explore if this will support engagement for the individual.

As part of the formulation process it is important to consider the role of shame and anticipate (perhaps by sharing with the team what is known about shame) its likely impact if it is possible to meet with the person. Gilbert (2010) recognises that when people are struggling with shame they can try to avoid the shame-evoking experiences by applying coping strategies which may have the unintended consequences of placing people in situations where the shaming experience reoccurs. Hagan and Gregory (2001) also demonstrate that people who have experienced abusive inter-personal relationships are likely to have developed 'lessons learned to survive'; that is, are likely to have developed a number of strategies to avoid situations where abuse is likely to re-occur or may have developed attributions to self about why they have been abused that can act to offer unusual presentations about the causes of events or difficulties. Abusive life experiences can shape personal understanding about capabilities and can generate causal attributions to self. Thus, when a person describes what is working, it is important to remain inquisitive and non-critical about coping strategies. Preparing for this meeting with the client may be seen as a pre-contemplative stage for the therapist and team.

The brief session

In this stage Motivational Interviewing questions (Miller & Rollnick, 1991) are used to explore contradictions in coping styles and can gently challenge attributions for difficulties that have been incorrectly attributed to self. Thus, it can be possible to support people to understand that their coping strategy may be the thing that is keeping the difficulty going and leaving the person stuck with their 'problem' as a means to be protected from a fear that has developed due to a significant life event. Listening to the person, allowing them to explain what they are struggling with, without judgements (blame, criticism or punishment) and allowing them to understand their own difficulty, without the need to try and fix the problem for the person, can help introduce a process of guided discovery (Padesky, 1993). The aim here is to explore how they arrived at the difficulty and generate solutions that can be more helpful.

Strategies and techniques

5Ps formulation model

Application of the 5Ps formulation model allows definition of the difficulty (the Presenting difficulty); where the difficulty began (the Predisposing factors); what might be happening to keep the difficulty going (the Perpetuating factors); exploration of stressors that make the difficulty worse (Precipitating factors) and exploration of skills and resources the person has to manage and resolve the difficulty (Protective factors). Involving professionals in its development can give insight into what a person may be struggling with, but also allow exploration of things that services may be struggling with too.

Interviewing style

Instead of adopting a deficit model that assumes the individual has something wrong with them, this brief therapy approach employs the principles first proposed by Kelly (1955), and later by Hagan and Gregory (2001) and Gilbert (2010), that individuals are doing the best they can and may need to share their life experiences and methods of coping in order to gain a different perspective and find different solutions.

Adopting the interviewing style developed by Miller and Rollnick (1991) allows respectful exploration. Interviewing should adhere to five principles: express empathy; develop discrepancy; avoid argumentation; roll with resistance and support self-efficacy. In applying these principles, it is possible to help an individual understand their own problem in greater detail and gain insight into some of the reasons why their own solutions may be blocked and explore opportunities to 'open up' blocked solutions so the problem state can change. This, coupled with Gilbert's (2010) environment for the expression of compassion (that is: being motivated to relieve suffering; noticing distress; having sympathy for what the distress feels like; having the ability to tolerate the distress; being empathic towards the distress and approaching the distress without judgement), can allow for the meaningful exploration of the difficulty.

Problem questions

The Tidal Model (Barker, 2005) offers some useful 'problem' questions, remembering that it is a collation of circumstances arriving at a point in time which lead to the problem. 'Why this? Why now?' allows exploration of the Presenting difficulty. The aim is to develop insight into what the person has tried in order to resolve the 'problem'. This promotes further insight into 'What works for the person?' The use of this question allows for an exploration of what resources/solutions the individual currently has at their disposal and what might be stopping them utilising these resources. When considering the 'What works for the person?', it can be possible to explore if the person is trying to achieve something or escape from the emotional distress of a situation (possibly linked to a trauma memory).

Case illustration: Paul

Paul was 30 years old at the time of brief intervention. He was troubled by psychotic experiences for many years and had rejected all previous attempts to provide help. He also used substances problematically (daily heroin use) and attended a Needle and Syringe Exchange (NSE) programme. Paul regularly missed appointments and when he did come to the NSE he said little, obtained clean syringes and left.

The 'problem' definition

In Paul's case, the 'problem' existed for a number of people and not necessarily for Paul. Concerns were raised about Paul from a number of sources, including the Police and Social Care (housing officers) regarding his general health and wellbeing and living situation, but Paul never asked for support or acknowledged that he needed it. Concerns continued to be expressed and a multi-professional–multi-agency meeting was arranged in order to share ideas and possible solutions. The 5Ps approach was suggested as a useful framework to support this. Present at the meeting were the local police Community Beat Officer; the Housing Officer from Social Care; the HIV Nurse from the local hospital, along with the NSE Tier II worker; NSE manager and the Clinical Psychologist (the chapter author).

Information from the NSE

Paul was injecting heroin daily, which put him in contact with individuals in society that may have exploited his vulnerability. He attended the NSE twice a week, when free fruit was distributed and on benefits day. He always collected clean injecting equipment and returned used equipment. The NSE worker reported that Paul was shy, avoided inter-personal contact and was a loner. He could often be seen walking miles away from his local area. Paul was typically not well kempt and experienced hearing voices. He was believed to be homeless/living rough.

Information from the HIV Nurse

Paul was known to be infected with HIV and Hepatitis C. This information had been gathered following an incident when he had been attacked whilst living rough and taken to the local hospital. Paul had attended to have his HIV and Hepatitis C status confirmed and had attended for some viral load monitoring, but when his viral load increased, he stopped attending. This had raised some Public Health concerns as Paul was living rough and when begging, he had contact with the public.

Information from the Police

Paul was known to the Police as he could sometimes be seen in public shouting at unseen stimuli, which led to increased public attention. He had been detained by the Police under Section 136 of the Mental Health Act (1983) on occasion but was not detained further once assessed as it was felt that he was experiencing Drug Induced Psychosis. He was not offered an intervention from Mental Health services, but instructed to stop his illicit drug use.

Paul would sometimes be found begging in the local town and was occasionally arrested for this. He was known to be homeless, which incurred Public Order offences and a criminal record. He was instructed to address his homelessness, but was perceived to have not taken action on this by the Police.

Paul had been involved in a number of assaults and had experienced bullying and intimidation from other people but had never pressed charges against other people for this. On one occasion, he had been assaulted which necessitated going to hospital. This resulted in the identification of HIV and Hepatitis C infection. Generally, Paul was non-violent, non-threatening and kept himself to himself.

Information from the Social Care Housing Officer

Paul had been re-housed by Social Care and was placed in shared accommodation. His tenancy agreement had been violated due to noise from Paul (believed to be him shouting at unseen stimuli and cleaning at unsociable hours); some rent arrears; and inviting people to the property that resulted in criminal activity and threats of violence. He had been offered accommodation in the local Hostel, but Paul had declined, preferring to live on the street. This information was used to generate the 5Ps shared formulation (see Figure 5.1).

The 5Ps formulation highlighted the symbiotic relationship between all of the presenting difficulties and how they were acting to generate a vicious cycle of coping that meant the 'problem' was difficult to resolve. This allowed all of the professionals involved to see how Paul was trying to resolve his difficulties (e.g. avoiding others, using heroin to cope) but how these solutions generated further problems. This engendered a more helpful and empathic response when professionals had contact with him.

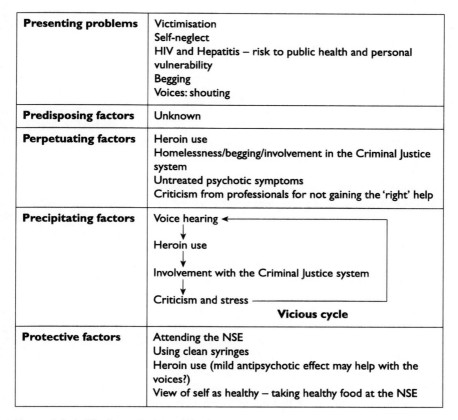

Presenting problems	Victimisation Self-neglect HIV and Hepatitis – risk to public health and personal vulnerability Begging Voices: shouting
Predisposing factors	Unknown
Perpetuating factors	Heroin use Homelessness/begging/involvement in the Criminal Justice system Untreated psychotic symptoms Criticism from professionals for not gaining the 'right' help
Precipitating factors	Voice hearing ← ↓ Heroin use ↓ Involvement with the Criminal Justice system ↓ Criticism and stress **Vicious cycle**
Protective factors	Attending the NSE Using clean syringes Heroin use (mild antipsychotic effect may help with the voices?) View of self as healthy – taking healthy food at the NSE

Figure 5.1 A 5Ps formulation of Paul

Drawing on Hagan and Gregory's (2001) 'Lessons Learned to Survive' Model, this suggests that Paul may have learnt that other people cannot cope with his distress. Others responding negatively to his experience of voice hearing and by his use of heroin may have perpetuated this. As an initial plan it was proposed that those involved might usefully build on Paul's Protective factors by offering a number of consistent responses whenever he had contact with each service.

1. Empathise with Paul's predicament;
2. Praise his attempts to live a healthy lifestyle;
3. Always offer help even if rejected.

This simple consistent response was an attempt to ensure that Paul gained concise instructions, which was important as his ability to think clearly was likely to be impeded by his experience of auditory hallucinations and drug use. This approach gradually increased his attendance at the NSE and opened up the possibility of engaging Paul in therapeutic contact.

Engagement with Paul

Being around in the Exchange allowed observation of Paul and his interactions with other people, as well as providing the opportunity for informal contacts and familiarisation with the Psychologist. Whenever these contacts occurred unconditional positive regard was offered along with questions about his healthy lifestyle and his attempts to remain healthy; for example, he was often asked how far he had walked and what he had seen on his travels. In a non-threatening way, Paul's life was explored and he began to get used to people asking after him and his wellbeing in a non-critical manner. Paul explained that he walked because he liked walking and that he was interested in maintaining his physical fitness. In this way, information was gathered to begin to compose a hypothesis about Paul's 'Personal Theory', that was, "I am a physically fit person". Furthermore, it was hypothesised that the answer offered by Paul may have given insight into the question 'What works for this person?' That was, he may have been using walking to help him regulate/distract himself from the 'voices' (a coping strategy).

This information formed the basis of a Motivational Interviewing approach to addressing the discrepancy between Paul's 'Personal Theory' and his untreated infectious disease status. Validation was offered to Paul about his 'Personal Theory' as comment was made about him coming to the Exchange on the days when free fruit was distributed. Linking the items of positive action together helped Paul to understand that many of his actions were positive and logical, thus promoting his self-efficacy. Paul then began to seek out the Psychologist to report how far he had walked. With interest being paid to Paul and offering positive affirmation related to Paul's skills and abilities that were not related specifically to his 'problem', it became apparent that Paul was willing to engage with professionals and offer further insight that could be used in a Motivational Interviewing approach. Interactions with Paul became opportunities to 'sow seeds' of engagement with Paul about how he might utilise his skills to make changes to his life. After having exposure to the Psychologist, Paul agreed to meet for a single session, to explore how he could improve his fitness.

The single session

Paul explained how he had been a soldier in the past and was due for active service in the Gulf War, but had been involved in a violent bullying attack by his army peers. From this time, he had strived to gain his peers' support, but to no avail, which had led to depression. He had been medically discharged from the army due to depression and this had destroyed his goal of gaining a medal. He reported that many of the voices he heard were related to criticism of his actions and some had 'flashback' qualities of his peers saying how terrible he was as a soldier.

At this point it was tempting to ask for more detail from Paul about the actions of his peers, in order to gain the full extent of the trauma he had experienced. However, to ask these questions may have been too invasive for Paul, with the possibility of evoking a sense of shame that may have made him want to end the session. The role of the intervention, as detailed by Hagan and Smail (1997b: 273), is to enable the individual to 'confront his/her abuser(s) in the real world, outside of the consultation room' rather than the role of the intervention being to confront inner painful memories. Instead, it was pertinent to validate Paul's experience (express empathy) as being very difficult to manage and to help him understand that his experiences can be managed and understood (distress tolerance).

The initial focus was on how Paul felt powerless to take action, noting that not acting was understandable in some situations (being outnumbered by peers) but emphasising where he had power to influence the situation in the present. It also emerged that Paul's voices undermined him by criticising him constantly for his actions past and present. We defined his problem as 'People keep hassling me!' From this statement, we drew out his attempts to stop people 'hassling' him and helped him to understand why his attempts to stop this had acted to keep the problem going, as depicted in Figure 5.2. Blocks and current solutions were identified.

This visual depiction was constructed in the session with Paul. It allowed him to understand why his actions had acted to keep the difficulties going. The discrepancy between the professional's perception of Paul's heroin use as being

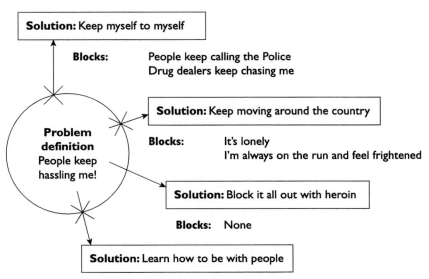

Figure 5.2 The 'problem' representation for Paul, with explorations of solutions and blocks to solutions

the 'problem' and Paul's use of heroin being the 'solution' was highlighted. For Paul, heroin use was a coping strategy to manage other difficulties in life. Gaining alternative 'solutions' that Paul generated to address his difficulties was therefore paramount for Paul to feel enabled to adopt and undertake the changes necessary to improve his situation.

We were then able to discuss alternative solutions to the 'problem'. We discussed how he might begin to change his dialogue with his voices: reminding the voices he had done the best he could to manage his situation. We next explored if Paul could gain some meaningful existence in his life, other than gaining a medal for a worthy cause. Again, using Paul's own Personal Theory, we discussed becoming a Gym Instructor or a Teacher as a means to maintain his physical fitness and help other people. This fitted Paul's Personal Theory as he thought that medals might be won for his athleticism. It was then possible to identify potential barriers to achieving this goal. This highlighted his opiate use and infectious disease status. Paul reported that he did use the heroin to control the voices and with a new strategy to control the voices, he felt he might get his heroin use under control. The best course of action was to be decided by Paul emphasising his personal power.

Outcomes for Paul

Paul did not volunteer for a further session but the fact that he engaged in a single session and identified some possible solutions was significant progress for him. He had also been more open about his difficulties than at any time previously. He did not feel judged, but listened to. He continued to attend the NSE. It is hoped that this positive experience of a therapeutic contact will encourage Paul to engage in obtaining further support. With Paul's permission these solutions were shared with others involved in the formulation process. In this way the simple consistent approach described earlier as a vehicle for engagement can be built upon; reminding Paul of his goals and solutions when opportunities are presented. Paul's recovery journey continues.

Reflecting on the case

There are a number of challenges to the use of single session interventions, but these are often conceptual, rather than actual. As Talmon (1990) points out, the use of single sessions are not amenable to the assessment of 'success' and can often be perceived by practitioners as 'failures'. There is a perception that a person with mental health difficulties not wanting more of any one intervention is related to the degree of success/usefulness that the intervention has to offer. Without a request for further contact, it may be perceived that a person may not want more or that the content was not useful and therefore failed. This may be a valid argument in a climate of outcome measures, evidence-based practice, clinical governance and ensuring that what we do with people works. However, this actually flies in the face of how we, as humans, solve problems. If one thinks of a time in life when one might feel stuck with a problem, we often turn to someone we know to discuss the problem and in so sharing the problem, find we had solutions for ourselves. It may not be that our confidant gave us good advice or told us what to do, but just sharing the problem and putting it in a format that allows it to be structured into a conversation could be solution enough. In such circumstances, it would be unusual for the other person to offer us a meeting in a week's time, to discuss the problem again – and bizarre for them to offer us a questionnaire to assess how useful the discussion was or to assess the outcome of our 'chat'! In a similar vein, it would be unrealistic to expect that one talk has 'solved' all of Paul's problems. All that was expected was some improved understanding of what he wanted to do next. The Tidal Model (Barker, 2005) recognises that our mental health 'ebbs and flows' over time, along with most aspects of power in our life (energy, money, strength, determination, inter-personal relationships, etc.). It may be difficult for mental health services to solve all of people's problems and often, when it tries to, it fails. To recognise what we, as individuals can do and what we cannot do and to accept that we cannot do what we can't do.

Conclusions and implications

The approach described in this chapter enables possible limited contact with people who may be difficult to engage in formal mental health settings. A limited contact can become a useful exercise, rather than being perceived as a 'failure' to engage. It also recognises that a single session or brief intervention will not resolve a person's difficulties overall, but can act to begin the process of enablement of change and the recognition that positive change can occur. The approach can also facilitate the communication of a consistent response for people involved with the person who is struggling with their mental health. This can enable the development of a useful communication between people, rather than the development of a blaming and critical interaction.

Adopting the role of facilitator for a person to explore their own understanding of their difficulties places the professional supporter in a different role. Rather than enabling a person to gain the insight and solution ideas from the professional, the meeting allows for the person to generate solutions to their own difficulties. This can mean that people are more likely to act upon solutions as they are self-generated. Thus, the meeting between professional and person has the potential to be an enabling relationship, rather than the person going away from a meeting with a list of 'things to do' and maybe feeling they will be criticised if they do not act upon the guidance from the professional. The approach also recognises that the person has solutions and supporting people to enable their own solutions can act to restore self-efficacy, self-confidence and self-esteem. These features can support the person's sense of personal power to control their own destiny.

References

Barker, P. (2005). *The Tidal Model: A guide for mental health professionals.* Hove, E. Sussex: Brunner-Routledge.

Boyle, M. (1990). *Schizophrenia: A scientific delusion?* London: Routledge.

Coles, S., Diamond, B. & Keenan, S. (2009). Clinical psychology in psychiatric services: The magician's assistant? *Clinical Psychology Forum, 198,* 5–10.

Corrigan, P., McCracken, S. & Holmes, E. (2001). Motivational Interviews as goal assessment for persons with psychiatric disability. *Community Mental Health Journal, 37,* 113–122.

Dillon, J., Johnstone, L. & Longden, E. (2012). Trauma, dissociation, attachment and neuroscience: A new paradigm for understanding severe mental distress. *The Journal of Critical Psychology, Counselling and Psychotherapy, September, 12,* 145–155.

Dudley, R. & Kuyken, W. (2014). Case formulation in cognitive behavioural therapy: A principle-driven approach. In L. Johnstone & R. Dallos (eds), *Formulation in psychology and psychotherapy: Making sense of people's problems* (2nd edn; pp. 18–44). London: Routledge.

Festinger, L. & Carlsmith, J. (1957). Cognitive consequences of forced compliance. *Journal of Abnormal and Social Psychology, 58,* 203–210.

Gilbert, P. (2000). The relationship of shame, social anxiety and depression: The role of evaluation of social rank. *Clinical Psychology and Psychotherapy, 7,* 174–189.

Gilbert, P. (2009). *The compassionate mind.* London: Constable & Robinson.

Gilbert, P. (2010). *Compassion Focused Therapy: the CBT distinctive features series.* London: Routledge.

Hagan, T. & Gregory, K. (2001). Group work with survivors of childhood sexual abuse. In P. Pollock (ed.), *Cognitive analytical therapy for adult survivors of childhood sexual abuse: Approaches to treatment and case management* (pp. 190–205). Chichester, Sussex: John Wiley and Sons.

Hagan, T. & Smail, D. (1997a). Power mapping-I. Background and basic methodology. *Journal of Community and Applied Social Psychology, 7,* 257–267.

Hagan, T. & Smail, D. (1997b). Power mapping-II. Practical application: The example of child sexual abuse. *Journal of Community and Applied Social Psychology, 7,* 269–284.

Johnstone, L. (2014). Using formulation in teams. In L. Johnstone & R. Dallos (eds.), *Formulation in psychology and psychotherapy: Making sense of people's problems* (2nd edn; pp. 216–242). Hove, E. Sussex: Routledge.

Kelly, G. (1955). *The psychology of personal constructs.* New York: Norton.

Larkin, W. & Morrison, A. (2006). *Trauma and psychosis: New directions for theory and therapy.* London: Routledge.

Masland, S., Hooley, J., Tully, L., Dearing, K. & Gotlib, I. (2014). Cognitive-processing biases in individuals high on perceived criticism. *Clinical Psychological Science, 28,* 1–12.

Meaden, A., Keen, N., Aston, R., Barton, K., & Bucci, S. (2012). *Cognitive therapy for command hallucinations: An advanced practical companion.* Hove, E. Sussex: Routledge.

Miller, W. & Rollnick, S. (1991) *Motivational Interviewing: Preparing people to change addictive behaviour.* New York: Guilford Press.

Murphy, J., Houston, J., Shevlin, M. & Adamson, G. (2013). Childhood sexual trauma, cannabis use and psychosis: Statistically controlling for pre-trauma psychosis and psychopathology. *Social Psychiatry and Psychiatric Epidemiology, 48,* 853–861.

Padesky, C. (1993). Socratic Questioning: Changing minds of guided discovery? Keynote address delivered at the European Congress of Behavioural and Cognitive Therapies, London, 24 September 1993. Accessed February 2014 from: padesky.com/newpad/wp-content/uploads/2012/11/socquest.pdf.

Pascal, B. (1958). *Pascal's pensées*. USA: E. P. Dutton & Co., Inc.

Read, J. & Gumley, A. (2008). Can attachment theory help explain the relationship between childhood adversity and psychosis? *Attachment: New Directions in Psychotherapy and Relational Psychoanalysis*, *2*, 1–35.

Rogers, C. (1967). *On becoming a person: A therapist's view of psychotherapy*. London: Constable & Co.

Smail, D. (2005). *Power, interest and psychology: Elements of a social materialist understanding of distress*. Ross-on-Wye, UK: PCCS Books.

Talmon, M. (1990). *Single session therapy: Maximising the effect of the first (and often only) therapeutic encounter*. San Francisco, CA: Jossey-Bass.

Turner, M., Bernard, M., Birchwood, M., Jackson, C. & Jones, C. (2013). The contribution of shame to post-psychotic trauma. *British Journal of Clinical Psychology*, *52*, 162–182.

White, R. & Gumley, A. (2009). Postpsychotic post traumatic stress disorder. Associations with fear of reoccurrence and intolerance of uncertainty. *The Journal of Nervous and Mental Disease*, *197*, 841–849.

Part II

Innovations in interventions for individuals

Chapter 6

Cognitive Behavioural Therapy for emotional dysfunction following psychosis

The role of emotional (dys)regulation

Mark Bernard, Chris Jackson and Max Birchwood

Introduction

There is a growing body of evidence to suggest that Cognitive Behavioural Therapy for psychosis (CBTp) is effective for reducing distress following psychosis and it is recommended as a treatment of choice (NICE, 2009). However, doubts about the efficacy of CBTp remain (e.g. Lynch *et al.*, 2010), and it has been argued that there is confusion regarding the choice of treatment targets (Birchwood & Trower, 2006). The present chapter aims to resolve some of this confusion by articulating a model of CBTp that focuses on targeting the emotional dysfunction often observed in psychosis (Birchwood, 2003).

Theoretical background and development: Cognitive Behavioural Therapy and psychosis

Evidence for the effectiveness of CBT in reducing delusional belief conviction and distress associated with delusional beliefs (Chadwick & Lowe, 1990) led to the application and development of CBTp and a proliferation of research studies. The updated NICE Guidelines for Schizophrenia (2009) found strong evidence that CBTp was effective in reducing the duration of hospital days, rates of re-hospitalisation and symptom severity. Robust small to medium effects were found for reductions in depression for CBT compared with both standard care and other active treatments and there was evidence of improvements in social functioning for up to twelve months. However, evidence for positive symptoms was less clear. Some data showed some effect for total severity of hallucinations at the end of treatment and there was limited but consistent evidence for CBTp on more symptom-specific measures including voice compliance, frequency of voices and believability. However, the evidence for CBT on delusions was inconsistent.

These sorts of inconsistencies have led to scepticism about the effectiveness of CBTp (Lynch *et al.*, 2010). Kingdon (2010) points out that studies where the effectiveness of CBTp is evaluated on a specific outcome such as command hallucinations (e.g. Trower *et al.*, 2004) show more promising findings with a bigger effect size (cf. Jackson *et al.*, 2009 for effectiveness of targeted CBT for post-psychotic trauma). Furthermore, Birchwood *et al.* (2004) pointed out that the primary outcome for the majority of CBTp trials has been positive symptoms of psychosis, as typically the primary dependent measure is a scale used in trials of neuroleptics such as the Positive and Negative Symptom Scale (PANSS; Kay *et al.*, 1987). Birchwood and Trower (2006) argue that, consistent with the developmental origins of CBT (Beck *et al.*, 1979), CBTp should focus on reducing emotional dysfunction by relieving distress, and that resolution of positive symptoms should be a secondary outcome. However, few trials of CBTp have used distress and emotional dysfunction as a secondary outcome let alone as a primary outcome (Wykes *et al.*, 2007; Jones *et al.*, 2012), which may be due to the historical divide between neuroses and psychosis influencing a neglect of the emotional experience of people with psychosis (Birchwood, 2003).

Emotional dysfunction and psychosis

A range of evidence now suggests that the separation of psychosis and emotion is misguided. High rates of affective symptoms are found in individuals diagnosed with affective and non-affective psychosis (van Os *et al.*, 2000), while a diagnosis of non-affective psychosis is often accompanied by a lifetime diagnosis of anxiety and mood disorders (Kendler *et al.*, 1996). There is evidence that individuals with a diagnosis of psychosis or a mood disorder do not differ in their experience of different types of emotional dysfunction (Livingston *et al.*, 2009). In addition, emotional dysfunction (e.g. anxiety, depression) is often implicated in the development (Hartley *et al.*, 2013), onset (Krabbendam & van Os, 2005), persistence (Myin-Germeys & van Os, 2007; Kramer *et al.*, 2013) and relapse (Birchwood, 2003; Gumley & Schwannauer, 2006) of psychosis. Finally, different types of emotional dysfunction including depression, social anxiety, post-traumatic stress disorder and shame are pervasive in first-episode samples (Birchwood, 2003). This has led to the idea that difficulties with affect dysregulation may underlie vulnerability to psychotic experiences (van Rossum *et al.*, 2011).

Implications for Cognitive Behavioural Therapy following psychosis

Based on a review of existing Randomised Controlled Trials following the original NICE Guidelines, Birchwood *et al.* (2004) highlighted the limited impact of CBT for psychosis on depression as only a few studies (with low effect sizes) found reductions in depression[1] (cf. Wykes *et al.*, 2007; Jones *et al.*, 2012). Birchwood *et al.* (2004) argued that the lack of change in depression following CBT for psychotic symptoms questions the assumption that reductions in distress and depression in psychosis will follow from the treatment of positive symptoms alone. Consequently, focussing solely on positive symptom reduction may mean that emotional dysfunction will not be addressed. To shed more light on why treatment of positive symptoms may be insufficient to ease emotional dysfunction,

Birchwood (2003) described three potential pathways to emotional dysfunction following psychosis.

Pathways to emotional dysfunction following psychosis

In the first pathway, emotional dysfunction is directly implicated in the experience of positive and negative symptoms of psychosis (Birchwood, 2003). This is based on evidence that depression can follow a similar course to positive symptoms (Birchwood et al., 2000; Hafner et al., 2005) and that high rates of co-morbid anxiety (46 per cent) are found in inpatients with psychosis (Cossof & Hafner, 1998). Similarly, social anxiety and associated social avoidance are commonly associated with positive symptoms such as threatening voices and paranoid delusions (Birchwood et al., 2004). In the second pathway, emotional dysfunction arises from a poor or dysfunctional psychological reaction to psychosis. This pathway is supported by evidence showing that emotional dysfunction is associated with negative appraisals of psychosis (including symptoms, treatment and diagnosis) such as it being stressful (Jackson et al., 2004), out of control (Birchwood et al., 2013) and shameful (Turner et al., 2013). In the final pathway, childhood trauma and developmental abnormalities can lead to the development of dysfunctional cognitive schemas or coping, which lead to poor adaptation to psychosis and its treatment (Birchwood, 2003). This pathway is supported by evidence that psychosis can have developmental antecedents such as trauma (Read et al., 2005), which affect biological, social and psychological development leading to low self-esteem, difficulties establishing relationships (Birchwood, 2003) and high emotional reactivity and susceptibility to stress later in life (Lardinois et al., 2011). Developmental trauma and susceptibility to stress may subsequently lead people vulnerable to psychosis if exposed to stressful environmental factors such as urban living, minority status and cannabis use (Birchwood, 2003; van Os et al., 2010).

Birchwood et al. (2004) demonstrated how consideration of these three pathways can inform CBT-based formulations and interventions with people experiencing psychosis. However, the three pathways to emotional dysfunction are not mutually exclusive (Birchwood, 2003), and all three may interact. In our clinical experience, there are often links between the second (reactions to psychosis) and third (developmental) pathways as service users with adverse developmental pathways often are vulnerable to persistent affective dysregulation in the post-psychotic phase due to unhelpful ways of regulating their emotions in the face of stressful daily life events and break-through psychotic symptoms.

Emotional regulation

Emotional regulation is a complex issue both conceptually and methodologically, which has been explored in a number of reviews (Gross, 2002; Kroole, 2009). In this chapter, we focus on aspects of emotional regulation that have implications for CBT and emotional dysfunction following psychosis. Emotional regulation can include conscious, effortful and deliberate processes aimed at overriding spontaneous emotional processes or unconscious, effortless and automatic processes (Kroole, 2009). Consequently, emotional regulation is the process by which individuals influence the emotions they experience, when they experience them and how they express them (Gross, 2002). The experience of emotion *per se* is not dysfunctional, as emotions often serve important functions such as motivational guides in the promotion of adaptive behaviours (e.g. approaching or avoiding stimuli) (Barlow, 2004; Phillips & Power, 2007; Mennin & Fresco, 2009). However, emotions may become dysfunctional if they are experienced to an excess; that is, if they are experienced too intensely, negatively and for too long (i.e. if they become dysregulated). Continuous emotional dysregulation may lead to different types of psychopathology such as anxiety, depression, trauma or borderline personality disorder (Kring & Sloan, 2010) and emotions may cease to function as reliable or functional motivational guides (Barlow, 2002; Phillips & Power, 2007; Mennin & Fresco, 2009).

Emotional regulation is also regarded as how easily people can leave any given emotional state (Kroole, 2009), which is determined by the degree to which a positive and negative emotion can be increased (up-regulated) or decreased (down-regulated) (Gross, 2002). This occurs through a range of different cognitive and behavioural emotional regulatory strategies (Aldao & Nolen-Hoeksema, 2010). One of the most influential models has been proposed by Gross and colleagues (Gross, 2002; John & Gross, 2004), which has focussed on two specific antecedent (re-appraisal) and response (suppression) strategies. In cognitive re-appraisal, the emotional impact of an event is reduced or modified by changing evaluations of the event; that is, the individual re-evaluates a potentially emotion-eliciting situation to order to modify its impact (Gross, 2002). Consistent with cognitive theories of distress (Beck *et al.*, 1979), the model emphasises that maladaptive appraisal processes drive emotional dysfunction such as anxiety and depression. Consequently, re-appraisal involves generating less maladaptive appraisals by reinterpreting situational or contextual aspects of stimuli – such as imagining a potentially upsetting image is fake or distancing oneself from stimuli by adopting a detached, third person perspective (Gross, 2002). In contrast, expressive suppression (e.g. keeping a straight face while lying), involves reducing emotionally expressive behaviour once the individual is already in an emotional state. Evidence supports the idea that certain emotional regulation strategies such as suppression and avoidance could be considered maladaptive and others such as re-appraisal could be considered adaptive due to respective negative and positive consequences (Aldao *et al.*, 2011; Gross, 2002; John & Gross, 2004).

Psychosis and emotional (dys)regulation

Evidence from a small number of studies does not equivocally support the idea that psychotic samples differ in their use of emotional regulation strategies compared with controls (Badcock *et al.*, 2011; Henry *et al.*, 2008; cf. Livingston *et al.*, 2009; van der Meer *et al.*, 2009), but the use of maladaptive strategies (e.g. avoidance, rumination and suppression) *within* psychotic samples is linked to more emotional dysfunction (Jackson *et al.*, in preparation) and other negative outcomes (Badcock *et al.*, 2011; Perry *et al.*, 2011). These findings are consistent with results from a large meta-analysis (Aldao *et al.*, 2011) and literature suggesting that deficits in emotional regulation are related to negative outcomes (Gross, 2002; John & Gross, 2004; Kroole, 2009; Mennin & Fresco, 2009). In addition, there is also evidence that emotional dysfunction across a range of different types of psychopathology is due to a latent transdiagnostic emotional regulation variable characterised by rumination, avoidance and low levels of re-appraisal (Aldao & Nolen-Hoeksema, 2010; Aldao *et al.*, 2011).

These findings may be particularly relevant to people who have experienced psychosis, as psychotic samples are particularly sensitive to stress in their daily lives as they react to daily life hassles with high levels of stress and negative affect (Myin-Germeys & van Os, 2007), so they could be said to have high levels of emotional sensitivity (Kroole, 2009). This susceptibility to stress is heightened for those who have experienced childhood trauma (Lardinois *et al.*, 2010), which supports the notion that emotional dysregulation has developmental antecedents. In addition, it is now well documented that emotional dysregulation is significantly implicated in different aspects of psychosis including the onset of psychosis and symptom formation (Hartley *et al.*, 2013), persistent psychotic symptoms (Myin-Germeys & van Os, 2007; Kramer *et al.*, 2013; van Rossum *et al.*, 2013), psychotic relapses (Gumley & Schwannauer, 2006) and different types of post-psychotic emotional dysfunction (Birchwood, 2003). The presence of maladaptive strategies like avoidance, rumination and low levels of re-appraisal (Aldao *et al.*, 2011) may then increase negative affect and emotional dysregulation, which may 'fuel' vicious cycles of persistent psychotic symptoms, relapses and a myriad of emotional dysfunction such as post-psychotic depression, anxiety and trauma. Thus, it may be possible to enhance the effectiveness for CBT for emotional dysfunction following psychosis through the combined effect of decreasing emotional sensitivity, reducing maladaptive emotional regulatory strategies and enhancing adaptive regulatory strategies (cf. Berking *et al.*, 2008; Gumley & Schwannauer, 2006; Tai & Turkington, 2009). This reasoning is consistent with recent developments in transdiagnostic approaches in the treatment of different types of emotional dysfunction (Mennin & Fresco, 2009; Barlow *et al.*, 2011) and could be done by placing more emphasis on emotional (dys)regulation in the assessment, formulation and intervention phases in CBT for emotional dysfunction following psychosis while also considering the three different pathways to emotional dysfunction identified by Birchwood (2003).

Aims, stages, strategies and techniques

Difficulties engaging service users who have experienced psychosis and with mental health services are well documented, and, in the last decade, adopting assertive outreach approaches has significantly improved engagement of young people with psychosis with mental health services (Tait *et al.*, 2010). However, people with adverse developmental trajectories often have understandable problems with trusting others, and may cope with emotional distress by avoiding it, ruminating on it or with other maladaptive emotional regulatory strategies like suppression and self-harm. These individuals may not have had much experience of talking about their emotional distress and may fail to make links between distress, thoughts and feelings, which can impact on engagement with services and therapy. Thus, for some service users it is important to engage them gently and encourage them to tell their life story leading up to their psychosis. From a service perspective, close working with the rest of the mental health team including their care coordinator and psychiatrist is important. Initial engagement may involve shorter sessions, greater flexibility in terms of location of sessions with majority of initial sessions occurring at the person's home and close working with other professionals (Tait *et al.*, 2010).

Assessment

Once engagement has been established, assessment with standardised measures can be used to inform the formulation. These measures can be used to normalise experiences by highlighting a range of difficulties that others also experience (the principle of 'universality', Yalom & Leszcz, 2005). Although many of the measures are self-report, it can often be more helpful to use them to guide an open-ended interview to assess distress and problems with emotional regulation.

Distress

Standardised measures of depression and anxiety are useful. However, we also find that more specific measures of social anxiety (Mattick & Clarke, 1998) are important due to the high rates of social anxiety in this group (Birchwood, 2003). In terms of trauma, the Impact of Event Scale–Revised (IES-R; Weiss & Marmar, 1997) is useful as it can be completed in relation to any stressful life event (e.g. childhood trauma; bullying in adolescence) but also to different distressing experiences associated with psychosis such as positive symptoms and negative treatment experiences (e.g. hospitalisations). The Basic Emotions Scale (BES; Phillips & Power, 2007) can be used to measure the experience of five basic emotions (anger, sadness, disgust, fear and happiness).

Emotional regulation

The majority of research studies assessing emotional regulation rely on the Emotional Regulation Questionnaire (ERQ; Gross & John, 2003). This is a short measure with good reliability and validity but assesses only two types of emotional regulation. However, other measures of emotional regulation have been developed (see Table 6.1). In one of our recent studies (Jackson *et al.*, in preparation), we used the Regulation of Emotions Questionnaire (REQ; Phillips & Power, 2007) and the ERQ and found that the dysfunctional strategies on the REQ had much higher correlations with different types of emotional dysfunction than the ERQ. We have also used this measure in many clinical cases as it assesses different types of emotional regulation including internal functional items (e.g. "I put the situation into perspective"), internal dysfunctional items (e.g. "I keep the feelings locked up inside"), external functional items (e.g. "I talk to someone about how I feel") and external dysfunctional items (e.g. "I try to make others feel bad"). These distinctions can be helpful to inform formulations and share with service users, carers and staff. The assessment of functional strategies also identifies existing (or lack) of helpful emotional regulatory strategies. If such strategies are present, there may be scope to increase the use of these or, if not present, these can be developed into therapeutic goals. Baseline and follow-up assessments can enable service users to monitor the extent to which they are letting go of unhelpful strategies and developing more helpful strategies.

Table 6.1 Measures of emotional regulation

Questionnaire	Authors	Items	Subscales	Assesses
Emotional Regulation (ERQ)	Gross & John (2003)	10	2	Cognitive re-appraisal and expressive suppression
Cognitive Emotional Regulation (CERQ)	Garnefski & Spinhoven (2001)	36	9	Self-blame; acceptance; rumination; positive re-focussing; refocus on planning; positive re-appraisal; putting into perspective; catastrophising; blaming others
Difficulties in Emotional Regulation (DERS)	Gratz & Roemer (2004)	36	6	Non-acceptance; goals; poor impulse control; lack of emotional awareness; limited emotional regulation strategies; lack of emotional clarity
Regulation of Emotions (REQ)	Phillips & Power (2007)	32	4	Internal and external functional and dysfunctional strategies
Affective Style (ASQ)	Hofman & Kashdan (2010)	20	3	Concealment; adjusting; tolerating

Psychotic experiences

Rather than relying on general measures of psychotic symptoms like the PANSS (Kay *et al.*, 1987), it is more helpful to use specific measures depending on what the person is experiencing. If they are experiencing voices and/or delusional beliefs, it can be useful to use the PSYRATS (psychotic symptom rating scales; Haddock *et al.*, 1999), as this measure captures a broader range of experiences (e.g. conviction, pre-occupation, frequency) than just symptom severity. The PSYRATS can be supplemented by additional measures such as the Beliefs About Voices Questionnaire–Revised (BAVQ-R; Chadwick *et al.*, 2000) to assess appraisals which may be contributing to distress associated with voices.

Psychotic illness-related appraisals

Emotional dysfunction following psychosis such as depression is often related to negative appraisals such as entrapment and isolation, which can be assessed with the Personal Beliefs about Illness Questionnaire–Revised (PBIQ-R; Birchwood *et al.*, 2003). We have also recently found that internal shame-based appraisals of psychosis are related to post-psychotic depression while external shame-based appraisals are related to post-psychotic trauma (Turner *et al.*, 2013). Therefore, assessing shame associated with psychosis may be important when intervening with emotional dysfunction following psychosis.

Formulation

Formulations can draw on the different pathways to emotional dysfunction outlined by Birchwood *et al.* (2004). However, the current approach places more emphasis on the relationships between the three different pathways while placing affective dysregulation at the centre of the formulation (see Figure 6.1). Furthermore, the current approach has integrated emotional regulation strategies into the formulation by linking their origins with developmental events and their current use with affective dysregulation and in turn with different types of post-psychotic emotional dysfunction and persistent psychotic experiences. This formulation also accommodates psychosis-related appraisals.

Interventions

The initial aim is to share the formulation with the service user to help them make sense of their distress. This can help normalise their experience and help them understand the origins of their current emotional regulatory strategies (both helpful and unhelpful). It can also facilitate the development of therapeutic goals. It can also be helpful to share a formulation with carers (if appropriate), care coordinators and psychiatrists to help them make sense of the service user's experiences of distress and their helpful and unhelpful regulatory strategies. One aim is to target unhelpful strategies and facilitate the development of more helpful strategies as this should help to reduce affective dysregulation and in turn reduce different types of post-psychotic emotional dysfunction and break-through psychotic symptoms. While this may involve more third wave interventions (Tai & Turkington, 2009) such as mindfulness and other distress tolerance skills, it still operates within a traditional CBT framework by developing behavioural experiments to see if newly developed skills (e.g. distress tolerance problem solving) are more effective in reducing distress and promoting functioning than their previous strategies (e.g. suppression, rumination). Consistent with traditional CBT (Beck *et al.*, 1979) there remains a strong emphasis on linking situations, thoughts and feelings, and modification of problematic thoughts and beliefs through evidence collecting. Some service users may have poor awareness of links between situations, thoughts, feelings, their unhelpful regulatory strategies and psychotic experiences, so the initial sessions may involve developing awareness of these links. Often the psychotic experience may be the most salient experience, and awareness of precipitating variables including affective dysregulation can be poor so initial sessions may involve developing awareness of links between situations, unhelpful regulatory strategies, affective dysregulation and psychotic experiences. If service users are motivated this can be set as homework between sessions with thought diaries but often it is necessary to repeatedly work through examples in the sessions. Once more helpful ways of regulating distress (e.g. re-appraisal, evidence gathering, distress tolerance) have been developed to provide some balance to unhelpful strategies (e.g. avoidance, suppression), behavioural experiments can be set to test out the efficacy of different ways of responding. If successful, this should provide a greater sense of control of stressful situations (including break-through psychotic symptoms) and reduce the chances of affective dysregulation.

Summary

Consistent with the approach outlined above, the primary aim of the intervention is to reduce current levels of distress by the reduction of maladaptive cognitive, emotional and behavioural regulatory strategies, followed by the development of more adaptive strategies, and finally by the modification of unhelpful post-psychotic appraisals. Consistent with Birchwood and Trower (2006) the primary outcome of the therapy is change in emotional distress. However, changes in emotional regulation strategies are important secondary outcomes. Finally, given the strong association between emotional distress and psychotic symptoms (Birchwood, 2003; Hartley *et al.*, 2013; Myin-Germeys & van Os, 2007; Kramer *et al.*, 2013; van Rossum *et al.*, 2013), it would not be unreasonable to expect reductions in psychotic experiences and future relapses if reductions in emotional distress are maintained through the use of more adaptive emotional regulatory strategies.

Case illustration: James

James is a 21-year-old man living with his girlfriend. He has been accepted by an Early Intervention Service following a psychotic breakdown when he presented with paranoia and auditory hallucinations. The severity of the hallucinations and paranoia has reduced with medication but he continues to experience some paranoia, voices and social anxiety. He has had no previous contact with mental health services despite a long history of low mood and anxiety. James spends most of his time in the house reading and using his computer. He avoids going out because of his anxiety, paranoia and low motivation due to low mood.

Psychology assessment of history

James reported a difficult childhood characterised by emotional deprivation and instability. He had spent periods away from the family home in the care of relatives following the birth of his sister when he was 4 years old. When he returned home he recalled feeling wary of his parents and scared of the dark. On one occasion, he felt sick and after vomiting felt less scared, which he then often used to reduce feelings of anxiety. At school he was sometimes bullied for not fitting in with others and often felt isolated, 'down' and anxious. Following school, he found a job in IT and was quickly promoted as he had used a personal computer for many years. He started a relationship and had joint friendships with his new girlfriend. However, he became worried about his abilities at work and made a few mistakes. His supervisor noticed these and suggested ways of helping but James felt he was being critical. He started to worry that his supervisor did not think he was good enough to do his job and was worried that his co-workers felt the same. He began to feel that his boss and all his co-workers were against him and started to worry that CCTV cameras at work were monitoring him. Over time, this worry developed into a fear that he was being watched by other cameras and he began hearing occasional critical voices. He left his job and subsequently became more preoccupied with his voices and beliefs. He believed that other people knew he had difficulties just by looking at him. His independent social functioning ceased. He stopped sleeping and after many months of keeping his concerns to himself finally informed his partner who sought help.

James reported that his partner would insist on them going out to see friends or shopping but most of the time he refused. Occasionally when he did go out he would avoid eye contact and avoid checking out his worries (that people were looking at him, talking about him). He remained worried about the dark and shadows at night but would hide under the duvet instead of checking them out. He was worried about showing his emotions to his partner or disclosing his worries as he believed she would leave him if he was upset. Thus, he tended to suppress his emotions and thoughts. On other occasions, he would make himself sick as this would help him feel temporarily better. However, this meant that he was sometimes underweight. James also reported he would spend many hours ruminating on past events (his treatment from his parents, bullying at school, leaving his job), which would leave him feeling distressed. He acknowledged that at these times his paranoia would increase and he would occasionally hear voices.

Standardised assessments

Emotional regulation

James scored very low on cognitive re-appraisal and moderately high on expressive suppression on the ERQ. On the REQ, he was low on internal functional regulation, as he did not attempt to review plans, goals or his thoughts, and lower on external functional regulation as he did not attempt to talk to others when upset. James scored low on external dysfunctional regulation as he rarely took his feelings out on others but he scored very high on internal dysfunctional regulation as he sometimes harmed and punished himself, dwelled on unhelpful thoughts and feelings and kept feelings locked inside. Finally, the CERQ revealed that he was very high on self-blame, rumination and catastrophising and very low on acceptance, positive refocus and putting things into perspective.

Post-psychotic reactions

The PBIQ-R revealed that James felt he had little control over his illness, ashamed, entrapped and socially marginalised.

Emotional dysfunction

James had depression at the lower end of the severe end, severe levels of social anxiety and moderately high levels of anger, sadness and disgust and low levels of happiness (as measured by the BES).

Formulation

From Figure 6.1, it can be seen that James's emotional dysfunction following his psychosis may be due to the three different pathways identified by Birchwood (2003). In relation to the first pathway, James may have experienced low mood and anxiety directly as the result of his experience of voices and paranoia during the acute phase. Consistent with the second pathway, it is likely that James's specific post-psychotic appraisals of entrapment, loss (e.g. of his job), shame and marginalisation were contributing to his post-psychotic depression and social anxiety. In addition, on days when his emotional dysfunction was more intense, his paranoia and voices increased, which exacerbated his low mood and anxiety. Consequently, the interaction between the first and second pathway was acting as a vicious cycle.

However, it is also likely that the third developmental pathway identified by Birchwood (2003) was playing a significant role in James's post-psychotic emotional dysfunction. Consistent with Barlow *et al.* (2011), James may have been born with an existing vulnerability to react to stress with a high level of emotional sensitivity or reactivity, which was activated in his early adverse environment. This may have led to the onset of prolonged negative affect, which he attempted to deal with through emotional regulatory strategies such as avoidance, rumination and other strategies (e.g. making himself sick), which resulted in the unintended consequences of causing additional emotional distress and emotional dysregulation. In addition, he did not gain the opportunity to develop more adaptive emotional regulatory strategies. This tendency to use maladaptive emotional regulation strategies may have increased in the context of later stressful life events (e.g. bullying at school and work distress), which may have contributed to the onset of low mood and anxiety. This emotional dysfunction may have been exacerbated by his use of maladaptive strategies and a lack of more adaptive strategies like seeking social support and attempting to re-appraise (cf. Gumley & Schwannauer, 2006). Following a more prolonged experience of negative affect he most likely entered an 'at risk mental state' (Yung *et al.*, 2005), which again he reacted to with maladaptive emotional regulation, exacerbating his emotional dysregulation and culminating in psychosis (Myin-Germeys & van Os, 2007). As mentioned above, the experience of psychosis could have directly caused emotional dysfunction, which was subsequently maintained by specific negative appraisals about his psychosis (Birchwood *et al.*, 2013). However, it is also likely that his pre-existing maladaptive emotional regulatory strategies exacerbated and maintained his post-psychotic emotional dysfunction even after the resolution of his acute positive symptoms. Finally, attempts to cope with this on-going emotional dysfunction (e.g. low mood and social anxiety) with maladaptive emotional regulation prolonged his distress and occasionally triggered break-through psychotic symptoms.

Intervention

James was encouraged to discuss his thoughts and feelings about his experiences, which he found difficult. However, his feelings were validated and he was given homework sheets to start identifying links between stressful situations, thoughts and emotions. Consistent with recent approaches to emotional regulation (Barlow *et al.*, 2011; Mennin & Fresco, 2009), James received psycho-education about the functions of emotions and about emotional regulation. There was an emphasis on the differential impact (e.g. positive or negative consequences) of adaptive and maladaptive strategies and James was given feedback about his use of strategies based on the assessments. Subsequent sessions focussed on reducing his use of maladaptive strategies by helping him to accept and tolerate his feelings through the use of mindfulness and distress tolerance techniques.

Following these sessions, the focus shifted to helping James increase more adaptive emotional regulation strategies including expressing his thoughts and feelings about stressful situations either by talking to his partner or by using written emotional expression (Pennebaker, 1997), which we have previously used with a psychotic sample (Bernard *et al.*, 2006) or by using problem solving to counteract rumination. Following this, traditional CBT was introduced, including re-appraisal through the ABC model. The five area model (Williams & Garland, 2002) was used to increase his awareness of links between situations, thoughts, feelings, physical sensations, behaviours and traditional techniques like reviewing evidence for and against thoughts were introduced. His specific post-psychotic negative appraisals involving entrapment, shame and loss were targeted using these techniques. In addition, he was encouraged to elicit social support from his partner and to reality check in stressful situations (e.g. when he was scared of the dark).

Over time, James reported improvements in his mood and general levels of anxiety, which appeared to result in less break-through symptoms of paranoia and

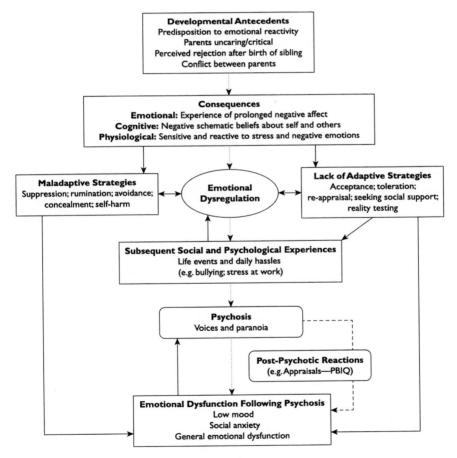

Figure 6.1 Formulation of emotional dysfunction following psychosis

voices. Thought records and behavioural experiments were reviewed so James could see how responding to stressful situations (including break-through voices and increases in paranoia) in a more helpful manner reduced the impact of these experiences due to eliciting less emotional distress. However, he remained socially avoidant and anxious. Consequently, a formulation for his social anxiety was used to guide a CBT-based exposure intervention (e.g. using behavioural experiments to drop safety behaviours and testing out negative beliefs about how he looked to others) with the support of the MDT. James was also encouraged to use his new adaptive emotional regulation strategies while doing the exposure work such as accepting and tolerating negative affect, disclosing his negative thoughts and feelings and re-appraising negative thoughts. Over time his social anxiety reduced, which enabled him to increase his independence and activity levels. This reduced his sense of social marginalisation and entrapment and along with his improved emotional regulation strategies improved his negative appraisals of control over his illness. Finally, work was done to help James challenge his negative beliefs about himself and others. In addition, based on Fennell (2009), James was encouraged to develop more adaptive beliefs about himself and others, and was set homework tasks to help him pay more attention to evidence inconsistent with his previous negative beliefs and consistent with his new adaptive beliefs.

Conclusions and implications

CBTp has evolved in recent years by incorporating research on post-psychotic emotional dysfunction (Birchwood, 2003), emotions (Hartley *et al.*, 2013), distress (Birchwood & Trower, 2006) and distress-focussed outcome measures (Trower *et al.*, 2004; Jackson *et al.*, 2009). In addition, it has incorporated 'third wave' CBT approaches (Tai & Turkington, 2009), which aim to improve emotion regulation through accepting rather than avoiding emotions. In the last fifteen years, research on emotions and emotional regulation has identified important individual differences in emotional regulation strategies (Gross & John, 2003) and that some strategies have more negative consequences than others (Gross, 2002; John & Gross, 2004). This is currently leading to the development of new treatments which either implement emotional regulation training prior to CBT (e.g. Berking *et al.*, 2008) or incorporate CBT techniques into an integrated treatment for emotional dysfunction (e.g. Mennin & Fresco, 2009; Barlow *et al.*, 2011). These interventions may be particularly suitable for individuals who have experienced psychosis due to high levels of emotional reactivity (Myin-Germeys & van Os, 2007), emotional dysfunction (Birchwood, 2003) and deficits in effective emotional regulation (Jackson *et al.*, in preparation) in psychotic samples. Consequently, the effectiveness of CBTp may be enhanced by placing more emphasis on emotional (dys)regulation in the assessment, formulation and intervention process.

Note

1 As reported above there have been more positive outcomes on depression following CBT for psychosis reported in NICE (2009).

References

Aldao, A. & Nolen-Hoeksema, S. (2010). Specificity of cognitive regulation strategies: A transdiagnostic examination. *Behaviour Research and Therapy*, *48*, 974–983.

Aldao, A., Nolen-Hoeksema, S. & Schweizer, S. (2011). Emotional-regulation strategies across psychopathology: A meta-analytic review. *Clinical Psychology Review*, *30*, 217–237.

Badcock, J. C., Paulik, G. & Maybery, M. T. (2011). The role of emotion regulation in auditory hallucinations. *Psychiatry Research*, *185*, 303–308.

Barlow, D. H. (2004). *Anxiety and its disorders: The nature and treatment of anxiety and panic*. New York: Guilford Press.

Barlow, D. H., Farchione, T. J., Fairholme, C. P., Ellard, K. K., Boisseau, C. L., Allen, L. B. & Ehrenreich-May, J. (2011). *The unified protocol for transdiagnostic treatment of emotional disorders: Therapist guide*. New York: Oxford University Press.

Beck, A. T., Rush, A. J., Shaw, B. F. & Emery, G. (1979). *Cognitive therapy of depression*. New York: Guilford Press.

Berking, M., Wupperman, P., Reichardt, A., Pejic, T., Dippel, A. & Znoj, H. (2008). General emotion-regulation skills as a treatment target in psychotherapy. *Behaviour Research and Therapy*, *46*, 1230–1237.

Bernard, M., Jackson, C. & Jones, C. (2006). Written emotional disclosure following first-episode psychosis: Effects on symptoms of post-traumatic stress disorder. *British Journal of Clinical Psychology*, *45*(3), 403–415.

Birchwood, M. (2003). Pathways to emotional dysfunction in first-episode psychosis. *British Journal of Psychiatry*, *182*, 373–375.

Birchwood, M. & Trower, P. (2006). The future of cognitive behaviour therapy for psychosis: Not a quasi-neuroleptic. *British Journal of Psychiatry*, *188*, 107–108.

Birchwood, M., Iqbal, Z., Chadwick, P. & Trower, P. (2000). Cognitive approach to depression and suicidal thinking in psychosis. I. Ontogeny of post-psychotic depression. *British Journal of Psychiatry*, *177*, 516–528.

Birchwood, M., Iqbal, Z., Jackson, C. & Hardy, K. (2004). Cognitive therapy and emotional dysfunction in early psychosis. In J. F. M Gleason & P. D. McGorry (eds), *Psychological interventions in early psychosis: A treatment handbook* (pp. 209–228). Chichester, Sussex: John Wiley & Sons.

Birchwood, M., Jackson, C., Brunet, K., Holden, J. & Barton, K. (2013). Personal Beliefs about Illness–Revised. *British Journal of Clinical Psychology*, *51*, 448–458.

Chadwick, P. D. & Lowe, C. F. (1990). Measurement and modification of delusional beliefs. *Journal of Consulting and Clinical Psychology*, *58*(2), 225–232.

Chadwick, P., Lees, S. & Birchwood, M. (2000). The revised Beliefs About Voices Questionnaire (BAV–Q). *British Journal of Psychiatry*, *177*, 229–232.

Cossof, J. & Hafner, R. (1998). The prevalence of comorbid anxiety in schizophrenia, schizoaffective disorder, and bipolar disorder. *Australian and New Zealand Journal of Psychiatry*, *32*, 67–72.

Fennell, M. (2009). *Overcoming low self-esteem*. London: Constable & Robinson.

Garnefski, N. & Spinhoven, K. P. (2001). Negative life events, cognitive emotional regulation, and emotional problems. *Personality and Individual Differences, 30*, 1311–1327.

Gratz, K. L. & Roemer, L. (2004). Multidimensional assessment of emotional regulation and dysregulation: Development, factor structure, and initial validation of the difficulties in emotional regulation scale. *Journal of Psychopathology and Behavioural Assessment, 24*, 41–54.

Gross, J. J. (2002). Emotion regulation: affective, cognitive, and social consequences. *Psychophysiology, 39*, 281–291.

Gross, J. J. & John, O. P. (2003). Individual differences in two emotion regulation processes: Implications for affect, relationships and well-being. *Journal of Personality and Social Psychology, 85*, 348–362.

Gumley, A. & Schwannauer, M. (2006). *Staying well after psychosis: A cognitive interpersonal approach to recovery and relapse prevention.* Chichester, Sussex: John Wiley & Sons.

Haddock, G., McCarron, J., Tarrier, N., Faragher, E. & Tarrier, N. (1999). Scales to measure dimensions of hallucinations and delusions: The psychotic symptom rating scales (PSYRATS). *Psychological Medicine, 29*(4), 879–889.

Hafner, H., Maurer, K., Trendler, G., An Der Heiden, W. & Schmidt, M. (2005). The early course of schizophrenia and depression. *European Archive of Psychiatry and Clinical Neuroscience, 255*, 167–173.

Hartley, S., Barrowclough, C. & Haddock, G. (2013). Anxiety and depression in psychosis: A systematic review of associations with positive psychotic symptoms. *Acta Psychiatrica Scandinavica, 128*, 327–346.

Henry, J. D., Rendell, P. G., Green, M. J., McDonald, K. & O'Donnell, M. (2008). Emotion regulation in schizophrenia: Affective, social, and clinical correlates of suppression and re-appraisal. *Journal of Abnormal Psychology, 117*(2), 473–478.

Hofman, S. G. & Kashdan, T. B. (2010). The affective style questionnaire: Development and psychometric properties. *Journal of Psychopathology, 32*, 255–263.

Jackson, C., Knott, C., Skeate, A. & Birchwood, M. (2004). The trauma of first episode psychosis: The role of cognitive mediation. *Australian and New Zealand Journal of Psychiatry, 38*, 327–333.

Jackson, C., Trower, P., Reid, I., Smith, J., Hall, M., Townend, M. . . . Birchwood, M. (2009). Improving psychological adjustment following a first episode of psychosis: A randomised control trial of cognitive therapy to reduce post psychotic trauma symptoms. *Behaviour Research and Therapy, 47*, 454–462.

Jackson, C., Bernard, M. & Birchwood, M. (in preparation). Emotional regulation and emotional dysfunction following first episode psychosis.

John, O. P. & Gross, J. J. (2004). Healthy and unhealthy emotional regulation: Personality processes, individual differences, and life-span development. *Journal of Personality, 72*, 1301–1333.

Jones, C., Hacker, D., Cormac, I., Meaden, A. & Irving, C. B. (2012). Cognitive behaviour therapy versus other psychosocial treatments for schizophrenia (Review). The Cochrane Collaboration. *Cochrane Database of Systematic Reviews*, issue 4, no. CD008712. doi: 10.1002/14651858.CD008712.pub2.

Kay, S. R., Fiszbein, A. & Opler, L. A. (1987). The Positive and Negative Syndrome Scale (PANSS) for schizophrenia. *Schizophrenia Bulletin, 13*, 261–269.

Kendler, K. S., Gallagher, T. J., Abelson, J. M. & Kessler, R. C. (1996). Lifetime prevalence, demographic risk factors and diagnostic validity of non-affective psychosis as assessed in US community sample. *Archives of General Psychiatry, 53*, 1022–1031.

Kingdon, D. (2010). Over-simplification and exclusion of non-conforming studies can demonstrate absence of effect: A lynching party? *Psychological Medicine, 40*, 25–27.

Krabbendam, L. & van Os, J. (2005). Affective processes in the onset and persistence of psychosis. *European Archives of Psychiatry and Clinical Neuroscience, 255*(3), 185–189.

Kramer, I., Simons., C. J. P., Wigman, J. T. W., Collip, D., Jacobs, N., Derom, C., . . . Wichers, M. (2013). Time-lagged moment to moment interplay between negative affect and paranoia: New insights in the affective pathway to psychosis. *Schizophrenia Bulletin* (Advance Access) 13 February.

Kring, A. M. & Sloan, D. M. (2010). *Emotion regulation in psychopathology: A transdiagnostic approach to etiology and treatment.* New York: Guilford Press.

Kroole, S. (2009). The psychology of emotional regulation: An integrative review. *Cognition and Emotion, 23*(1), 4–41.

Lardinois, M., Lataster, T., Mengelers, R., van Os, J., & Myin-Germeys, I. (2011). Childhood trauma and increased stress sensitivity in psychosis. *Acta Psychiatrica Scandinavica, 123*(1), 28–35.

Livingston, K., Harper, S. & Gillanders, D. (2009). An exploration of emotion regulation in psychosis. *Clinical Psychology and Psychotherapy, 16*, 418–430.

Lynch, D., Laws, K. R. & McKenna, P. J. (2010). Cognitive behaviour therapy for major psychiatric disorder: does it really work? A meta-analytical review of well controlled trials. *Psychological Medicine, 40*, 9–24.

Mattick, R. P. & Clarke, J. C. (1998). Development and validation of measures of social phobia scrutiny and social interaction anxiety. *Behaviour Research and Therapy, 36*, 455–470.

Mennin, D. S. & Fresco, D. M. (2009). Emotion regulation as an integrative framework for understanding and treating psychopathology. In A. M. Kring & D. M. Sloan (eds), *Emotion regulation in psychopathology: A transdiagnostic approach to etiology and treatment* (pp. 356–379). New York: Guilford Press.

Myin-Germeys, I. & van Os, J. (2007). Stress-reactivity in psychosis: Evidence for an affective pathway to psychosis. *Clinical Psychology Review, 27*, 409–424.

National Institute for Health and Care Excellence (2009) *Schizophrenia: Core interventions in the treatment and management of schizophrenia in adults in primary and secondary care.* NICE clinical guideline 82. London: NICE.

Pennebaker, J. W. (1997). Writing about emotional experiences as a therapeutic process. *Psychological Science, 8*, 162–166.

Perry, Y., Henry, J. D. & Grisham, J. R. (2011). The habitual use of emotional regulation strategies in schizophrenia. *British Journal of Clinical Psychology, 50*, 217–222.

Phillips, K. F. V. & Power, M. (2007). A new self-report measure of emotion regulation in adolescents: The regulation of emotions questionnaire. *Clinical Psychology & Psychotherapy, 14*, 145–156.

Read, J., van Os, J., Morrison, A. P. & Ross, C. A. (2005). Childhood trauma, psychosis and schizophrenia: A literature review with theoretical and clinical implications. *Acta Psychiatrica Scandinavica, 112*, 330–350.

Tai, S. & Turkington, D. (2009). The evolution of cognitive behaviour therapy for schizophrenia: Current practice and recent developments. *Schizophrenia Bulletin, 35*(5), 865–873.

Tait, L., Ryles, D. & Sidwell, A. (2010). Strategies for engagement. In P. French, J. Smith, D. Shiers, M. Reed & M. Rayne (eds), *Promoting recovery in early psychosis: A practice manual* (pp. 35–44). London: Blackwell.

Trower, P., Birchwood, M., Meaden, A., Byrne, S., Nelson, A. & Ross, K. (2004). Cognitive therapy for command hallucinations: A randomised control trial. *British Journal of Psychiatry, 184*, 312–320.

Turner, M., Bernard, M., Birchwood, M., Jackson, C. & Jones, C. (2013). The contribution of shame to post-psychotic trauma. *British Journal of Clinical Psychology, 52*, 162–182.

van der Meer, L., van't Wout, M. & Aleman, A. (2009). Emotion regulation strategies in patients with schizophrenia. *Psychiatry Research, 170*, 108–113.

van, Os, J., Gilvarry, C., Bale, R., van Horn, E., Tattan, T., White, I. & Murray, R. (2000). Diagnostic value of the DSM and ICD categories of psychosis. An evidence based approach. *Social Psychiatry and Psychiatric Epidemiology, 35*, 305–311.

van Os., J., Kenis, G. & Rutten, B. P. F. (2010). The environment and schizophrenia. *Nature, 468*, 203–212.

van Rossum, I., Dominguez, M. D., Lieb, R., Wittchen, H. U., & van Os, J. (2011). Affective dysregulation and reality distortion: A 10-year prospective study of their association and clinical relevance. *Schizophrenia Bulletin, 37*(3), 561–571.

Weiss, D. S. & Marmar, C. R. (1997). The Impact of Event Scale–Revised. In J. P. Wilson & T. M. Keane (eds), *Assessing psychological trauma and PTSD: A handbook for practitioners* (pp. 399–411). New York: Guilford Press.

Williams, C. J. & Garland, A. (2002). A cognitive–behavioral therapy assessment model for use in everyday clinical practice. *Advances in Psychiatric Treatment, 8*, 172–179.

Wykes, T., Steel, C., Everitt, B. & Tarrier, N. (2007). Cognitive behaviour therapy for schizophrenia: Effect sizes, clinical models, and methodological rigor. *Schizophrenia Bulletin, 34*(3), 523–537.

Yalom, I. D. & Leszcz, M. (2005). *Theory and practice of group psychotherapy.* New York: Basic Books.

Yung, A. R., Yuen, H. P., McGorry, P. D., Phillips, L. J., Kelly, D., Dell'Olio, M. . . . Buckby, J. (2005). Mapping the onset of psychosis: The Comprehensive Assessment of At-Risk Mental States. *Australian and New Zealand Journal of Psychiatry, 39*(11–12), 964–971.

Chapter 7

Compassion Focused Therapy for people experiencing psychosis

Sophie L. Mayhew

Introduction

Evidence suggests that experiences of psychosis are associated with shame and self-criticism (e.g. Romme & Escher, 1989; Turner et al., 2013). Compassion Focused Therapy (CFT; Gilbert, 1992, 2000, 2010a; Gilbert & Irons, 2005) is an approach developed to reduce shame and self-criticism. This chapter outlines CFT theory, considers some of the difficulties people with psychosis experience and discusses how CFT may be used to understand these. A case study illustrates how this approach can be utilised in people with psychosis who may be difficult to reach.

Theoretical background and development: the evolution of CFT

Individuals who have come from neglectful, critical or abusive backgrounds often find it difficult to self-soothe and have high levels of shame and self-critical thinking (Gilbert et al., 2004). Compassion Focused Therapy aims to 'tone down' the person's self-critical relationship with themselves and facilitate the development of a new relationship based on care, concern and self-soothing. It de-shames and de-pathologises difficulties, fostering an understanding of these difficulties in terms of 'survival strategies' and supports the person to develop tolerance and become compassionate towards themselves.

Although CFT was developed for non-psychotic individuals (Gilbert & Procter, 2006), there is growing evidence for its use in psychosis (Braehler et al., 2013; Gumley et al., 2010; Johnson et al., 2011; Laithwaite et al., 2009; Lincoln et al., 2013; Mayhew & Gilbert, 2008). CFT and Compassionate Mind Training (CMT; the *techniques* used within CFT used to develop compassion) were both developed to help people cope with chronic feelings of shame (Gilbert, 1992, 1997, 2000; Gilbert & Irons, 2005).

Understanding shame and self-critical thinking

CFT draws upon evolutionary psychology, attachment theory, Cognitive Behavioural Therapy, neurophysiology and Buddhist insights (Gilbert, 2009a). It takes the position that individuals are 'thrown' into the world and have to cope the best they can with the circumstances they find themselves in (Gilbert, 2009a). The human brain and its associated functions, motives and competencies are explicitly viewed as products of evolution created to operate in certain ways. CFT uses this notion to support people to let go of self-blame and self-criticism and view their difficulties as unique but limited coping strategies that can be replaced with more helpful strategies grounded in the notion of compassion.

Shame is a socially mediated emotion about the self which can be thought of as part of a threat detection system that warns individuals of the possibility of negative evaluation in the minds of others (Gilbert, 2009a). Shame links threat-based emotions such as anger, anxiety and disgust into the experience of self. Common behaviours resulting from feelings of shame may be attack, submissive appeasement, escape, apologetic denial or self-harm (Gilbert, 2009a).

Internal shame involves negative self-evaluation, while external shame involves the perception of negative self-evaluation in the mind of the other. Shame functions to modify behaviour and is experienced as highly unpleasant and aversive. The common response to shame is disconnection from others as an attempt to escape from the feelings of negative evaluation. However, if the shame is internal shame (i.e. negative self-evaluation), then social isolation will not necessarily reduce the feeling of shame, and individuals may develop other ways of coping. Early experiences of shame are often linked with powerful, hostile or rejecting others and shame-based memories can be considered traumatic in that they are experienced as powerful, intrusive and reoccurring (Gilbert, 2009a).

Gilbert and Irons (2005) suggest that people who are self-critical (i.e. have a tendency towards negative self-evaluation) are less able to stimulate brain pathways associated with feelings of safeness, they often are unable to self-soothe and have a relatively stable (internally generated) sense of threat – they struggle to be 'at peace'. To be soothed or reassured by a thought (e.g. "I am lovable") this thought needs to link with an associated *emotional experience* (e.g. of 'being lovable'). People who have few memories or experiences of being lovable or soothed may therefore struggle to feel reassured by the generation of plausible non-critical thoughts alone (Gilbert, 2009a). Developing the experience of compassion towards oneself provides a link to positive emotional experience and increases the ability of the person to self-soothe.

Shame, self-criticism and psychosis

Experiences of bullying, humiliation, trauma, shame and loss are associated with an increased risk of developing psychosis (Bebbington *et al.*, 2004; Campbell & Morrison, 2007; Romme & Escher, 1989). Post-psychotic trauma symptoms are correlated with shame related to psychosis (Turner *et al.*, 2013) and there are numerous potential sources of shame following a psychotic episode. Turner *et al.* (2013) suggest that internal shame related to psychotic experiences may lead to vulnerability to depression following a psychotic episode.

Malevolent voices can be perceived as powerful and omnipotent, resembling the way self-critical thoughts are perceived by people with depression (Gilbert *et al.*, 2001). People who hear malevolent voices perceive the attacks as more external and more insulting than self-critical thoughts alone (Gilbert *et al.*, 2001). It has been suggested that the pseudo-social nature of the relationship with voices triggers internal *and* external shame (Gilbert & Irons, 2005). A feeling of reassurance can therefore be difficult to obtain in people who are self-critical and those who are persecuted by malevolent voices.

Psychosis is characterised by a high sense of external threat and fear of others (Freeman & Garety, 2003) and threat-based emotions such as fear, anxiety and anger may contribute to paranoid delusions and hallucinations (Freeman & Garety, 2003). Mills *et al.* (2007, cited in Hutton *et al.*, 2012) suggest that hateful self-criticism may lead to a heightened sense of threat and a misattribution of the actions of others, leading to the development of paranoia. People with persecutory delusions engage in more hateful self-criticism and less self-reassurance than a healthy population, which may serve to maintain delusions (Hutton *et al.*, 2012). Furthermore, people with psychosis often display concerns about how they are perceived by others (Kingdon *et al.*, 2011; Lysaker *et al.*, 2010) and have a high sense of external threat (Freeman & Garety, 2003), which may contribute to an increased vulnerability to feelings of shame. Given that shame is typically associated with social withdrawal, this can make the development of therapeutic relationships difficult.

Connor and Birchwood (2013) found that voice hearers' self-critical thoughts reflect the relationship they have with their voice and suggest that being able to self-reassure may act as a protective factor, resulting in more benign, less shaming voice content. This was found to be the case in a pilot of CMT with people who heard malevolent voices; following CMT their voices became less malevolent and more reassuring (Mayhew & Gilbert, 2008). Eicher *et al.* (2013) also found higher self-compassion is linked to decreased positive psychotic symptoms. Early studies have showed promising results for compassion based approaches for psychosis (Braehler *et al.*, 2013; Gumley *et al.*, 2010; Johnson *et al.*, 2011; Laithwaite *et al.*, 2009; Lincoln *et al.*, 2013; Mayhew & Gilbert, 2008).

CFT is specifically designed to reduce critical factors underlying limited 'engagement' in terms of helping people address their key fears or threats, strengthen their ability to self-soothe, develop courage and do what is most helpful for them to move forward. There is often a high level of emotional turbulence in the period before, during and following the acute phase of psychosis, so being able to access the soothing system to regulate affect is important with regards to relapse and recovery (Laithwaite *et al.*, 2009). CFT provides an interpersonally and developmentally sensitive approach to recovery from psychosis (Gumley *et al.*, 2010) that focuses on increasing the capacity for improved social relating.

Aims, stages, strategies and techniques

CFT aims to reduce shame and self-critical thinking, change unhelpful behaviours and unwanted consequences arising from these, plus build capacity for compassion and self-soothing. Clients with psychosis who experience shame or self-critical thinking may have other issues to address including trauma or abuse, difficulties in mentalising, attachment difficulties, self-harming, alexithymia or substance abuse. Such issues can be incorporated into the CFT formulation and therapy.

The therapist needs to model compassion, and it is helpful for the therapist to practise compassion and the skills training. It is essential that the therapeutic relationship is a compassionate one and that therapy is a safe space for the client. This may be the only safe place they have and, as such, may initially be the only place that they can access their soothing system. In highly threat-focused clients, consideration needs to be given to gradually desensitising them to the experience of affiliative positive affect. For them, stimulation of the soothing system is likely to also activate their threat system (i.e. they perceive it as 'dangerous to let their guard down'). This is tackled by the therapist having an open discussion with the client that the therapeutic relationship *itself*, as it develops, may trigger the client's threat system. The explanation to the client of why this may happen can help prevent disengagement (as it is not an unpleasant surprise when it occurs) and initiates the CFT psychoeducation and self-soothing work relating to emotions. During sessions the pace is measured, allowing time to be able to *feel*, name, discuss and work with emotional processes that are occurring during the session.

Assessment

Initial assessment is a standard psychological assessment of difficulties including psychotic symptoms, shame, self-critical thoughts or voices. Background including any trauma should also be assessed. Assessment examines the intensity, frequency, content and distress relating to these difficulties as well as assessing any coping strategies. In CFT, the person's difficulties are understood as coping or survival strategies they employ to protect them against their fears, which in turn arise from their previous experiences. Language used in assessment is very much related to this and terms such as 'survival strategies' are used instead of 'symptoms'. Assessment considers the 'unintended consequences' arising from the use of safety behaviours and any efforts the client makes to cope with these consequences. The key theme in CFT is that as humans, we are 'all in the same boat' trying to survive whatever challenges life may throw at us. Again, during assessment, this idea is shared with the client to start the process of de-shaming. Various measures may be completed to assess shame (eg: Goss, Gilbert & Allan, 1994), compassion (Hacker, 2008; Neff, 2003) or self criticism (Gilbert et al, 2004).

When working with people with psychosis who are hard to reach, CFT typically takes at least forty 60-minute sessions over the course of a year. CFT in itself is not a manualised approach that follows a regimented protocol, but a collaborative and flexible approach adapting to the client's needs. Certain critical elements are always present, including psychoeducation, formulation and skills training, but there is no set formula as to what particular order these are delivered.

In each session it is helpful to agree an 'escape clause', emphasising that the client can choose how long they stay in the room and that they may have comfort breaks (whatever makes them feel at ease). The client is reminded that they are 'in charge' of the session in terms of what they feel able to discuss. The session location is agreed prior to therapy, with consideration given to where the client feels safest. Clients may wish to meet informally at first, perhaps at a community art project or at a drop-in. In short, extensive consideration is given to the reduction of potential engagement barriers.

Addressing concerns and fears: psychoeducation in CFT

Early dialogue to elicit fears or concerns the client has about CFT offers opportunity for psychoeducation. The client's understanding of compassion and their fears of developing it are discussed, including fears of compassion from others, towards others and towards the self. Anxieties may include such misconceptions as "If I'm compassionate to others they'll see me as weak", "self-compassion will let me off the hook for my bad behaviour", "compassion from others is dangerous because they have ulterior motives". Constant vigilance for threat may have been functional for clients, so feeling safe may be an alien experience. Clients may fear their own emotions and of feeling unfamiliar emotions. In those who have been abused, to feel self-compassion may have another challenge – "what does it mean (about the world/my care givers) if it *wasn't* my fault"? The Fears of Compassion Scale (Gilbert *et al.*, 2011) is a useful assessment tool to promote discussion and normalise client concerns.

The principles of CFT are discussed with clients to socialise them to the model. The key message is that much of what occurs to us (particularly our early life) is not our fault or of our choosing. Attention is also drawn to our innate complexity: we have complex brains, emotions and motives. CFT refers to humans having an 'old brain' and a 'new brain' (see Figure 7.1). The old brain is concerned with threat-based emotions and behaviour: fight, flight, withdraw/engage, sex, status, attachment and tribalism. The new brain's functions are more cognitive: imagination, fantasising, planning, ruminating and the integration of mental abilities. When self-monitoring thoughts, it is the new brain that is used. In people with psychosis, the 'new brain' would be recruited for thoughts about the hallucinatory experiences experienced. The old brain is in action when feeling threatened, for example by voice content. Clear diagrams are used to illustrate this (see Figure 7.1). The old brain–new brain concept aids understanding

Interaction of old and new psychologies

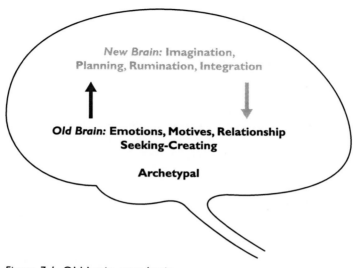

Figure 7.1 Old brain–new brain

From Gilbert & Choden (2013). Reproduced with kind permission Constable & Robinson.

Types of Affect Regulator Systems

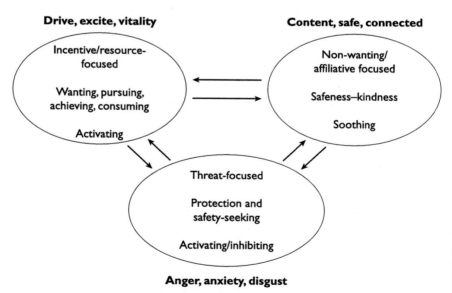

Figure 7.2 Three Circles Model of affect regulation

From Gilbert (2009a). Reproduced with kind permission Constable & Robinson.

of a complex system and helps patients 'make sense' of difficulties in a de-shaming way.

The Three Circles Model (Figure 7.2) outlines three important affect regulation systems in our brain, and it primes discussion about what activates the systems. CFT aims to help clients build capacity to self-soothe and regulate these systems (see Figure 7.2). These three types of emotion regulation systems focus on: threat and self-protection (threat system), doing and achieving (drive system) and contentment and feeling safe (soothing system).

Co-formulation: validating, de-shaming and making sense of 'safety behaviours'

It is helpful to have a formulation on paper so it can be easily referred to each session. The formulation is reworked and reformulated as new material comes to light and new insights are made. People with high shame may be fearful of disclosing personal information, while in psychosis, there may be added factors such as malevolent voices warning them not to disclose certain information, or paranoid ideation about what may happen if they do tell the therapist. As such, it often takes longer to formulate with this client group. A key aspect of formulating using the CFT model is that the process of formulation itself is a way to start de-shaming the client by understanding difficulties as 'survival strategies' (employed to protect against their fears materialising) or 'unintended consequences' from these strategies.

Survival strategies

These are understood as 'better safe than sorry' actions that individuals may engage in to protect them from perceived risks; for example, avoiding engaging in conversation to protect themselves from being thought of as boring. However, behaviours will have unwanted 'side effects'. It is helpful to use examples to illustrate this. The therapist may use cognitive and/or behavioural exercises to help the client to address fears underlying their coping behaviour. Clients are not asked to give up these strategies; rather they are supported to become more compassionate so they no longer need their survival strategies.

Formulation

The CFT formulation (see Figure 7.4 Maggie's formulation) identifies the client's key fears and critical beliefs (the 'inner bully') and the function of this is explored (e.g. self-improvement or punishment). Significant background events are gathered, particularly those relating to early attachment, trauma and experiences of being soothed or threatened by others. The formulation is contextual rather than symptom-focused and validates difficulties in the context of life events. There is a focus on courage, asserting that many of life's circumstances are not under a person's control and are not their fault – they are just doing the best they can.

Working with emotions

Compassion is linked to soothing, which involves engaging with pain and suffering with kindness and support. Central to CFT is the importance of courage and learning how to tolerate and face up to difficult situations and emotions. The complexity of emotions and associated desires, thoughts and behaviours is discovered using chair work. In the 'compassion chair' the client reflects on their emotions, motives and thoughts from a compassionate perspective to help them validate and have empathy for their emotions [refer to Gilbert (2009b) for further details on CFT chair work].

Key skills in Compassionate Mind Training

Throughout CFT the therapist guides the client in developing compassion skills: from self to others, self to self, and from others to self (the compassion 'flow'). The skills training outlined below is referred to as Compassionate Mind Training (CMT). CMT refers to techniques that can be used to help people experience compassion (Gilbert & Irons, 2005). Clients have likened this to 'physiotherapy for the brain' as it stimulates a new way of thinking that strengthens capacity for self-soothing and aids development of a more compassionate way of self-relating. Through practice, the client develops empathy and sympathy for their distress, is more able to be aware of their emotions and thoughts without judgement or blame and more easily able to self-soothe and regulate emotions.

Compassion qualities and the skills training to develop them are illustrated in Figure 7.3. The attributes of compassion are viewed as: sensitivity (to distress), distress tolerance, empathy, sympathy, warmth, non-judgement and care for the wellbeing of self or others. These attributes can be developed and strengthened by skills training using imagery, reasoning, behaviour change, sensory focus, becoming more aware of feelings and attentional exercises. Compassion is a combination of these and the therapist supports and encourages practice. The importance of courage is stressed when developing compassion: courage to take actions needed to promote the flourishing and wellbeing of ourselves and others. If clients struggle with the concept of compassion (and even the concept of emotions) some preliminary psychoeducational and experiential work on emotions will need to be completed prior to CFT.

Compassionate attention

This is learning to attend differently to the environment using compassion to organise the mind and the different aspects and parts of the self. It is about helping the client shift their attention, reasoning, thinking and focus onto what is helpful

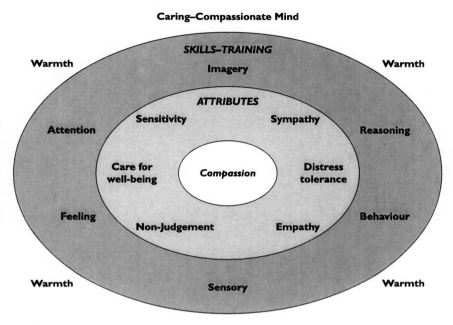

Figure 7.3 Compassion Circle

From Gilbert (2009a). Reproduced with kind permission Constable & Robinson.

for them. The client is encouraged from a position of being threatened by their internal world to be motivated to bring compassion to it. This may involve training clients to attend to people who are supportive rather than those who are dismissive or hostile, or learning to attend to kind facial expressions. This shifts attention away from stimuli that trigger the threat-affect system to those that stimulate the soothing-affect system.

Mindfulness techniques enable clients to notice the state of their mind and emotions. Mindfulness is a useful skill in itself (Chadwick, 2006), but is also a helpful first place to start with a client in CFT, to get them used to the process of observing. Certain skills are also taught, including breathing exercises to trigger a relaxed state and the feeling of safeness (Gilbert, 2009a).

Compassionate imagery

Compassionate imagery is a large component of the CMT exercises used to facilitate stimulation of the soothing-affect system. There are various exercises, including imagining a 'compassionate other' or 'perfect nurturer' (Lee, 2009) who directs compassion towards them.

Safe place imagery is guided discovery incorporating all the senses, where the client imagines themselves being in a place that feels safe, and either real or imagined. It is a place of *safeness*, rather than one of *safety* (which is associated with the threat system). Initially it may be helpful for the therapist to suggest they can see a beach or forest for example. Once the client finds their own safe place attention is focused on what it *feels like* to be in their safe place. It is helpful to intertwine qualities of compassion into this exercise, suggesting that the safe place feels welcoming or has an element of warmth.

'Focusing on the compassionate part of the self' exercise asks the client to imagine themselves at 'their best' and to bring to mind what posture they adopted, their facial expression, voice tone and what they said or did. Guided discovery can be used to help cue people into compassionate qualities such as an open posture, warm voice tone and so forth. Similarly, role play can be used. A client can *imagine* themselves with the qualities of compassion and *imagine* compassion flowing out to others. This exercise is helpful if clients do not feel they have any compassionate qualities or cannot recall any times they have been compassionate to others. It may start with them imagining compassion flowing towards someone (a person or animal) who is cared about. As this client group are frequently socially isolated and without family, this may be a pet, or they may choose a person in the media who they feel needs compassion.

The compassionate colour exercise is a guided exercise that asks clients to close their eyes and bring to mind a compassionate colour. The colour needs to have the qualities of warmth (so the therapist may suggest a 'warm' colour), qualities of acceptance and friendliness and its sole purpose is to 'help you and heal you'. The therapist can help guide the imagery by suggesting the colour may feel warm on the person's skin and so forth. If, and only if, the client feels comfortable with it, the therapist can suggest the colour moves towards the person and either surrounds them or enters through their skin and flows around their body, filling them with warmth and compassion. For those who are very threat focused, this exercise (like all the others) can be developed at the client's pace; allowing them to look at the colour, then walk towards it, then it moves towards them, then it surrounds them.

The key point of all these exercises is to stimulate the soothing system and develop compassionate qualities, so it does not really matter what stage of the exercise is reached as long as it 'does the job' (i.e. the client feels compassion). The exercises are like a 'tool box' in that the therapist and client can choose which ones to use; some will be preferred or more effective than others.

Compassionate thinking

Various exercises can be used including compassion-focused thought diaries or compassionate letters written by the client to themselves. The focus is on helping the person acknowledge their emotional distress, validate it, have empathy for it and be able to consider what may help them to move forward. The client is encouraged to think in a kinder and less self-critical way. The function of self-criticism is again considered alongside the fears of letting this inner critic go. Clients may start by writing an (unsent) letter to a friend, or even write to themselves from the perspective of a compassionate other (prior to writing to themselves from themselves).

Compassionate behaviours

A key focus is finding for the client what is experienced as helpful, kind and supportive in this moment. Compassionate behaviours are often not easy, as they can require strength and courage. A compassionate behaviour for a person in an abusive relationship may be to leave. A compassionate behaviour for a person with psychosis may be to seek therapy to help them increase their feelings of control over the voices. The aim is engagement in a behaviour that can help the person to move forward and flourish, and the therapist can draw attention to instances of compassion when the client finds these difficult to identify.

Case illustration: Maggie

Maggie is 46 and lives alone. She hears critical voices, experiences visual and tactile hallucinations and believes she is being poisoned by nurses. She experiences social anxiety, low mood and frequent suicidal ideation. She worries about therapy for fear of what others may think. Maggie has physically assaulted people, including staff, and spent several months stalking a woman who she believed had rejected her.

Maggie experiences shame regarding her psychosis, being detained for compulsory hospital treatment, past abuse and weight gain. She uses alcohol problematically and used to inject heroin; she is currently receiving methadone treatment. Initial assessment suggests she has poor emotional literacy, difficulty recognising emotions in others and limited mentalisation (Fonagy & Bateman, 2006) abilities. Maggie has difficulty trusting others which has been a barrier to seeking therapy. She fears breaches in confidentiality, negative appraisal and abandonment by the therapist, yet also fears dependency. Radical collaboration has been used initially to develop the therapeutic relationship, which involves active listening, supported discovery, clear discussions about confidentiality, responsibility and choice (Chadwick, 2006).

Assessment and engagement issues

Maggie's alexithymia was recognised as a potential therapy block as she struggled to identify and name emotions. She dreaded her emotions spiralling out of control and feared 'failing' CFT. Maggie worried that if compassionate, she would let her 'guard down' and others would victimise her. She was wary of accepting others' compassion, and suspicious of their motives. She feared self-compassion and letting go of self-blame for the abuse she experienced.

Developing the CFT formulation

The CFT formulation was developed and modified as information came to light, trust grew and insights were made (see Figures 7.4 and 7.5). The formulation was used to help Maggie understand her problems were not her fault; rather, they were linked to her attempts to cope with her fears. Key influences and experiences were elicited along with related fears. Survival strategies used to protect Maggie against these fears and the resulting unwanted consequences were explored. For example, Maggie's substance use was understood as a way of emotional control, with side effects of addiction and not understanding her emotional landscape. Opportunities to de-shame and orientate her to CFT, using terminology such as 'survival strategy' and 'unwanted side effects' as opposed to 'problem behaviours' and 'symptoms' were used. Maggie's shame relating to her early experiences, how it blocked social connection, increased social anxiety and repeatedly triggered her threat system were explored. Example (fictitious) 'case studies' were used to illustrate the model and to de-stigmatise and normalise her fears and survival strategies.

Socialising Maggie to CFT: understanding motives and emotions

The 'Three Circles Model' (Figure 7.2) illustrates the relationship between the threat, soothing and drive-affect systems. Maggie knew her childhood experiences led her to develop a highly sensitive threat system and understood this could be activated when she starts to feel safe or soothed. This led to anxiety, hallucinations, irritability and shame related thoughts, feelings and behaviour. Maggie's soothing system was poorly developed, as she had few experiences of feeling safe or soothed. She recognised her drive system could go into 'overdrive' where she would write prolifically; when depressed this system was underactive, leading to low motivation and feeling flat.

Figure 7.1 (the old brain–new brain) was used to explain in a straightforward, de-shaming way, why human brains and emotions behave the way they do with a focus on the 'threat system'. In the context of psychosis, it was discussed how Maggie's 'new brain' consciously tried to make sense of her hallucinations and the 'old brain' was triggered into action when she felt threatened by these.

Psychoeducation

Preliminary work focused on developing Maggie's ability to recognise emotions using photos, role play, experiential exercises and diary keeping. Psychoeducation also provided information about the links between her thinking, emotions and behaviour (see CFT workbook by Gilbert, 2010b). Maggie kept a written and

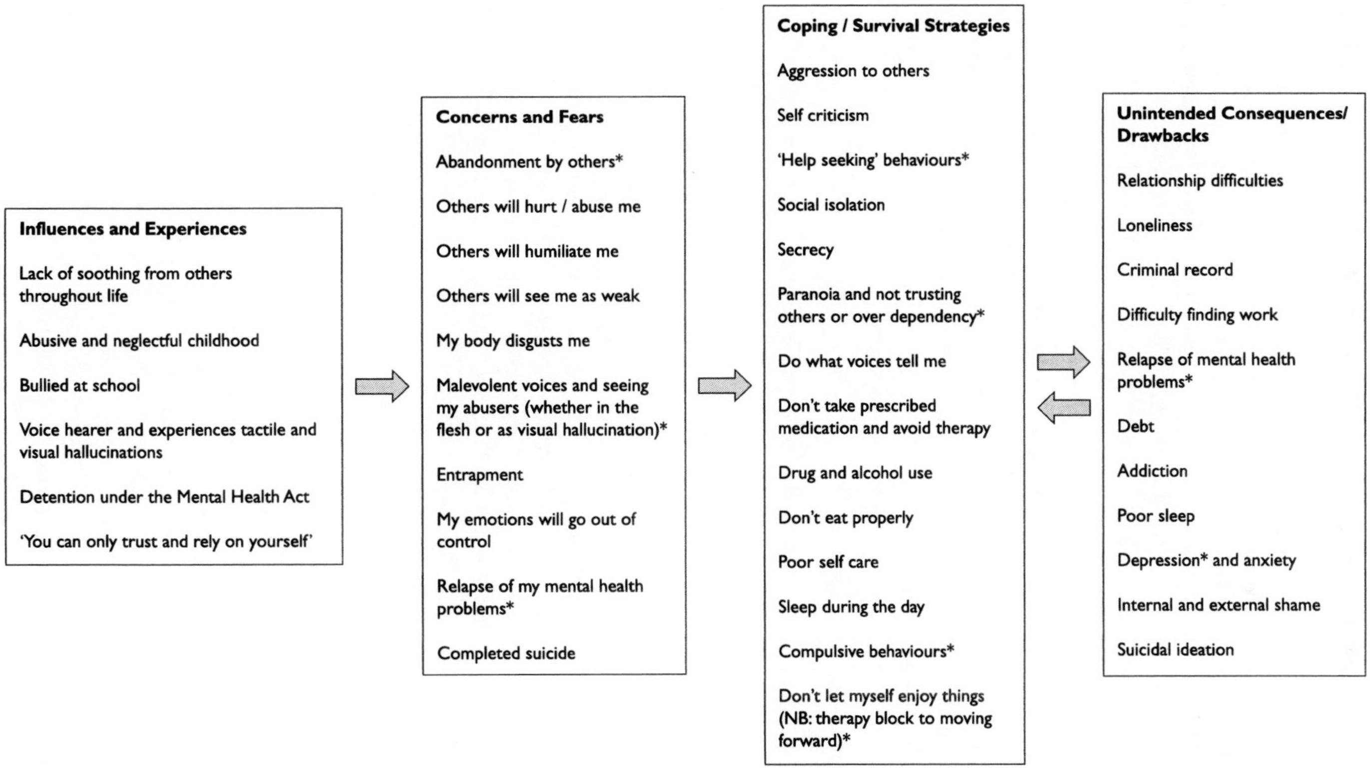

Influences and Experiences

Lack of soothing from others throughout life

Abusive and neglectful childhood

Bullied at school

Voice hearer and experiences tactile and visual hallucinations

Detention under the Mental Health Act

'You can only trust and rely on yourself'

Concerns and Fears

Abandonment by others*

Others will hurt / abuse me

Others will humiliate me

Others will see me as weak

My body disgusts me

Malevolent voices and seeing my abusers (whether in the flesh or as visual hallucination)*

Entrapment

My emotions will go out of control

Relapse of my mental health problems*

Completed suicide

Coping / Survival Strategies

Aggression to others

Self criticism

'Help seeking' behaviours*

Social isolation

Secrecy

Paranoia and not trusting others or over dependency*

Do what voices tell me

Don't take prescribed medication and avoid therapy

Drug and alcohol use

Don't eat properly

Poor self care

Sleep during the day

Compulsive behaviours*

Don't let myself enjoy things (NB: therapy block to moving forward)*

Unintended Consequences/ Drawbacks

Relationship difficulties

Loneliness

Criminal record

Difficulty finding work

Relapse of mental health problems*

Debt

Addiction

Poor sleep

Depression* and anxiety

Internal and external shame

Suicidal ideation

Figure 7.4 Maggie's formulation (* disclosed later during work)

audio diary to support her to notice, name and respond to her emotions and their patterns.

In terms of fears, blocks and resistance to CFT, psychoeducation addressed how CFT would help Maggie manage emotions. Qualities of compassion were explored, alongside a discussion of how compassion would increase her skills and develop courage to explore her fears and emotions. Maggie's concerns were normalised and the idea that 'it's understandable why you feel that/why you would do that, given your life circumstances' was used to model compassion and de-shaming.

Maggie found the old brain–new brain (Figure 7.1) explained links between anxiety and self-criticism and her appraisals of the hallucinations and her abuse. She also found it powerfully de-shaming as she realised her feelings were not 'abnormal' or her fault. Maggie liked the description of how the 'new brain' can be harnessed to think more compassionately about her difficulties to gain more control over her emotions.

CMT experiential exercises

Maggie was supported in session to complete CMT exercises and was also texted weekly 'practice reminders'.

Chair work

Maggie identified a 'head–heart lag' (Lee, 2005): she was able to cognitively *understand* emotions but unable to link this with the *experience* of emotions. Early in therapy Maggie viewed a recording of chair work to help her conceptualise it and afterwards her concerns were dealt with before agreeing to start. The chair work related to Maggie's emotional responses to the voices as well as other situations arising. Maggie was not left in any one chair for *too* long as this can be aversive for those who struggle considerably with their emotions. However, Maggie was there long enough to be able to *feel* each emotional response to her voices and consider the thoughts and behaviours linked to it.

Compassionate attention

Maggie needed support to recognise warmth. Photos and film clips were used to practise attending to others' facial expressions, body posture, gestures and voice tone. Maggie was able to recall memories of kindness to others and some memories of others being kind to her (though the latter needed more assistance) and was supported to connect with the feelings of kindness in these memories. When Maggie raised any threatening situations (typically involving social situations where she perceived others were thinking negatively towards her) this was an opportunity to practise connecting with her developing sense of compassion.

Compassionate imagery

Initially, soothing rhythm breathing was used along with mindfulness to calm body and mind, using smooth pebbles to practise in session. Maggie chose to take a pebble home as a transitional object to use for mindful practice but was soon using numerous environmental stimuli. Maggie chose the imagery exercises that she found most effective at stimulating her soothing system. She found a Safe Place easy to bring to mind (woodland), but partway through the exercise Maggie felt she was being followed by a 'bad person' through the wood. When the Safe Place felt unsafe, the exercise was paused, Maggie was supported to engage in soothing rhythm breathing and the exercise tried again. With practice, the feeling of threat disappeared. Interestingly, Maggie found the same element of threat appeared in the Compassionate Colour exercise in that the colour tried to smother her, rather than surround her with warmth. Using Maggie's feedback, the wording of the exercise was modified so that she approached the colour to feel its warmth (rather than the other way around). The tendency to perceive threat in the exercises was understood with Maggie as her internal threat system automatically inserting an element of danger into her internal world.

Following the development of trust, Maggie began to talk more about herself. When she felt able to discuss her compassion to others she was supported to imagine her compassion flowing to someone she cared for (she chose her dog). This exercise also elicited sadness from Maggie, which clinical experience suggests is not uncommon, particularly if people have had little compassion in their lives. Maggie said that she found it helpful to identify this and wanted to 'feed the seed of compassion'. Maggie also developed an image of a compassionate other (Aslan from *The Lion, The Witch and The Wardrobe*) that embodied warmth, strength, wisdom and acceptance.

Compassionate thinking

A number of sessions focused on compassionate letter writing in session and then at home. Maggie started by writing to another in need, then writing to herself from the perspective of her compassionate other (Aslan) and, lastly, writing to herself from the compassionate part of herself. Therapeutic letters from the therapist were used to model compassion and to help her attend compassionately to her progress and her difficulties. Ways that Maggie could cognitively reduce the power of the hallucinations were also discussed (Meaden *et al.*, 2012), along with ways to soothe and ground herself.

Compassionate behaviour

Maggie was supported with compassionate self-behaviours, including courage, practising CMT exercises, self-care, working to reduce the power of her voices, allowing herself to enjoy activities and getting out of the house to meet people.

Behavioural activation (Martell *et al.*, 2001) was used to stimulate the drive-affect system, boost energy levels, motivation and mood. The importance of recognising when the drive system was overactive and how to calm it was also discussed.

Reformulation

This reformulation process (see Figure 7.5) outlined how the unwanted consequences of Maggie's survival strategies reinforced many of her fears, particularly relationship anxieties and her shame-based thinking. CFT helped Maggie identify her strengths and qualities which became the compassionate focus for her and gave hope for a more positive future.

Progress and outcomes

Maggie's depression reduced and her anxiety and self-reported shame diminished. Maggie's self-view appeared to change through the process of reformulating and she was able to think more self-compassionately. The voices remained but she better understood them and they did not trigger self-critical thoughts or coping strategies (such as social isolation). Maggie became able to recognise and express emotions in herself and others. Her confidence in trying new helpful behaviours grew, including joining a creative writing group. Instead of shutting away memories and feelings, Maggie became aware of these, which enabled her to develop ways of responding to them in a compassionate and understanding way. Maggie requested and was subsequently referred for therapy related to her history of abuse and problematic substance use.

Conclusions and implications

Individuals who come from neglectful, critical or abusive backgrounds often find it difficult to self-soothe (Gilbert & Irons, 2004) including many with psychosis. CFT activates and strengthens the soothing affect system, which may not be easily accessible in this population (Gumley *et al.*, 2010) so therapy may be slower than with other client groups. It is important to be open and create safeness in the therapy room when using CFT and this is particularly important when working with psychosis, as there is often a high sense of external threat and fear of others. It is helpful to ask clients what voices may be saying about the therapy and what the voices' fears are, in order to de-shame, normalise and tackle fears, blocks or resistance early.

The development of a therapeutic relationship may trigger a sensitive threat system so this needs to be given attention and openly discussed at the outset. When engaging clients it is helpful to understand where the client may become stuck and which CMT skills or attributes may be difficult – the Fears of Compassion Scale can be a useful aid. It is also critical to address therapists'

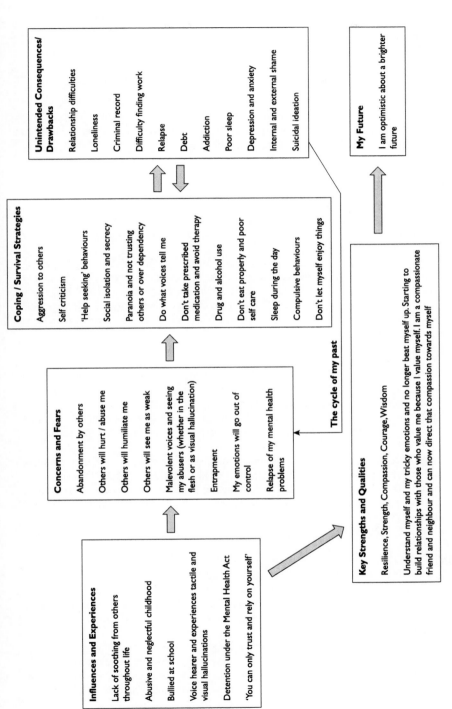

Influences and Experiences

Lack of soothing from others throughout life

Abusive and neglectful childhood

Bullied at school

Voice hearer and experiences tactile and visual hallucinations

Detention under the Mental Health Act

'You can only trust and rely on yourself'

Concerns and Fears

Abandonment by others

Others will hurt / abuse me

Others will humiliate me

Others will see me as weak

Malevolent voices and seeing my abusers (whether in the flesh or as visual hallucination)

Entrapment

My emotions will go out of control

Relapse of my mental health problems

Coping / Survival Strategies

Aggression to others

Self criticism

'Help seeking' behaviours

Social isolation and secrecy

Paranoia and not trusting others or over dependency

Do what voices tell me

Don't take prescribed medication and avoid therapy

Drug and alcohol use

Don't eat properly and poor self care

Sleep during the day

Compulsive behaviours

Don't let myself enjoy things

Unintended Consequences/ Drawbacks

Relationship difficulties

Loneliness

Criminal record

Difficulty finding work

Relapse

Debt

Addiction

Poor sleep

Depression and anxiety

Internal and external shame

Suicidal ideation

The cycle of my past

Key Strengths and Qualities

Resilience, Strength, Compassion, Courage, Wisdom

Understand myself and my tricky emotions and no longer beat myself up. Starting to build relationships with those who value me because I value myself. I am a compassionate friend and neighbour and can now direct that compassion towards myself

My Future

I am optimistic about a brighter future

Figure 7.5 Maggie's reformulation

concerns in supervision (see also Chadwick, 2006) as therapists themselves need to remain open with an active soothing system so they may actively practise compassion themselves.

CFT is an approach to working with shame that is in the early stages of developing an evidence base for use in people who experience psychosis (Braehler *et al.*, 2013). It lends itself particularly for use in psychosis where it can additionally target the emotional impact of symptoms and social relating to reduce the risk of relapse and improve quality of life.

References

Bebbington, P. E., Bhugra, D., Brugha, T., Singleton, N., Farrell, M., Jenkins, R. . . . Meltzer, H. (2004). Psychosis victimisation and childhood disadvantage: Evidence from the second British National Survey of Psychiatric Morbidity. *British Journal of Psychiatry*, *185*, 220–226.

Braehler, C., Gumley, A., Harper, J., Wallace, S., Norrie, J. & Gilbert, P. (2013). Exploring change processes in compassion focused therapy in psychosis: Results of a feasibility randomized controlled trial. *British Journal of Clinical Psychology*, *52*(2), 199–214.

Campbell, M. L. & Morrison, A. P. (2007). The relationship between bullying, psychotic like experiences and appraisals in 14–16 year olds. *Behaviour Research and Therapy*, *45*, 1579–1591.

Chadwick, P. (2006). *Person-based cognitive therapy for distressing psychosis*. Chichester, Sussex: John Wiley & Sons.

Connor, C. & Birchwood, M. (2013). Through the looking glass: Self reassuring meta-cognitive capacity and its relationship with the thematic content of voices. *Frontiers in Human Neuroscience*, *7*, 213. doi: 10.3389/fnhum.2013.00213.

Eicher, A.C., Davis, L.W. & Lysaker, P. H. (2013) Self-compassion: A novel link with symptoms in schizophrenia? *The Journal of Nervous and Mental Disease*, *201*, 389–393.

Fonagy, P. & Bateman, A. (2006). Mechanism of change in mentalisation based treatment of borderline personality disorder. *Journal of Clinical Psychology*, *62*, 411–430.

Freeman, D. & Garety, P. A. (2003). Connecting neurosis and psychosis: The direct influence of emotion on delusions and hallucinations. *Behaviour Research and Therapy*, *41*(8), 923–947.

Gilbert, P. (1992). *Depression: The evolution of powerlessness*. Hove, E. Sussex: Lawrence Erlbaum.

Gilbert, P. (1997). The evolution of social attractiveness and its role in shame, humiliation, guilt and therapy. *British Journal of Medical Psychology*, *70*(2), 113–147.

Gilbert, P. (2000). Social mentalities: Internal 'social' conflicts and the role of inner warmth and compassion in cognitive therapy. In, P. Gilbert & K. G. Bailey (eds), *Genes on the couch: Explorations in evolutionary psychotherapy*. Hove, E. Sussex: Brunner-Routledge.

Gilbert, P. (2009a). *The compassionate mind*. London: Constable & Robinson.

Gilbert, P. (2009b). An introduction to the theory and practice of Compassion Focused Therapy and Compassionate Mind Training for shame based difficulties. Available at: http://www.compassionatemind.co.uk/downloads/training_materials/4.%20New_one-two_day_handout.pdf (accessed 6 October 2014).

Gilbert, P. (2010a). *Compassion Focused Therapy: The CBT distinctive features series.* W. Dryden (ed.). London: Routledge.

Gilbert, P. (2010b). *Training our minds in, with and for compassion. An introduction to concepts and compassion-focused exercises* [online]. Available at http://www.compassionatemind.co.uk/ (accessed 8 May 2014).

Gilbert, P., Birchwood, M., Gilbert, J., Trower, P., Hay, J., & Murray, B. . . . Miles, J. N. (2001). An exploration of evolved mental mechanisms for dominant and subordinate behaviour in relation to auditory hallucinations in schizophrenia and critical thoughts in depression. *Psychological Medicine, 31*(6), 1117–1127.

Gilbert, P. & Choden (2013). Mindful compassion; using the power of mindfulness and compassion to transform our lives. London, Robinson.

Gilbert, P., Clarke, M., Hempel, S., Miles, J. N. & Irons, C. (2004). Criticising and reassuring oneself: An exploration of forms and reasons in female students. *British Journal of Clinical Psychology, 43*, 31–50.

Gilbert, P. & Irons, C. (2004). A pilot exploration of the use of compassionate images in a group of self-critical people. *Memory, 12*(4), 507–516.

Gilbert, P. & Irons, C. (2005). Focused therapies and compassionate mind training for shame and self-attacking. In P. Gilbert (ed.), *Compassion: Conceptualisations, research and use in psychotherapy*. London: Routledge.

Gilbert, P., McEwan, K., Matos, M. & Rivis, A. (2011). Fears of compassion: Development of three self-report measures. *Psychology and Psychotherapy: Theory, Research and Practice, 84*(3), 239–255.

Gilbert, P. & Procter, S. (2006). Compassionate mind training for people with high shame and self criticism: Overview and pilot study of a group approach. *Clinical Psychology and Psychotherapy, 13*, 353–379.

Goss, K., Gilbert, P. & Allan, S. (1994). An exploration of shame measures: I: The 'other as shamer' scale. Personality and Individual Differences, 17, 713–717.

Gumley, A., Braehler, C., Laithwaite, H., Macbeth, A. & Gilbert, P. (2010). A compassion focused model of recovery after psychosis. *International Journal of Cognitive Therapy, 3*(2), 186–201.

Hacker, Thomas (2008). The relational compassion scale: development and validation of a new self rated scale for the assessment of self-other compassion. D Clin Psy thesis, University of Glasgow.

Hutton, P., Kelly, J., Lowens, I., Taylor, P. J. & Tai, S. (2012). Self-attacking and self-reassurance in persecutory delusions: A comparison of healthy, depressed and paranoid individuals. *Psychiatry Research*, http://dx.doi.org/10.1016/j.psychres.2012.08.010.

Johnson, D. P., Penn, D. L., Fredrickson, B. L., Kring, A. M., Meyer, P. S., Catalino, L. I. & Brantley, M. (2011). A pilot study of loving-kindness meditation for the negative symptoms of schizophrenia. *Schizophrenia Research, 129*(2), 137–140.

Kingdon, D., Kinoshita, K., Kinoshita, Y., Saka, K., Arisue, Y., Dayson, D. . . . Furukawa, T. A. (2011). Fear of negative evaluation is associated with delusional ideation in non-clinical population and patients with schizophrenia. *Social Psychiatry and Psychiatric Epidemiology, 46*(8), 703–710.

Laithwaite, H., O'Hanlon, M., Collins, P., Doyle, P., Abraham, L., Porter, S. & Gumley, A. (2009). Recovery After Psychosis (RAP): A compassion focused programme for individuals residing in high security settings. *Behavioural and Cognitive Psychotherapy, 37*, 511–526.

Lee, D. (2009). The perfect nurturer: a model to develop a compassionate mind within the context of cognitive therapy. In P. Gilbert (ed.), *Compassion: Conceptualisations, research and use in psychotherapy* (pp. 326–351). Hove, E. Sussex: Routledge.

Lincoln, T., Hohenhaus, F., & Hartmann, M. (2013). Can paranoid thoughts be reduced by targeting negative emotions and self-esteem? An experimental investigation of a brief compassion-focused intervention. *Cognitive Therapy and Research, 37*(2), 390–402.

Lysaker, P. H., Yanos, P. T., Outcalf, J. & Roe, D. (2010). Association of stigma, self-esteem, and symptoms with concurrent and prospective assessment of social anxiety in schizophrenia. *Clinical Schizophrenia and Related Psychoses, 4*(1), 41–48.

Martell, C. R., Addis, M. E. & Jacobson, N. S. (2001). *Depression in context: Strategies for guided action.* New York: Norton and Company.

Mayhew, S. L. & Gilbert, P. (2008). Compassionate mind training with people who hear malevolent voices: A case series report. *Clinical Psychology and Psychotherapy, 15*(2), 113–138.

Meaden, A., Keen, N., Aston, R., Karen, B. & Bucci, S. (2012). *Cognitive therapy for command hallucinations: An advanced practical companion.* Hove, E. Sussex: Routledge.

Mills, A., Gilbert, P., Bellew, R., McEwan, K. & Gale, C. (2007). Paranoid beliefs and self-criticism in students. *Clinical Psychology and Psychotherapy, 14*, 358–364.

Neff, K. D. (2003). Development and validation of a scale to measure self-compassion. Self and Identity, 2, 223–250.

Romme, M. A. J. & Escher, A. D. (1989). Hearing voices. *Schizophrenia Bulletin, 15*, 209–216.

Turner, M., Bernard, M., Birchwood, M., Jackson, C. & Jones, C. (2013). The contribution of shame to post-psychotic trauma. *British Journal of Clinical Psychology, 52*(2), 115–234.

Chapter 8

An existential approach to therapy

Core values and therapeutic principles

Catherine Amphlett

> (I)f real success is to attend to the effort to bring a man to a definite position, one must first of all take pains to find him where he is and begin there. This is the secret of the art of helping others.
>
> (Kierkegaard, 1848: 334)
>
> we owe it to our clients to keep cleansing the lenses through which we look at the world.
>
> (van Deurzen, 2012: 172)

Introduction

Values provide a foundation, helping us to gain a sense of who we are and to connect with others. As therapists, our values, as well as those of the contexts we are embedded in, guide our practice. Whatever our approach, whilst we often reflect with clients on their values and beliefs, our own and those of the services we work in are rarely made explicit. In this chapter, a way of working with people who have experiences labelled as 'psychosis' will be described, one which is grounded in existential values. After clarifying these values, some principles of existential practice will be identified as a basis for therapeutic work with this client group, particularly those who are reluctant to engage with mental health services. It is argued that adopting an existential attitude – acknowledging universal aspects of life alongside the uniqueness of individual experience – can facilitate development of a strong therapeutic alliance and provide a basis upon which other psychosocial interventions might be integrated.

Theoretical background and development: The existential approach

The existential approach to therapy is philosophical, involving exploration of what it means to be alive. Reflection upon these universal issues within therapy is carried out with an open mind and an attempt to avoid the application of pre-established categories or interpretations. As such, existential practitioners are concerned with description and clarification of the different levels of experience and existence that people are confronted with (e.g. van Deurzen, 2002).

Two complementary philosophies, Existentialism and Phenomenology, have informed the development of a range of existential therapies in Europe and the USA. *Existentialism* is concerned with the subjective dimension of human existence, describing the 'givens' of life (e.g. meaninglessness, death, isolation, freedom and responsibility) and how we experience these. Key existential philosophers include Kierkegaard (1813–1855), Nietzsche (1844–1900), Buber (1878–1965), Tillich (1886–1965), Heidegger (1889–1976) and Sartre (1905–1980). *Phenomenology* is the study of phenomena (the appearance of things) as they present to our consciousness. Husserl (1859–1938) advanced the phenomenological method by evolving the idea of intentionality, describing how our sense of reality is experienced and shaped through our consciousness reaching-out to the world. Phenomenology emphasises absence of an objective or true reality, arguing that we have only our uniquely interpreted one (Spinelli, 1996).

Existential therapy is concerned with how the givens of existence are negotiated by a client, through the interpretations and meanings they assign to their experience (Milton *et al.*, 2002). An individual's difficulties are regarded as attempts to resist or deny the angst and uncertainty demanded by authentic living in the face of life's limitations (Spinelli, 1989). For further description of the philosophical background and development of existential therapies, see Cooper (2003), Spinelli (2007) and van Deurzen and Adams (2011). In this chapter, the work of R. D. Laing will be considered in more depth as aspects of his work informed the development of the British School of Existential Analysis. Laing also had much to say about understanding and working therapeutically with people experiencing psychosis.

R. D. Laing: An existential-phenomenological understanding of the experience of 'psychosis'

Laing's book, *The Divided Self: An Existential Study in Sanity and Madness* (1960), remains a key existential-phenomenological text and the ideas contained within it are still being developed and debated. The influences on Laing's thinking and approach to therapy were many, his ideas evolved over time and he avoided delineating his therapeutic approach for fear of it being corrupted, meaning that it has been difficult to characterise his work (Cooper, 2003).

As a trainee psychiatrist in the 1950s, Laing came to reject the predominance of biological models of distress. He saw psychiatrists as excessively powerful and the psychiatric system as dehumanising and dismissive of those it claimed to help. In his clinical work he therefore attempted to eliminate the gulf between the client and therapist by emphasising the importance of behaving 'in such a way that reassures one's patients that they are in the presence of another human being like themselves' (Thompson, 1997: 596).

Laing's work was rooted in phenomenology, stressing the existence of a world of immediate or 'lived' experience. The aim of phenomenological inquiry is to reveal the minutiae of experience in a descriptive fashion, rather than to *explain* it in causal terms, in order to come to a better understanding of its essence. Laing extended the work of earlier existential-phenomenological practitioners (Cooper, 2003: 95), arguing that when a therapist enters into their client's phenomenologically lived world, meaning can always be found. He asserted that all thoughts, feelings and behaviours were valid and intelligible from the client's perspective and encouraged therapists to consider a client's experiences as meaningful attempts to deal with their world.

Whilst emphasising the importance of an interpersonal, phenomenological approach, Laing (1960) also offered an intrapersonal theory of how psychosis might emerge. First he described the concept of 'ontological security' in which a person will:

> experience his own being as real, alive, whole; as differentiated from the rest of the world in ordinary circumstances so clearly that his identity and autonomy are never in question; as a continuum in time; as having an inner consistency, substantiality, genuineness, and worth
>
> (Laing, 1960: 41)

This existential position was described by Laing as developing in childhood and as enabling a person to face life's challenges without losing a sense of reality. Whilst extreme stress might prompt such a loss, an ontologically secure person will only temporarily experience this.

Laing hypothesised that the roots of psychosis lay in ontological *insecurity* – a partial or almost total absence of the assurances derived from ontological security due to adverse early experiences. If a person is ontologically insecure, he argued, the world and other people become threatening. Laing (1960) outlined a process by which an individual attempts to cope with this threat by splitting into a 'true self', which retreats inwards for protection, and a 'false self', offered to the world. He theorised that psychosis develops as an individual's real self withdraws from their body and other people, and opportunities for genuine relatedness become restricted. Laing drew here on a psychoanalytic concept of the self as an object, rather than the existential view of self as a process and, as will be described, his deterministic view of psychosis has since been challenged by existential practitioners (e.g. van Deurzen, 1998). Through his case descriptions, however, Laing illustrated how an individual's need for meaningful relatedness could not be satisfied if he or she feared loss of their personal identity and his approach to therapy was more holistic.

Putting theory into practice: Laing's therapeutic approach

Laing described the aim of therapy as to discover the meaning behind the beliefs and behaviour of people experiencing psychosis. He saw himself as an 'attendant' in this process:

> Rather than intervene, dispute the individual's claims or numb the fears with medication, Laing observed and provided ... empathy so that he could

eventually reconstruct the individual's situation and understand the fears being defended against.

(Evans, 1976: 141)

Regardless of how strange, confused or destructive an individual's actions might appear, Laing saw them as attempts at self-survival. He argued that individuals experiencing psychosis needed support to help face their anxiety so they were able to break down defensive reactions and foster a more authentic way of being.

For Laing, the role of the therapist was to help clients untie the 'knots' they were in, believing that the best way to do this was by doing the opposite of what they had experienced, through dysfunctional communication patterns, in childhood (Laing, 1970). To facilitate disentanglement he treated his clients as authentically as he could. Thus, Thompson (1995: 93) described Laing's conception of therapy as an 'obstinate attempt by two human beings to be perfectly honest with each other, knowing they will never entirely succeed'. Laing believed that a client's capacity for relatedness could be restored through the therapeutic encounter and that this would facilitate their ability to meet other existential needs, including self-disclosure, relatedness and an experience of ontological security. He adopted a non-invasive approach to therapy, involving a sense of communion, to aid recovery and re-integration.

Laing (1967) believed that anything we are capable of experiencing cannot in itself be toxic, no matter how distressing, and always has a meaningful purpose – *denial* of experience is what gives rise to difficulties. He therefore decided that attending to experience, recognising its revelatory aspects and engaging with it fully, was a vehicle for change. According to Thompson (1997), the emphasis on the transformative nature of experience as a therapeutic tool characterises the existential component of Laing's clinical work and, furthermore, he suggests 'fidelity to experience' is the agent of change in every successful therapy, regardless of the model being adopted.

Criticism and development of Laing's approach

The idea of ontological security can be found in the earlier writings of Tillich (1995/2000). However, Tillich writes that whilst anxiety of fate and death produces a striving for security, no absolute security is possible as 'life demands again and again the courage to surrender some or even all security for the sake of full self-affirmation' (Tillich, 2000: 74). Indeed, Laing has been criticised for not recognising the basic human experience of existential anxiety and for attaching it to psychosis via the concept of 'ontological insecurity' (van Deurzen-Smith, 1991). In addition, drawing on her clinical experience at one of Laing's therapeutic communities, van Deurzen-Smith (1991) has argued that their paradigm failed to give residents an alternative philosophical examination of their situation.

Van Deurzen (1998) has gone on to develop the existential aspects of Laing's approach, asserting that psychosis might emerge following intense prolonged exposure to existential anxiety, which appears to offer a link with the role of early trauma (e.g. Read & Bentall, 2012). Van Deurzen (1998: 11) describes the experience of psychosis as 'an extreme form of the core human experience of being insecure: deeply and totally essentially insecure' and the notion of ontological insecurity as at the heart of existential philosophy. Her starting point for therapy with all clients is the belief that 'life is an endless struggle where moments of ease and happiness are the exception rather than the rule' (1998: 132) but recognises that due to the degree of their sensitivity to interpersonal threat a skilled and sustained approach to therapy is needed with people experiencing psychosis.

A values-based approach

Existential practitioners place much importance on values as these are seen to play a key role in determining purposeful action. Valuing a person's freedom to choose, existential therapists encourage clients to work towards self-examination and self-determination.

Jacobsen (2005) describes how change elicited in the client's value structure and belief system is regarded as an outcome of existential therapy:

> Traditional therapy helps 'the functional man' to function still better, whereas existential therapy helps the individual to find his or her roots and define the value base of the life he or she chooses to live.
>
> (Jacobsen, 2005: 237)

Similarly, van Deurzen (2012) identifies the aim of existential therapy as to assist clients to gain clarity about their beliefs and ideals and to develop a flexible, coherent and resilient values system.

As described, there is great diversity in the practice of existential therapy and many factors influence how an existential therapist chooses to work, including the stage of therapy, what the client wants from therapy, the therapist's experience, the client's disposition and how therapy is proceeding (Cooper, 2003). Jacobsen (2005: 237) attempts to find some common values within the field suggesting, as summarised here, that most existential therapists would agree it is a good thing to:

- listen openly and carefully;
- respect the other person's autonomy and dignity;
- communicate clearly and openly;
- show generosity and social conscience;
- allow the other person to be different from oneself;
- take every human life and every life question very seriously.

The existential approach as a basis for therapeutic integration

Milton *et al.* (2002) argue that existential therapy has the potential to enhance and deepen narrower epistemological frameworks by offering an understanding of what it means to be human, forming a basis for therapeutic integration and bringing a 'soulfulness' to therapy. Broadly, adopting an existential stance involves paying attention to anxiety, self-construction, interpersonal threat, dilemmas and values. It involves embracing uncertainty and turning towards difficulty, emphasising the shared human condition whilst acknowledging the uniqueness of individual experience. Clients bring explicit and implicit existential concerns into therapy and openness to these allows engagement with them in a meaningful way. Some clients have reported such issues to have previously been dismissed or pathologised within mental health services.

In the next section, the work of Laing (1960) and other practitioners will be drawn on to describe an approach to therapy involving principles congruent with existential values. Thus a basis for therapeutic integration will be introduced which can be used when working with individuals experiencing visions, voices and fixed beliefs who are distressed by their experiences and have previously had difficulty forming trusting relationships and therefore engaging with services.

Aims, stages, strategies and techniques

When working with people who are 'hard to reach', the first aim of existentially based therapy is to make a connection, from where trust can be built and the aims of therapy agreed. Just as there is no one existential therapy, no particular protocol, process or techniques will be outlined here. Rather, some ways in which a therapist can hold a sense of direction will be described. Similarly, the stages of therapy will vary for each individual but clarification of experiences is a key objective from the beginning and particular attention is paid to anxiety and other existential concerns. Following on from this, the person's values can be explored to help identify goals for therapy which are meaningful, drawing on congruent psychosocial interventions when addressing these.

Some key existential principles can be integrated into clinical practice, reflecting the values and approach outlined in the preceding section. These may be grouped into five themes (Amphlett, 2009):

1. Clarifying meaning;
2. Entering the lived-world of the client;
3. Attending to anxiety;
4. Recognising the potential for personal growth and recovery;
5. Meeting person-to-person.

1. Clarifying meaning

Laing (1960) encouraged therapists to trust their clients' experiences as meaningful attempts to deal with their worlds. In line with Jacobsen's (2005) value of allowing the other person to be different, a key existential principle is thus 'assume intelligibility unless proved otherwise' (Cooper, 2003: 95). As described earlier, existential therapists attempt to approach therapy with an attitude of un-knowing (Spinelli, 1997) and to 'bracket' their own assumptions in order to be more open and able to clarify meaning with the client.

> *Clinical illustration*
> A client would occasionally 'escape into another world', assuming an alternative identity or ascribing different identities to those around her. Whilst others saw this as evidence for her relapsing, she described this as means of self-protection. She feared condemnation and, when feeling anxious about this occurring, took flight into an alternative realm which was familiar and of comfort.

As therapists we also need to be aware of the judgements attached when people are referred to us – to 'bracket' others' assumptions. It is important to listen to and accept clients' experiences of mental health services, their understanding of their difficulties and what they find helpful. Clients entering therapy will have differing attitudes towards their psychosis – some may find their experiences frightening and confusing whilst others find comfort in the sense of certainty they bring. Some will want to alter their beliefs, perceptions or relationship with their voices, whilst others will want to retain the status quo, to preserve their experiences at all costs (Spinelli, 2001).

2. Entering the lived-world of the client

Laing (1960) saw meaning within the language and behaviour of people experiencing psychosis, entering into the client's world to uncover this alongside them. Laing (1967) thus emphasised the importance of 'fidelity to experience', adopting an open and honest approach with clients to help them illuminate their world-view. This phenomenological method involves staying at the level of description and taking a neutral but empathic stance, adopting the values of listening and communicating clearly. Rather than accepting or directly challenging a client's beliefs or values, this approach encourages dialogue, reflection and flexibility (Hulme, 1999).

Five principles to facilitate entering the lived-world of the client are:

i. *Allow space for co-creation of understanding.*

> *Clinical illustration*
> The following exchange took place with the client described earlier on an acute ward:

> Client: I keep thinking you're Gina
> Therapist: Gina?
> Client: Gina, from my class. Are you Gina? You look and sound like her.
> Therapist: Like her?
> Client: She was my friend, she helped me.
> Therapist: How did she help you?
> Client: She talked to me, helped me sort things out. Are you sure you're not her? I think you might be.
> Therapist: Because I'm here to talk to you, to help you?
> Client: Yes, maybe [*leans forward and studies my face intently*]. Actually, you can't be Gina because you haven't got lots of earrings. You remind me of her though. You really are Catherine, aren't you?
> Therapist: Yes.
> Client: I feel like I'm in school. It's nearly time for afternoon break isn't it? The teachers bring tea at three.

The client was experiencing the ward, its hierarchy and routine, as a school and relating to others accordingly. On reflection, this was later seen by her to be a way of surviving her hospital admission and distancing herself from events leading up to it.

ii. *Take a phenomenological approach: clarify, keep an open mind, accept the client's beliefs whilst encouraging reflection and flexibility.*

> *Clinical illustration*
> A client recounted having been assaulted by a "government rapist". It was important to him that I believed this had occurred and, whilst he could not remember the event, we spent time discussing the reasons he believed it had happened. His preoccupations and attributions were explored, looking for the meaning in terms of his life experience. Several months on we discussed the subject again and he reflected that there were three possible explanations: 1. The assault had occurred and was a random attack. 2. He had not been assaulted, but was experiencing distressing psychosis at the time. 3. The assault had happened as he had initially

believed. In any case, he came to see himself as having survived a traumatic ordeal and described feeling stronger and less shame related to this experience.

iii. *Be honest: develop trust so there is room for challenge*

Clinical illustration
A client described feeling lonely and stated that others avoided her. We clarified her fears of being controlled by others and how she coped by using aggression at times to maintain interpersonal distance. As our therapeutic relationship developed, she occasionally became hostile in sessions. Because trust had developed between us, I was able to challenge and discuss this with her. In this way we used our relationship to identify when she felt the presence of interpersonal threat and how she might chose to respond when it occurred.

iv. *Be courageous: create a space where the client feels able to be candid*

Clinical illustration
A client on a ward was extremely distressed, talking angrily about 'black magic' that was being conducted against her. During our conversation she described terrifying visions and acted some of these out in the room. After our discussion, the client said she did not want to meet again as she had no need of mental health services. However, a few months later she engaged in therapy and recalled our conversation. She stated that because I had listened to her she felt confident I could 'handle' what she might want to discuss. Thus by adopting an attentive stance, as well as drawing upon courage and being mindful of personal safety, a connection was made with someone in a highly distressed state.

v. *Be present in the encounter: treat everything as equally relevant*
It is important to attend to what a client, who may be disorientated or confused, is saying and to keep hold of different strands, clarifying and bringing these together.

Clinical illustration
A client stated at the beginning of a session that he was 'fine' but had the occasional 'worrying thought'. Although initially adamant that he did not want to share these thoughts, later he quickly mentioned something that seemed troubling and moved on. When the opportunity arose, I reminded him of what he had said and asked if this was one such 'worrying thought'. He replied: "So you do really do want to know what's going on in my head?" and went on to describe the experiences causing him distress.

3. Attending to anxiety

According to van Deurzen-Smith (1991), resonance with existential anxiety can contribute to psychosis but also to engagement with the vital issues of life and death. She argues that the task of therapy with any client is not to achieve ontological security, but to harness their anxiety and find more flexible and personally fulfilling ways-of-being. In this way a client may be assisted to find the value in their experience, clarifying what is of most importance to them in the social, personal, spiritual and physical dimensions of their existence (van Deurzen & Arnold-Baker, 2005).

The following three principles relate to attendance to anxiety when working with people experiencing psychosis:

i. *Invite exploration of fears: reflect on existential anxiety and be aware of interpersonal threat*

   Clinical illustration
   A client entered the therapy room asking: "Do you think I'm a bad person? Do you hate me? Does everyone hate me? Am I really a bad person?" She often sought reassurance from others about how they viewed her, but received only temporary relief from this. We talked about her strong fear of being rejected by others and how she had come to see the world and other people as threatening in this way.

ii. *Explore how the person's beliefs and experiences developed: be aware of the potential conflicting needs to escape from and to preserve selfhood*
   If a client is distracted, disconnected or distressed, describing and reflecting on emotions being experienced by the client and therapist can facilitate understanding of their situation and implicit values. Clarifying how the experience of visions, voices or distressing beliefs developed and are being maintained can indicate a way forward.

   Clinical illustration
   A client heard several voices and when we first met she was very distressed by them. Over time she came to recognise that when her voices were persecutory, they reflected underlying anxieties and decided to use this to identify issues to bring to therapy. The way she related to her voices changed over time as she came to see them as less malevolent.

iii. *See the person in context*
   When exploring with a client how their difficulties arose and are being maintained, it is important to do this in the context of their past and present relationships, their environment and the socio-political climate. Similarly, what values a person holds will depend on their circumstances and the level of anxiety they are experiencing.

Clinical illustration

During an acute admission a service user was observed by staff to have made good progress and plans were made for his discharge. Soon after, however, he refused medication, damaged property and assaulted a nurse. He was transferred to a locked ward and continued to be challenging in his behaviour. This man had previously expressed anxiety about living 'out there, in the real world' to his named nurse, and appeared to value the security of the ward over his personal freedom. Other clients in the same environment, however, will have a different experience, valuing freedom more highly.

4. Recognising the potential for personal growth and recovery

As described, Laing (1967) believed that denial of experience led to difficulties. He asserted that engaging fully with experience facilitated change and argued that individuals needed support to help them face their anxiety to foster a more integrated and authentic way of being. Therapists thus need to be aware of the potentially transformative nature of psychosis and the possibility that people can draw positively on their experience (e.g. Kiser, 2004).

As described in the following case study, a client can deconstruct their world and be assisted to generate new meanings and a value base that allows them to find a satisfying way to live in the world (Milton, 2005). In therapy, clients might also explore ways to integrate their experience of the psychiatric system and to reclaim their right to self-definition. Clients who are 'hard to reach' have often felt particularly disempowered within services, but can be supported to find a voice, individually and through groups such as the Hearing Voices Network (Dillon & May, 2002).

5. Meeting person-to-person

Laing upheld the value of respecting a client's autonomy and dignity and his genuineness meant that at times he did not adopt the strict boundaries of the 'therapeutic hour', for example working with clients outside the therapy room.

Three principles are useful to consider:

i.   *Do not take responsibility for the client or action over his or her life*
     This stance can be difficult to maintain in statutory services, particularly when issues of risk are involved and where sharing of information is important.

     Clinical illustration
     A client had stopped smoking cannabis in the past few months. In a session he revealed that he had felt pressured into this decision by his care

coordinator and disagreed with her view of the impact of his drug use. He confided that he intended to smoke cannabis with friends that weekend and we agreed to reflect on the impact this choice had on his wellbeing in our next session. When this issue was later discussed as a team, the need to take a non-judgemental stance to foster a collaborative relationship with this client was agreed.

ii. *Be aware of one's own position in the mental health service and issues of freedom and choice*
This is particularly important in a setting in which it may be necessary to defend a client's autonomy against the status quo.

Clinical illustration
A colleague suggested that therapy be made a condition of a client's treatment under the Mental Health Act. This client had requested therapy but was considered by others to be unable to commit to this. I pointed out that to compel the person to comply with this aspect of their care plan was to remove personal responsibility and freedom and would be counter-therapeutic.

As well as overt pressure being asserted on clients in this way, it is important to explore any covert pressure the client is under to engage in therapy. It is also important to be candid about one's own position and responsibilities within the service.

iii. *Be aware of expectations, limitations and resonances with the client's existential concerns*
From an existential perspective the experience of visions, voices and the holding of fixed beliefs are regarded as ways-of-being and, as such, not things to be 'cured'. Similarly, the task of therapy is not to help a client achieve ontological security, but to address or harness their existential anxiety and find more flexible and fulfilling ways-of-being.

Clinical illustration
A client described regular 'visitations from God' in the form of a vision. He gained a sense of importance from this, but also felt overwhelmed at times and anxious about what he believed might be expected of him. He feared that this special relationship would end and his life would cease to have meaning. In sessions, alongside exploration of his spiritual experiences and beliefs, we clarified his values in other domains of existence and how he might focus upon these to gain a broader sense of life being worthwhile.

The task of existential therapy is inevitably anxiety provoking as it aims to help clients confront their world-view and potential for non-being. Therapists must themselves be aware of their own existential concerns and, in addition to supervision, personal therapy is indicated when working this way.

Integrating existential values and principles with a recovery approach

There are parallels between the values underlying an existential approach to therapy and recovery-oriented services for people with mental health difficulties (e.g. *Guiding Statement on Recovery*, NIMHE, 2005). In particular, both are non-pathologising, respect difference, emphasise individual experience, autonomy and responsibility and place importance on the search for fulfilment and meaning in life. Engaging in existentially based therapy can thus support a client in their recovery.

Whilst as practitioners we may share the values identified by Jacobsen (2005), they are not always easily applicable in the contexts in which we work. The biological model of distress, which Laing critiqued in the 1960s, is still a strong presence. Dillon and May (2002: 25) describe how their attempts to find 'meaningful ways to live in an often distressing and confusing world' were not understood as human responses, but that they were pathologised and labelled, an approach clearly at odds with existential and recovery-oriented values. The dominant values of services can also impact negatively on the relationship between client and therapist. For example, there is often a tension between respecting a person's autonomy and restricting their freedom using the Mental Health Act – clients who experience a team as coercive may lose trust in the service and the therapist working within it.

The current emphasis on risk management and standardised treatment protocols for people who experience psychosis also make it difficult, at times, to work creatively with this client group and those of us who want to adopt a broader approach to therapy will occasionally meet resistance. However, through observing the way clients have engaged in and reported benefits from therapy, colleagues have come to value an existentially informed way of working. Other practitioners have also successfully applied existential ideas in their therapeutic work with people who experience psychosis (e.g. Chadwick, 2006; Hulme, 1999; Trower & Chadwick, 1995; Chapter 9).

Case illustration: Sarah

Therapy with Sarah occurred over two years whilst she was being seen by an Assertive Outreach Team (AOT). She was referred for psychological intervention because team members were concerned about her risk of suicide, requesting that I work with her to clarify her difficulties and support her recovery.

Background

Sarah is in her late thirties, has experienced eleven admissions to acute mental health units and has a diagnosis of 'schizoaffective disorder'. Until recently, Sarah lived with her mother and they were very close but she found it very difficult to trust people outside of this relationship.

Sarah was admitted to an acute unit after she became distressed, experiencing voices and feelings of paranoia. The onset of these experiences was rapid and Sarah saw concern about her mother's poor physical health as triggering their emergence. After a two month admission Sarah was discharged home but several weeks later her mother was admitted to general hospital, dying soon after. Sarah appeared to AOT members as coping well with her feelings of grief but after two months made a suicide attempt, cutting her throat with a razor blade. Sarah did not lose consciousness and when the pain became unbearable, she rang a priest who accessed help. She was admitted to hospital and from there to the acute mental health unit, where we met for the first time.

Initial meetings

Sarah expressed remorse about her suicide attempt: she had wanted to join her mother in heaven but concluded she would have gone to hell had she ended her life. Prior to her bereavement she felt low in mood, sensing that life was passing her by. She expressed regret about the circumstances of her mother's sudden death and a sense of profound loss, recounting how prior to her suicide attempt she had been hearing a voice she identified as her mother commanding her to join her. Sarah described feeling alone and anxious about the future and her ability to cope.

I continued to meet with Sarah during and after her inpatient stay. In early sessions we focussed on her experience of loss, clarifying her presenting difficulties as feelings of emptiness, isolation, anxiety and hopelessness. The voice Sarah had heard ceased after her suicide attempt but she was concerned this and her suicidal ideation might return. We also reflected on Sarah's reluctance to engage with mental health professionals as related to previous experiences of feeling alienated and dismissed. She recounted that she had lost trust in her own ability to gauge her wellbeing and we identified the main aim of therapy as to assist her in developing confidence to look after her wellbeing and assert her needs. Taking a phenomenological approach, we clarified that Sarah had seen suicide as an escape from feelings of meaninglessness and isolation, as she had hoped to be reunited with her mother. In addition, whilst finding some meaning in her role as carer for her mother, she had been feeling directionless and low in mood prior to her bereavement.

Sarah understood her previous experiences of psychosis as part of an illness triggered by stress. She chose to focus in therapy on recovering her wellbeing, rather than reflect on the potential meaning within her past experiences. I respected this viewpoint whilst attending to opportunities to explore it further. Thus, for example, we were able to discuss how Sarah's experience of hearing her mother's voice was understandable in the context of her grief.

Supporting recovery

Initially, Sarah attempted to address feelings of emptiness and isolation by filling her time with activities. However, anxiety soon pulled her in the opposite direction as she started to avoid engagement in life, wanting to prevent stress and potential relapse. With reference to the four domains of existence – physical, personal, social and spiritual (van Deurzen & Arnold-Baker, 2005) – Sarah and I developed goals for therapy and her recovery. We began in the physical and personal domain by completing early signs work with the aim of enhancing her sense of control over her wellbeing. As Sarah gained confidence in this area, focus shifted towards the social domain, building on existing relationships and engaging with the wider community through some voluntary work.

After a year, Sarah described 'treading water' and we reflected on her sense of self, clarifying what she valued and wanted to direct her efforts towards. In this context, we explored her fear of intrusion by others, relating this to past experiences of emotional abuse and Sarah identified that she needed to find courage to face the anxiety she experienced when in relation to others. She therefore set herself some challenges, visiting relatives in different parts of the country and developing assertiveness skills. Sarah also started to make longer term plans to access education and employment.

Towards the end of our contact, we reflected on how Sarah had remained well:

Sarah: I think getting over my mum's death and what happened after made me stronger, more able to deal with things. When she died, I thought my mental health would get worse, not *better*. My cousin thinks I'm better because she isn't around to stress me out, but it isn't that. I think I've just got stronger.

Therapist: You're feeling more resilient. Although you've tried to keep stress to a minimum over the past year or so, you've dealt with some very difficult situations . . .

Sarah: Yes and I *didn't get sick*. I might have got sick over those things before, but coming through what I have has made me more able to deal with things. I feel more confident in myself.

Therapist: And you feel ready to take more on now, starting your course, for example.

Sarah: Yes, I'm more ready than I've ever been before.

Over the course of therapy, Sarah faced the task of grieving for her mother and constructing a more secure sense of self. Her emotions, existential concerns, values and hopes were explored and her autonomy grew as she began to feel more resilient and new possibilities opened up.

By the end of therapy, Sarah reflected that surviving the suicide attempt had brought the opportunity of accessing support to recover her wellbeing. After facing death, she appeared determined to embrace life, searching with vigour for meaning and purpose. From an existential perspective, it might be hypothesised that as Sarah developed a more secure sense of self, guided by her values, her experience of existential anxiety became less intense and the likelihood of experiences of 'psychosis' emerging reduced. Over the next few years we met for occasional follow up sessions and Sarah came to see herself as a strong individual who had survived much adversity, her fear of 'relapse' diminishing as she continued to cope with life's ups and downs.

Conclusions and implications

Adopting an existential approach to therapy encourages us to see the person first and connect with them on the basis of the shared experience of being human whilst respecting the uniqueness of their situation. This respect for the other person is shown through meeting person-to-person and adopting a phenomenological method, starting from where the client is at (Kierkegaard, 1848: 334). Co-creating meaning in the experiences of distressing psychosis facilitates understanding and clarifying values can assist in finding ways forward for recovery which feel authentic to the individual. Alongside this, other interventions such as early signs work (see Chapter 4) or mindfulness (Chadwick, 2006) can be drawn upon and integrated into therapy. Often it is experience of trauma in early life or within mental health services which undermines an individual's ability to trust others and it is the therapist's role to offer an opportunity for a relationship which supports the client to reach out to others and services in ways that are beneficial to their wellbeing.

Whilst many studies have demonstrated the therapeutic relationship and client variables have the greatest impact on outcome (Cooper, 2008), there is a need for robust research to demonstrate the critical ingredients and effectiveness of existential therapies. Finlay (2012) argues that practice-based evidence, involving small-scale practitioner research in clinical settings, such as case studies, offers a natural extension of an existential therapist's usual reflective approach. Interpretative phenomenological analysis (IPA) provides a structured method to explore lived-experience, which is rooted in existential values, and this methodology is growing in prominence in the UK (Smith *et al.*, 2009). As Finlay (2012) asserts, the challenge is to engage in research in ways that are authentic but also widely accepted and respected.

There are many different existential therapies and this chapter has offered an account of how to work therapeutically with people who experience psychosis which is in keeping with the values existential practitioners often hold. At times, it is challenging to exist in a context where one's values might not be widely shared and there is a need for dialogue within services, so different values can be made explicit and common ground be found. Van Deurzen (2005) highlights the need for individuals to be self-reflective, to critically evaluate their values and world-view. She describes how therapy is often geared towards fitting people back into an established ideology. An existential approach contests this and 'calls people to wake up, claim their freedom and rethink their own ideology' (van Deurzen, 2005: 266). This chapter has attempted to introduce some existential values and principles that can, despite the challenges, be adopted when working psychologically with people who experience psychosis and are reluctant to engage with services.

References

Amphlett, C. (2009). An existential approach to working with people who experience psychosis: Core values and therapeutic principles. *Special Issue: Faculty for Complex Mental Health and Psychosis, Clinical Psychology Forum, 196*, 22–26.

Chadwick, P. D. J. (2006). *Person-based cognitive therapy for distressing psychosis.* Chichester, Sussex: John Wiley & Sons.

Cooper, M. (2003). *Existential therapies.* London: Sage.

Cooper, M. (2008). *Essential research findings in counselling and psychotherapy: The facts are friendly.* London: Sage.

van Deurzen, E. (1998). *Paradox and passion in psychotherapy.* Chichester, Sussex: John Wiley & Sons.

van Deurzen, E. (2002). *Existential counselling and psychotherapy in practice* (2nd edn). London: Sage.

van Deurzen, E. (2005). A new ideology. In E. van Deurzen & C. Arnold-Baker (eds), *Existential perspectives on human issues.* Basingstoke, Hants: Palgrave Macmillan.

van Deurzen, E. (2012). Reasons for living: Existential therapy and spirituality. In L. Barnett & G. Madison (eds), *Existential therapy: Legacy, vibrancy and dialogue.* Hove, E. Sussex: Routledge.

van Deurzen, E. & Adams, M. (2011). *Skills in existential counselling and psychotherapy.* London: Sage.

van Deurzen, E. & Arnold-Baker, C. (eds). (2005). *Existential perspectives on human issues.* Basingstoke, Hants: Palgrave Macmillan.

van Deurzen-Smith, E. (1991). Ontological insecurity revisited. *Journal of the Society of Existential Analysis, 2*, 38–48.

Dillon, J. & May, R. (2002). Reclaiming experience. *Clinical Psychology, 17*, 25–28.

Evans, R. I. (1976/1981). *Dialogue with R. D. Laing.* New York: Praeger.

Finlay, L. (2012). Research: An existential predicament for our profession? In L. Barnett & G. Madison (eds), *Existential therapy: Legacy, vibrancy and dialogue.* Hove, E. Sussex: Routledge.

Hulme, P. (1999). Collaborative conversation. In C. Newnes, G. Holmes & C. Dunn (eds), *This is madness: A critical look at psychiatry and the future of mental health services.* Ross-on-Wye, UK: PCCS Books.

Jacobsen, B. (2005). Values and beliefs. In E. van Deurzen & C. Arnold-Baker (eds), *Existential perspectives on human issues.* Basingstoke, Hants: Palgrave Macmillan.

Kierkegaard, S. (1848) The point of view, trans. W. Lowrie. In R. Bretall (ed.), *A Kierkegaard anthology*, 1946. Princeton, NJ: Princeton University Press.

Kiser, S. (2004). An existential case study of madness: Encounters with divine affliction. *Journal of Humanistic Psychology, 44*(4), 431–454.

Laing, R. D. (1960). *The divided self: An existential study in sanity and madness.* London: Tavistock; published 1990, Harmondsworth: Pelican Books.

Laing, R. D. (1967). *The politics of experience and the bird of paradise*. Harmondsworth: Penguin.

Laing, R. D. (1970). *Knots*. London: Penguin.

Milton, M. (2005). Political and ideological issues. In E. van Deurzen & C. Arnold-Baker (eds), *Existential perspectives on human issues*. Basingstoke, Hants: Palgrave Macmillan.

Milton, M., Charles, L., Judd, D., O'Brien, M., Tipney, A. & Turner, A. (2002). Extended paper. The existential-phenomenological paradigm: The importance for psychotherapy integration. *Counselling Psychology Review*, *17*(2), 4–20.

National Institute for Mental Health in England (2005). *Guiding statement on recovery*. London: Department of Health.

Read, J. & Bentall, R. (2012). Negative childhood experiences and mental health: Theoretical, clinical and primary prevention implications. *British Journal of Psychiatry*, *200*, 89–91.

Smith, J. A., Flowers, P. & Larkin, M. (2009). *Interpretative phenomenological analysis: Theory, method and research*. London: Sage.

Spinelli, E. (1989). *The interpreted world: An introduction to phenomenological psychology*. London: Sage.

Spinelli, E. (1996). The existential-phenomenological paradigm. In R. Woolfe & W. Dryden (eds), *Handbook of counselling psychology*. London: Sage.

Spinelli, E (1997). *Tales of un-knowing: Therapeutic encounters from an existential perspective*. London: Duckworth.

Spinelli, E. (2001). Psychosis: New existential, systemic and cognitive-behavioural developments. *Journal of Contemporary Psychotherapy*, *31*(1), 61–67.

Spinelli, E. (2007). *Practicing existential psychotherapy: The relational world*. London: Sage.

Thompson, M. G. (1995). Deception, mystification, trauma: Laing and Freud. *Journal of the Society for Existential Analysis*, *6.1*, 79–94.

Thompson, M. G. (1997). The fidelity to experience in RD Laing's treatment philosophy. *Contemporary Psychoanalysis*, *33*(4), 595–614.

Tillich, P. (1995/2000). *The courage to be* (2nd edn). New Haven, CT: Yale University Press.

Trower, P. & Chadwick, P. D. J. (1995). Pathways to defence of the self: A theory of two types of paranoia. *Clinical Psychology: Science and Practice*, *2*, 263–278.

Chapter 9

Enhancing social participation and recovery through a cognitive-developmental approach

Andrew Fox and Chris Harrop

Introduction

This chapter develops the approach first outlined by Harrop and Trower (2003) who argue that individuals with psychotic experiences often miss out on important developmental experiences of adolescence (e.g. separation–individuation from parents, development of coherent self-identity, peer group socialisation, exploration of romantic dyads, etc). Current interventions for people with psychotic difficulties do not explicitly take into account the needs that result from these disruptions to psychosocial development. This chapter aims to offer an integrative framework for structuring interventions to address these needs, based on an understanding of the social and cognitive-developmental aspects of their difficulties. The aims are to increase social participation and achieve personally meaningful recovery goals.

Theoretical background and development

Adolescence is an important period of self-development, where possible selves are explored and beliefs about the individual self are developed through repeated social experience (Harter, 1999). Research has demonstrated that adolescents have particular styles of beliefs that reflect this developmental stage (e.g. Frankenberger, 2000) while more recent research has investigated the role these beliefs play in young adult psychopathology (e.g. Fox, 2007; Fox *et al.*, 2009).

Harrop and Trower (2003) note that many of the transitory experiences of adolescence are similar to experiences of psychosis (e.g. self-consciousness, social withdrawal, unusual beliefs, paranoia) and suggest that the onset of psychosis disrupts typical adolescent development. Consequently, individuals with psychosis continue to demonstrate excessively 'adolescent' ways of behaving and relating to others. Socialisation is therefore critical in helping people with psychosis to progress through the adolescent developmental stages they may have missed out on and to reduce some of the distressing experiences of psychosis.

Outline of normative adolescence

Amongst the various psychological considerations of adolescence, the theme of egocentricity (i.e. the tendency for self-focus and to view the world from one's own perspective) has received a large amount of theoretical and empirical attention. Egocentricity has been deconstructed into two separate but linked patterns of thought: the 'imaginary audience' (the belief that others are always watching) and the 'personal fable' (the self as unique, invulnerable and omnipotent) (Elkind, 1967; Vartanian, 2000). Vartanian (2000) suggests that these can be understood as social-cognitive aspects of adolescent development. The 'new look' approach to adolescent egocentricity (Lapsley, 1993) considers the accumulated interpersonal experiences of adolescents, and how these are related to identity development beyond the imaginary audience and personal fable, particularly when considering the process of 'separation–individuation'.

The original conceptualisation of separation–individuation refers to the process by which human infants develop a sense of separateness from the physical world, yet retain a sense of relatedness towards it (Kroger, 1996; Mahler et al., 1975). Blos (1962) suggested that a second individuation process (encountered during adolescence) involves the development of an individual sense of self that is separate from the family and yet retains a sense of connectedness with them. At the start of adolescence the individual is physically independent from their parents but they have yet to psychologically separate from the internalised parent. A belief in an imaginary audience and personal fable aid the psychological process of individuation as the adolescent imagines themselves in interpersonal situations and practises and develops their concept of self and other (Vartanian, 2000). As such, the imaginary audience and the personal fable appear to be critical aspects in the process of the second individuation and the development of a model of self.

Adolescence, self-development and psychosis

Harrop and Trower (2003) suggest that the beliefs and implicit assumptions regarding the self which are developed during childhood and adolescence are particularly important when considering the onset and experience of psychosis. Indeed, Harvey (2013) found that adolescent egocentrism moderated the relationship between early emotional trauma, attachment difficulties and psychosis. Some of our own research with young adult students suggests that adolescent egocentrism (the personal fable) is associated with paranoid ideation and psychoticism (Fox, 2007). Furthermore, it is also apparent that young people with experiences of psychosis struggle to access the same level of social resources as that of their peers (Hirshfeld et al., 2005; Redmond et al., 2010).

There is now a consistent body of evidence that indicates that people with psychosis have difficulties in social domains and this is linked to poorer functional outcome – both in terms of social skills (Bellack et al., 2004) and social cognition (Couture et al., 2006). The current framework proposes that the development and experience of the self is an intrinsically social process (Harrop & Trower, 2003). Adolescence is an important period for the development of social skills, social functioning and social networks (Bijstra *et al.*, 1994); during this period the concept of self develops and the interpersonal focus shifts onto that of peers and romantic partners (Collins, 2003; Waldinger *et al.*, 2002). The individual develops beliefs and interactional styles that will influence future relationships and the development of support networks. Therefore, mental health difficulties that have their onset during or around adolescence and early adulthood (such as psychosis; Gogtay *et al.*, 2011) along with the disruptions observed in social skills, beliefs, networks and cognition can be understood as disruptions in normative adolescent development and the ability to construct a self (Harrop & Trower, 2003).

Other models of therapy for psychosis, such as Person-Based Cognitive Therapy (PBCT; Chadwick, 2006) incorporate an understanding of self-processes in people with psychosis, but do not integrate this within an understanding of the broader social-developmental factors that are associated with the experience of psychosis. From this perspective, supporting people to progress through the disrupted social-developmental processes in order to facilitate healthy self-construction is a key component of any therapeutic work, and is the rationale for the basis of the therapeutic framework discussed in this chapter.

Aims, stages, strategies and techniques

The overall strategy is one of remediating blocks to healthy self-construction, and, through this, facilitating the achievement of personally meaningful life goals and social participation. When discussing goals with individuals with psychosis we often find that they place much less emphasis (compared with professionals) on reducing symptoms, or mastering daily living skills and rather more on social goals: getting a partner, having a family and friends. Therapeutic work can accordingly be targeted at five key domains:

Self-construction
Social skills
Social beliefs
Social cognition
Social networks.

Table 9.1 lists some resources that may be useful when developing a formulation.

Self-construction

Understanding difficulties that arise in the process of constructing and experiencing a self is viewed as the organising concept that links all the other domains discussed in the current framework. Drawing on the work of our colleague, Peter Trower, we take the view that the self is created through

Table 9.1 Summary of useful resources

Name	Area assessed	Source
Evaluative Beliefs Scale	Negative views of own self and other's self	Chadwick, P., Trower, P. & Dagnan, D. (1999). Measuring negative person evaluations: The Evaluative Beliefs Scale. *Cognitive Therapy and Research*, 23, 549–559.
The Awareness of Social Inference Test	Emotion recognition and theory of mind	McDonald, S., Flanagan, S. & Rollins, J. (2002). *The Awareness of Social Inference Test*. Suffolk, UK: Thames Valley Test Co., Ltd.
Adolescent Invulnerability Scale	Beliefs regarding invulnerability to threat or harm	http://www3.nd.edu/~dlapsle1/Lab/Scales.html
Dysfunctional Separation–Individuation Scale	Beliefs regarding separation-individuation	http://www3.nd.edu/~dlapsle1/Lab/Scales.html
Subjective Omnipotence Scale	A measure of typical adolescent narcissism	http://www3.nd.edu/~dlapsle1/Lab/Scales.html
Personal Uniqueness Scale	Beliefs regarding individual uniqueness of experience and individuality	http://www3.nd.edu/~dlapsle1/Lab/Scales.html
Self and Other Scale	Threats to self-construction	Dagnan, D., Trower, P. & Gilbert, P. (2002). Measuring vulnerability to threats to self-construction: The Self and Other Scale. *Psychology and Psychotherapy: Theory, Research and Practice*, 75, 279–293.
Chapter 3: Assessment of Social Skills (pp. 30–45)	Social skills	Bellack, A. S., Mueser, K. T., Gingerich, S. L. & Agresta, J. (2004). *Social skills training for schizophrenia: A step-by-step guide*. New York: Guilford Press.
Self-Consciousness Scale	Public and private self-consciousness and social anxiety	Scheier, M. F. & Carver, C. S. (1985). The Self-Consciousness Scale: A revised version for use with general populations. *Journal of Applied Social Psychology*, 15, 687–699.
Romantic Beliefs Inventory	Unhelpful romanticised relationship beliefs	Eidelson, R. J. & Epstein, N. (1982). Cognition and relationship maladjustment: Development of a measure of dysfunctional relationship beliefs. *Journal of Consulting and Clinical Psychology*, 50, 715–720.

interactions with others. The self is viewed as a process rather than a fixed object (Chadwick, 2006; Harrop & Trower, 2003; Trower & Chadwick, 1995), and needs to be socially presented, recognised and accepted through moment-to-moment interactions with the other. The necessary conditions for self-construction are a subjective agent who presents a possible self, and an observing other who is able to accept (or reject) this self-presentation. There are three main ways that people experience self-construction difficulties (Harrop & Trower, 2003: 80):

1. Difficulties in constructing a self due to limitations in social skills, social knowledge or social cognitive abilities (the 'Insufficient Self');
2. Fearing that the desired self will not be recognised by the other (the 'Insecure Self');
3. Fearing that only a particular unwanted self will be accepted by the other (the 'Alienated Self').

In this chapter we are referring to people who fall under the category of the Insufficient Self: due to difficulties across the other four domains (social skills, social beliefs, social cognition and social networks) they struggle to construct a self. Once these difficulties are addressed, if needed, work can be focussed on the Insecure or Alienated Self (Harrop & Trower, 2003: 80–89). A measure of vulnerability to these two areas of difficulty in self-construction, the Self and Other Scale (Dagnan et al., 2002), has been developed.

Social skills

Social skills encompass all of the abilities and behavioural repertoires required by people to function within a social environment. Some may have learned and lost these skills; others may have never mastered them. Assessment should show in which particular areas there are strengths, and which will need further work. Social skills can be assessed through some of the measures provided by Bellack et al. (2004). Liaison with Occupational Therapy colleagues can also be helpful in assessing what aspects of social skills may be more or less problematic in the individual's daily life.

Social beliefs

Social beliefs appear to be modified through learning experiences provided by interactions with others. Given the socially isolating aspects of psychosis it is perhaps not surprising that some people with psychosis hold social beliefs more usually associated with adolescence (Fox, 2007). These can take many possible forms, such as beliefs about personal uniqueness (e.g. "no-one can possibly understand me") or heightened self-consciousness. Typically they are unrealistic and can act as unhelpful barriers to the achievement of life goals. As such, many of the measures used in the adolescent and young adult literature can be useful in offering an insight into people's beliefs and knowledge about the social world.

Limited friendships and limited romantic relationships are common in people with psychosis (Buchanan, 1995), and they often see themselves as lower in social rank or subordinate to their peers (Allison *et al.*, 2013). Fewer social experiences may mean that many people with psychosis have little opportunity to practise the skills associated with relationships. Additionally they may have developed naïve or unhelpful beliefs about social interactions that limit the chances for successful social interaction and relationship development (Redmond *et al.*, 2010). It can therefore be helpful to assess beliefs and knowledge about friendships and romantic relationships in order to ascertain whether there are any unhelpful beliefs that may restrict the development of social networks.

Social cognition

People with psychosis often have particular difficulty dealing with social information (Couture *et al.*, 2006), with a minority qualifying for a diagnosis of Asperger's Syndrome (Andrews, 2007). The ability to effectively and accurately process social information is of critical importance when negotiating life areas such as work, friendships, activities of daily living and training. Domains likely to be impaired in people with psychosis can include, but are not limited to: theory of mind, emotion recognition, jumping to conclusions and attribution bias (Couture *et al.*, 2006). Social cognition can now be assessed with a range of measures (see Table 9.1). Another important area is an awareness of the properties of others, their tendencies and habits. In our experience, many of our clients with psychosis demonstrate a chronic tendency for self-focus (linked, perhaps, to adolescent egocentricity). Therefore, supporting them to switch from a chronic self-focus to being more other-focussed can be helpful as it starts them thinking about the role of the other, rather than just themselves. This is linked to the previously discussed role of the other in self-construction.

Social networks

Many people with psychosis have restricted social networks (Allison *et al.*, 2013) and may be limited to family or mental health professionals. They may lack pro-social associates, a factor likely to reduce opportunities for recovery and increase risk (Webster *et al.*, 2004). Assessing this area may simply involve the use of a genogram or eco-map that identifies the important people within an individual's life. Discussion can then be focussed around the potential to develop or change these networks and any goals associated with this (e.g. to make friends outside of mental health services).

An important aspect of this area of work is to appreciate the limited opportunities faced by people to develop their social networks. Impairment in social skills, self-beliefs, social beliefs and social cognitive difficulties, along with external factors such as stigma and social exclusion all limit social networks. The latter will be factors that limit the development of social networks quite independently of any intrapersonal factors.

General strategy

As Chadwick (2006) has noted, therapeutic engagement is a critical factor when working with people with psychosis, and this holds true for those who are treatment resistant or difficult to reach. Our 'hook' to motivate people to engage in work targeted at improving their social networks is the identification of important life-goals: making friends; feeling comfortable with themselves; meeting potential romantic partners ('mates and dates'). In this way therapeutic goals can be collaboratively agreed that focus on meaningful outcomes. The small steps that are needed to achieve these goals can then be elucidated through traditional assessment techniques. An additional motivator is our focus on the barriers that are posed to life-goals rather than on symptoms. However, it is worth bearing in mind that 'negative symptoms' (i.e. behavioural deficits) may act to impede the ability of people to engage with peers and achieve friendships and romantic relationships. A thorough discussion of this is outside the scope of this chapter; however, there is a promising and developing evidence-base for the use of psychological therapies for negative symptoms (e.g. Grant *et al.*, 2012; see Chapter 14).

Another point when working with people who may be difficult to reach is that intervention is resource intensive. Where possible, it can be helpful to involve other people working with the client (e.g. family, friends or professionals) in achieving these goals. This can also ensure that therapeutic work is delivered *in vivo* and provides much greater opportunity to offer timely support in personally meaningful situations. Our approach may also be usefully be incorporated within the Shared Assessment, Formulation and Education (SAFE; Meaden & Hacker, 2010) framework to facilitate a collaborative understanding of the client's difficulties and goals and identify factors that may impede or facilitate social competencies.

Formulation

The framework described in this chapter proposes that difficulties in some or all of the five domains (i.e. self-construction, social skills, social beliefs, social cognition and social networks) contribute to limited access to desired life-goals, such as work, romantic relationships or friendships. The formulation brings together the assessment findings from these areas and highlights treatment targets. This may or may not incorporate an explicit consideration of psychotic symptoms depending upon the individual. It is of course possible to integrate the assessment information into existing formulation models developed by other authors.

We take no particular stance on the longitudinal aspect of the formulation – where the difficulties came from, or how they started. Rather, our focus is on the way in which difficulties in these areas continue to limit the person's abilities to access goals and opportunities. The aim of intervention is therefore to help the person overcome these difficulties and increase their access to their desired goals. If the person has particular strengths in these domains that have been identified through assessment, these can then be included in any intervention plan. An example outline for structuring the formulation is illustrated below in our case study. We place self-construction at the centre of the formulation, as it is our view that this is the critical function that all the other domains contribute to. Social skills are important in being able to articulate and negotiate self-constructions; social beliefs form an understanding of the self in relation to others; social cognition is the process through which self-referent information is dealt with; while social networks are the substrate through which self is constructed and experienced. In essence, it is difficulties in the experience of self that limit the person's ability to achieve their desired goals.

Techniques

Given the broad framework, it should be clear by now that interventions could be as varied as the client and clinician wish them to be; our conceptual framework which guides assessment and supports formulation is the key. Accordingly, information from assessment can easily be integrated within existing formulations from whichever therapeutic modality the client and clinician are operating within. We believe that there are, however, several particular techniques and approaches that can be particularly helpful when working to address difficulties identified in each of the different domains. It is also important to note that once progress has been made in one domain, this may facilitate progress in others. It is often helpful to revisit the formulation (with the client, where possible) in order to reassess, evaluate progress and reformulate.

Social skills training

Ability in this area is critical for negotiating social interactions, and, as such, we often start by addressing any difficulties here. Bellack *et al.* (2004) offer a comprehensive assessment and treatment guide for this area. They note that social skills involve less therapeutic discussion with more emphasis on practice. We would echo this, encouraging practice in a safe environment before expanding this into real social situations and scenarios. This also sets the scene for engaging in behavioural experiments that can be used to 'reality test' social knowledge and beliefs.

Social beliefs

Limited social experience and knowledge is often associated with unrealistic social beliefs, including, but not limited to, beliefs about parents, autonomy, personal uniqueness and self-consciousness. These can be discussed in the context of a collaborative therapeutic relationship and targeted through traditional cognitive techniques such as Socratic questioning, guided discovery and, when appropriate, addressed more directly through didactic disputation. Combining this with gathering observations from the local environment in order to widen social knowledge is helpful. Very often, for example, we will spend time in the local community with clients, testing out their beliefs that others will pay particular attention to them (self-consciousness). When we unobtrusively watch others we usually note very quickly that others are generally more preoccupied with their own activities than ours.

More active forms of enquiry about these beliefs can test their social validity: are other people really as clients think they are? According to the theoretical framework, this involves supporting clients to complete their socialisation and gather the social knowledge that they did not have (or lost) when they were younger. We have noted that clients can sometimes hold unrealistic beliefs about their parents or significant others, particularly if they are viewed as important. Helping clients to see them as human beings with hopes, dreams, histories (and even flaws!), can often be very powerful in helping them to develop more realistic understanding of their social world. Supporting clients to ask these important people normalising questions about their lives and experiences is often useful – asking parents, for example: what are they most proud of? What sort of things do they worry about? Are they a morning person or an evening person? What is their most embarrassing memory from being a teenager? This has two primary functions: it increases client's knowledge about important others so they have a greater understanding of the other (who is so important in self-construction) and it starts to shift the focus from themselves onto others. Clearly it may be helpful for clinicians to discuss the rationale for this work with family members, staff and others beforehand, but with their help, this can be a useful first step of helping to question unhelpful assumptions about the social world, and start the process of switching from a chronic self-focussed style of attention (see also Harrop & Trower (2003) Chapter 15).

Romantic relationships

Romantic relationships have received relatively little attention within the research literature on psychosis. While many people with psychosis have successful love-lives, it remains true that on the whole, they are less likely to date, and much less likely to get married (Jablensky *et al.*, 1992) – particularly men. They typically name it as one of their highest priorities, but also one of their greatest fears (Redmond *et al.*, 2010), as well as often having little hope it will happen (Hirschfeld *et al.*, 2005).

Starting dating is a distinctive part of life that can only be learnt through trial and error, with inevitable mistakes and failures along the way, and this is as true for people with psychosis as it is for everyone else. It is also one of the most exciting and potentially rewarding. Successful dating in adolescents brings about self-esteem, status and cognitive development (Furman *et al.*, 2007). For most of us, during adolescence/early adulthood, we have confidants or friends we can discuss dating ideas with (Furman & Buhrmester, 1992). People with psychosis report that they have no such sources of information, ideas and support about dating (Redmond *et al.*, 2010). Such normalising information is particularly important: "What is a good chat up line?", "How long should a first date be?", "How should I respond if they get aggressive with/reject me?"

We are developing interventions based around dating skills and support; for example, in Hounslow (West London) Early Intervention Service, the second author has developed a 'Lads Group' whose main objective is 'to get the participants a girlfriend', working through a mix of group-discussions and 'in-field' training sessions (for example, where the objective is to talk to girls). An emphasis is placed on being able to discuss, collaborate and practise together. We have plans to start a 'Ladies Group', and a gay/lesbian group if there is demand for it. Individual work has encouraged the use of dating agencies as ways to gain experiences, so that when the right person comes along, they have already learnt the skills necessary. The approach has been very successful in terms of motivation; the service users and their families have been very keen; for example, some of the young men attending the 'in-field' training sessions who usually have poor self-care were extremely smartly turned out for potentially meeting girls. It is worth reporting we have already had two marriages through this, to non-service-user partners!

A key aspect of this sort of work is ensuring that the person remains safe – many people with psychosis can be vulnerable to exploitation from others (Brekke *et al.*, 2001), so risk-awareness training on this area, along with assertiveness training (as part of social skills), is often a necessary precursor. Risk assessment should also be considered; Meaden and Hacker (2010) offer a detailed yet flexible approach to assessing and formulating risk that encourages positive risk taking.

Negotiating relationships can be precarious at the best of times, and there are often particular skills that can help people and beliefs that can hinder them. Practising social skills in this area requires that the basic skills are mastered. These can then be applied in the various social settings available to the person, including while out with any friends that have been acquired during the course of the work. Widening social networks to gain access to potential friends or romantic partners is usually difficult but necessary (see the following section for ideas on how to address limited social networks). Finally, targeting unhelpful romantic beliefs and understandings identified in the initial assessment can be a helpful first step in working in this area. The Romantic Beliefs Inventory is designed primarily from a cognitive therapy orientation (Edelson & Epstein, 1982) and can be useful in this regard.

Social cognition

Remediation of cognitive difficulties has in the past few years received a great deal of attention (Wykes *et al.*, 2011). This has also focussed on the social domains of cognition with recent meta-analyses of social cognitive treatments suggesting promising benefits (Fett *et al.*, 2011). Several group-based interventions for social cognition are available, including Metacognitive Training (MCT; Moritz *et al.*, 2013) and Social Cognitive Interaction Training (SCIT; Roberts & Penn, 2009). Interventions can be adapted from these approaches for individuals with social-cognitive deficits. Particular areas that appear to be helpful to consider include theory of mind, emotion recognition, jumping to conclusions and interpersonal attributions.

Of these, theory of mind seems most critical, as it not only reflects the ability to accurately interpret potentially ambiguous social information, but it involves a focus on the other. Encouraging people to think about other people's motivations, hopes and dreams is one aspect where this process can be started (as mentioned under the Social Beliefs section). Helping the individual to understand and practise thinking about others and putting themselves in their shoes is important. As friendships develop, so too does the opportunity for practising theory of mind skills, along with the motivation to achieve a solid understating of others' perspectives.

Social networks

This is perhaps the most difficult area in which to complete successful work. Clinical experience suggests that while many clients may be happy to socialise with other users of mental health services, many others are not. Recovery principles suggest that a preferable self-sustaining social network is one that does not revolve just around professional services (Deegan, 2002). Social networks may include college, work, voluntary jobs and religious communities. Classes can include learning a new sport, language, playing instruments, dance or singing. Very often, a trip down to the library or an Internet search can help people identify local community networks, although they may need support to access these. A relatively new phenomenon is the rise of online social networking. Sites such as www.meetup.com can be helpful in identifying possible social networks, including ones specifically for people with similar interests or things in common (including online groups for people with social anxiety).

A typical experience for our service users is that, at first sight, a group or class does not seem to have any kindred spirits or potential friends in, but if they persevere they do make some friends. To help people persevere, social events like these can be seen as exposure tasks, getting clients used to being in social situations as a therapeutic goal in itself. Social anxiety often serves to make clients want to avoid social events, and we emphasise that social contact in itself is usually beneficial and therapeutic.

An alternative approach is to nurture or resurrect established friendships. Often people had friends at school but contact dwindled over the years after school (see Brand *et al.*, 2011). After interviewing friends who have managed to stay in contact with their psychosis-suffering pals, it became clear that more friendships could survive psychosis if the friends had more support (e.g. knowledge about psychosis and how to react). Often these friends have a life-long investment in the psychosis-suffering person, and remain keen to meet (Brand *et al.*, 2011). In this spirit, we have been conducting 'Friends Interventions', in a way analogous to 'Family Interventions'. Initial meetings are low-key, normalising, possibly away from healthcare premises, either with a single best friend or partner, or alternatively with a group of friends (obviously, always including the client). Psychoeducation is given, and an opportunity to ask questions. Discussion and negotiation is encouraged between the person with psychosis and the friend(s). They are usually very helpful, for example, providing an alternative to substance-using peers or being understanding about social avoidance. They are also often very insightful about the beginning of their friend's problems and spotting future triggers (see Harrop *et al.*, 2014).

Shared formulation with key others increases the scope of these interventions to times when the primary clinician is simply not present and into daily activities. Using staff to deliver interventions, for example, can be an effective use of resources, but it also serves to apply skills and insights outside of the therapeutic relationship and widen their use into the 'real world'. Having separate but related therapeutic relationships will support the generalisation of achievements made within this model.

Case Illustration: Harold

Harold is a 40-year-old man who lives alone in the rural suburbs of a large city. Harold has reported hearing voices on and off for many years, he has a history of poor engagement with services and receives care from the local Assertive Outreach Team. He recently spent 2 months in an acute psychiatric hospital; prior to the voluntary admission he had been feeling anxious about the belief that others were entering his house and meddling with the furniture, TV channels and water. He became verbally hostile and threatening to his neighbours, believing that they had a key to the house and were trying spy on him. He agreed to a voluntary admission to the local acute mental health unit, and then to an admission to a psychiatric rehabilitation unit.

Assessment and formulation

Harold was initially reluctant to engage with psychology and said that he had 'nothing to talk about'. In a goal-planning group, it was noted by the nursing staff that Harold found it difficult to identify particular goals and aspirations. His named nurse was concerned about him returning to his house and remaining socially isolated. Harold agreed that spending lots of time on his own exacerbated feelings of low mood and suspiciousness and that he tended to ruminate on thoughts about himself. When the notion of working on his social isolation was introduced Harold agreed to do some goal-planning work with psychology and identified that he would like to make some more friends, feel more confident around others, and possibly meet a girlfriend. Harold said that he had a few friends at school, but he was no longer in touch with any of them. He once had a girlfriend when he was at local college, but he believed that she got 'bored' and left him for somebody else. Harold completed a number of assessments with the psychologist, the findings of which are summarised in a formulation in Figure 9.1.

Intervention

Harold agreed that he would like to be able to get around the local area, but was reluctant to give up his car. It was agreed that while he was unable to drive (his licence had been handed in to the DVLA), getting a bus pass could allow him to travel around the area and widen his social networks. However, he was concerned about talking with other people ("I won't know what to talk about"). He described the belief that other people staring at him meant that they wanted to engage in conversation with him, that if this happened, then he would mess this up, the other person would get upset, and want to fight him.

Prior to starting bus travel, Harold and the therapist practised some social skills sessions (role plays) based around basic interactions and conversations in session, taken from Bellack *et al.* (2004). Once he felt ready, Harold agreed to go with the therapist on the bus to various parts of the local area. On the bus, behavioural experiments were used to test whether people were staring at him (the therapist's observations were that they were not) and whether he would get into fights with others (he did not). Harold's hypervigilance decreased, and he started to use more eye contact (following the reasoning that it is helpful to look at people to read their body language). As Harold's confidence increased, he went on the buses himself.

Following this, Harold joined an inpatient group where he could practise his social skills with other service users from different local areas. Harold was reluctant to take part in role plays with others until it was pointed out that this was a good opportunity to practise these skills in a 'safe' group setting before trying to use them in public. Once he started practising role plays with the group, his social skills improved. In the group, members were encouraged to focus on other members as they interacted and they generated topics of conversation for the group to practise. Staff at the rehabilitation Unit reported that they had noticed Harold practising his new skills and holding conversations with others. Harold

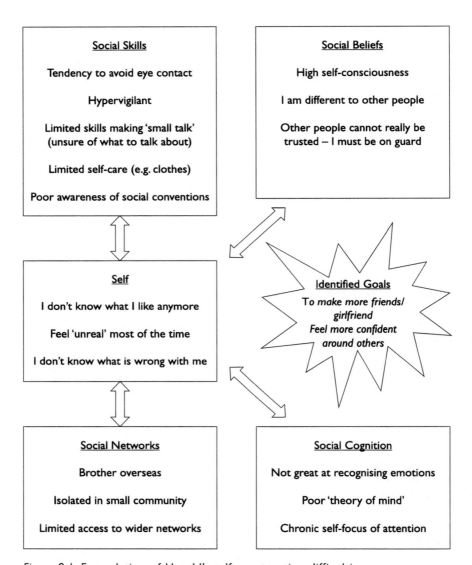

Figure 9.1 Formulation of Harold's self-construction difficulties

explained that he believed his ability to engage in 'small talk' was improving (which nursing staff agreed with).

Harold made friends with another resident of the Unit and together they attended a local 'cinema club' once a week, watching a film and then going for a drink to socialise afterwards. At first, Harold expressed anxiety, so in-session role plays were used to help him to practise starting conversations with others and maintaining these. He subsequently found it possible to attend the cinema club. Harold's conviction in the belief that he was different to others decreased, as did his self-consciousness, and self-focussed attention.

In 1:1 sessions, The Awareness of Social Inference Test (McDonald *et al.*, 2002) DVD was used to identify and work out different emotions shown by others: the video clips were rewound, paused and reviewed to differentiate the different emotions and explicitly understand the different types of social cues in the clips. This was in an attempt to improve Harold's awareness of social emotions and social conventions, and to facilitate practice of other-focussed attention. This triggered conversation about Harold's self-care, how others might think and feel if his self-care was poor, and what effect that might have on his social interactions. Staff reported that since Harold had been going to the cinema club with his friend, his self-care had improved, and Harold reported that he now felt it was easier to remember to attend to these aspects of his routine.

Progress and reflections

After 6 months Harold had booked a place to complete a maths access course at the local college, and was continuing to meet up with his friend to attend the cinema, often using buses to get around the local area. Harold had not explicitly covered any of the self-construction aspects of his difficulties in therapeutic sessions before discharge. While this remains a possible area of focus for future intervention, it seemed that for Harold it was not the right time. He had achieved his goal of widening his circle of friends and was now equipped with the skills and confidence to continue this in the community, possibly even going on to meet a romantic partner, if he still wished.

At no point in the therapy was the subject of symptoms of mental health discussed. This was not viewed as important by Harold to his goals of making friends. The therapeutic relationship was used to focus on the barriers to this goal, which, for Harold, did not at this moment in time include psychiatric symptoms. It may be that this emphasis on important goals increased the chances of Harold engaging with the therapist as he was motivated by a shared goal that had personal meaning for him, worked at collaboratively.

Conclusions and implications

In this chapter we have attempted to outline a framework for conducting work with people that addresses the impact that self-construction difficulties can have upon the achievement of life goals. An important aspect of this work is that it is focussed on normalised goals that many people tend to share: the experience of a positive sense of self. Blocks to this are then identified and targeted systematically to increase the chances of the person achieving this positive sense of self. Because symptoms are not necessarily the focus, this approach can be used to work with people who otherwise may not choose to engage with mental health services.

This chapter has not articulated explicit mechanisms for dealing with other aspects of difficult self-experience, such as the Alienated or Insecure Self. It remains important that the clinician remains aware of any difficulties experienced in this domain, and should shift focus onto this area should that appear helpful (Harrop & Trower, 2003). However, by removing blocks to healthy self-construction, there is an increased chance of people being able to continue to develop their own sense of self in a manner that they may never have fully experienced before. This returns us to the aim of the approach: to support people to access important social-developmental experiences so that they may experience a positive sense of self.

References

Allison, G., Harrop, C. & Ellett, L. (2013). Perception of peer group rank of individuals with early psychosis. *British Journal of Clinical Psychology, 52*, 1–11.

Andrews, K. (2007). *An empirical investigation of autistic spectrum traits in a sample of individuals at risk of psychosis.* Unpublished ClinPsyD manuscript, Birmingham University, UK.

Bellack, A. S., Mueser, K. T., Gingerich, S. L. & Agresta, J. (2004). *Social skills training for schizophrenia: A step-by-step guide.* London: Guilford Press.

Bijstra, J. O., Bosma, H. A. & Jackson, S. (1994). The relationship between social skills and psycho-social functioning in early adolescence. *Personality and Individual Differences, 16*(5), 767–776.

Blos, P. (1962). *On adolescence.* London: Collier-Macmillan.

Brand, R. M., Harrop, C. & Ellett, L. (2011). What is it like to be friends with a young person with psychosis? A qualitative study. *Psychosis, 3*(3), 205–215.

Brekke, J. S., Prindle, C., Bae, S. W. & Long, J. D. (2001). Risks for individuals with schizophrenia who are living in the community. *Psychiatric Services, 52*(10), 1358–1366.

Buchanan, J. (1995). Social support and schizophrenia: A review of the literature. *Archives of Psychiatric Nursing, 9*, 68–76.

Chadwick, P. (2006). *Person-based cognitive therapy for distressing psychosis.* Chichester, Sussex: John Wiley & Sons.

Chadwick, P., Trower, P. & Dagnan, D. (1999). Measuring negative person evaluations: The Evaluative Beliefs Scale. *Cognitive Therapy and Research, 23*, 549–559.

Collins, W. A. W. (2003). More than myth: The developmental significance of romantic relationships during adolescence. *Journal of Research on Adolescence, 13*, 1–24.

Couture, S. M., Penn, D. L. & Roberts, D. L. (2006). The functional significance of social cognition in schizophrenia: A review. *Schizophrenia Bulletin, 32*(Suppl. 1), S44–S63.

Dagnan, D., Trower, P. & Gilbert, P. (2002). Measuring vulnerability to threats to self-construction: The Self and Other Scale. *Psychology and Psychotherapy: Theory, Research and Practice, 75*, 279–293.

Deegan, P. E. (2002). Recovery as a self-directed process of healing and transformation. *Occupational Therapy in Mental Health, 17*(3–4), 5–21.

Eidelson, R. J. & Epstein, N. (1982). Cognition and relationship maladjustment: Development of a measure of dysfunctional relationship beliefs. *Journal of Consulting and Clinical Psychology, 50,* 715–720.

Elkind, D. (1967). Egocentrism in adolescence. *Child Development, 38,* 1025–1034.

Fett, A. J., Viechtbauer, W., Dominguez, M., Penn, D. L., van Os, J. & Krabbendam, L. (2011). The relationship between neurocognition and social cognition with functional outcomes in schizophrenia: A meta-analysis. *Neuroscience & Biobehavioral Reviews, 35,* 573–588.

Fox, A. P. (2007). *Adolescent self-development and psychopathology: Anorexia nervosa and psychosis.* Unpublished doctoral dissertation, University of Birmingham, UK.

Fox, A., Harrop, C., Trower, P. & Leung, N. (2009). A consideration of developmental egocentrism in anorexia nervosa. *Eating Behaviors, 10,* 10–15.

Frankenberger, K. D. (2000). Adolescent egocentrism: A comparison among adolescents and adults. *Journal of Adolescence, 23,* 343–354.

Furman, W. & Buhrmester, D. (1992). Age and sex differences in perceptions of networks of personal relationships. *Child Development, 63,* 103–115.

Furman, W., Ho, M. J. & Low, S. (2007). The rocky road of adolescent romantic experience: Dating and adjustment. In C. M. E. Engels, M. Kerr & H. Stattin (eds), *Friends, lovers and groups: Key relationships in adolescence* (pp. 61–80). New York: John Wiley & Sons.

Gogtay, N., Vyas, N. S., Testa, R., Wood, S. J. & Pantelis, C. (2011). Age of onset of schizophrenia: perspectives from structural neuroimaging studies. *Schizophrenia Bulletin, 37*(3), 504–513.

Grant, P. M., Huh, G. A., Perivoliotis, D., Stolar, N. M. & Beck, A. T. (2012). Randomized trial to evaluate the efficacy of cognitive therapy for low-functioning patients with schizophrenia. *Archives of General Psychiatry, 69*(2), 121–127.

Harrop, C. & Trower, P. (2003). *Why does schizophrenia develop at late adolescence? A cognitive-developmental approach to psychosis.* Chichester, Sussex: John Wiley & Sons.

Harrop, C., Ellett, L., Brand, R. & Lobban, F. (2014). Friends interventions in early psychosis: A narrative review and call to action. *Early Intervention in Psychiatry.* doi: 10.1111/eip.12172.

Harter, S. (1999). *The construction of the self: A developmental perspective.* New York: Guilford Press.

Harvey, A. M. (2013). *Adolescent egocentrism and psychosis.* Unpublished doctoral dissertation, University of Birmingham, UK.

Hirschfeld, R., Smith, J., Trower, P. & Griffin, C. (2005). What do psychotic experiences mean for young men? A qualitative investigation. *Psychology and Psychotherapy: Theory Research and Practice, 78,* 249–270.

Jablensky, A., Sartorius, N., Ernberg, G., Anker, M. & Cooper, J. E. (1992). Schizophrenia: manifestations, incidence, and course in different cultures – a World Health Organisation 10 country study. *Psychological Medical Monograph Supplement 20,* 1–97.

Kroger, J. (1996). *Identity in adolescence: The balance between self and other.* London: Routledge.

Lapsley, D. K. (1993). Toward an integrated theory of adolescent ego development: The 'new look' at adolescent egocentrism. *American Journal of Orthopsychiatry, 63,* 562–571.

McDonald, S. Flanagan, S. & Rollins, J. (2002). *The Awareness of Social Inference Test.* Suffolk, UK: Thames Valley Test Co., Ltd.

Mahler, M. S., Pine, F. & Bergman, A. (1975). *The psychological birth of the human infant.* New York: Basic Books.

Meaden, A. & Hacker, D. (2010). *Problematic and risk behaviours in psychosis: A shared formulation approach.* London: Routledge.

Moritz, S., Veckenstedt, R., Bohn. F., Köther, U. & Woodward, T. S. (2013). Metacognitive training in schizophrenia. Theoretical rationale and administration. In D. L. Roberts & D. L. Penn (eds), *Social cognition in schizophrenia. From evidence to treatment* (pp. 358–383). New York: Oxford University Press.

Redmond, C., Larkin, M. & Harrop, C. (2010). The personal meaning of romantic relationships for young people with psychosis. *Clinical Child Psychology and Psychiatry, 15*(2), 151–170.

Roberts, D. L. & Penn, D. L. (2009). Social cognition and interaction training (SCIT) for outpatients with schizophrenia: A preliminary study. *Psychiatry Research, 166*(2), 141–147.

Scheier, M. F. & Carver, C. S. (1985). The Self-Consciousness Scale: A revised version for use with general populations. *Journal of Applied Social Psychology, 15*, 687–699.

Trower, P. & Chadwick, P. (1995). Pathways to defense of the self: A theory of two types of paranoia. *Clinical Psychology: Science and Practice, 2*(3), 263–278.

Vartanian, L. R. (2000). Revisiting the imaginary audience and personal fable constructs of adolescent egocentrism: A conceptual review. *Adolescence, 35*, 639–661.

Waldinger, R. J., Diguer, L., Guastella, F., Lefebvre, R., Allen, J. P., Luborsky, L. & Hauser, S. T. (2002). The same old song? – Stability and change in relationship schemas from adolescence to young adulthood. *Journal of Youth and Adolescence, 31*(1), 17–29.

Webster, C. D., Martin, M., Brink, J., Nicholls, T. L. & Middleton, C. (2004). *Short-Term Assessment of Risk and Treatability (START).* Hamilton, ON and Coquitlam, BC: St. Joseph's Healthcare and British Columbia Mental Health and Addiction Services.

Wykes, T., Huddy, V., Cellard, C., McGurk, S. R. & Czobor, P. (2011). A meta-analysis of cognitive remediation for schizophrenia: Methodology and effect sizes. *American Journal of Psychiatry, 168*(5), 472–485.

Chapter 10

Telling stories and re-authoring lives

A narrative approach to individuals with psychosis

Helen Hewson

Introduction

A growing body of literature comments upon the use of narrative interventions for psychosis (Bargenquast & Schweitzer, 2013; Prasko *et al.*, 2010; Roberts, 2000; Rhodes & Jakes, 2009). Therapists working with 'hard to engage' client groups report that the approach supports engagement and can be usefully integrated alongside other evidence-based therapies (Lysaker *et al.*, 2010; Rhodes & Jakes, 2009). Whilst many have commented on the relevance of narrative theory for a thorough understanding of psychotic experience, few have attempted to describe a therapeutic approach. Rhodes and Jakes's (2009) description of narrative ideas can be used to support cognitive behavioural interventions in order to target distress associated with psychotic symptoms. The current chapter emphasises the use of White's (2007) narrative therapy. The telling of stories, deconstruction and re-authorship of problem-saturated stories is presented as a more general approach to working with the problems raised by individuals with psychosis (depression, powerlessness, self-esteem, stigma, voices and unusual beliefs). This is intended to provide an introduction and flexible guide to starting out and engaging clients with the use of a narrative approach.

Theoretical background and development: Narrative ideas and their relevance to individuals with psychosis

Narrative Therapy builds upon the philosophical principles of social constructionism. Knowledge is understood to emerge as the product of self-referential construction whereby new insights rely upon existing understandings of the world. All interpretations of 'reality' are mediated by social processes such as language, discourse and the social construction of meaning (Burr, 1995, 2003; Gergen, 1992). Constructionism challenges structuralist claims regarding the objectivity of a scientific approach (Burr, 1995, 2003). Instead, approaches to research and intervention are guided by the belief that all interpretations of 'reality' and human experience are shaped by language, narrative and story (Sarbin, 1986). Sarbin's

(1986) text, 'The storied nature of human conduct', has argued that narrative should represent a root metaphor for psychology with a focus on narrative replacing a natural science approach. Throughout the current chapter the terms 'story' and 'script' are used to describe the concept of 'narrative'.

According to Narrative Psychology humans are interpretative beings that make sense of experience by listening to the stories told by others and constructing more personal narratives (Bruner, 1990; Polkinghorne, 1988). Stories and scripts originating from families, cultural groups and other social systems are believed to directly influence individual interpretations of the world (White, 2007). The term 'narrative' refers to the temporal ordering of interpretations, intentions, values and events typical when telling a story about the world. As individuals, the construction of narrative helps us to describe and 'make sense' of ourselves, others and the world (Bruner, 1990). Without this, dialogue appears fragmented, incoherent or barren and without meaning (Lysaker & Lysaker, 2006). Narratives that communicate intentions and values transform lists of actions and experiences into meaningful stories that involve a beginning, middle and an end (White, 2007). Bruner (1990) argues that it is the capacity for 'narrative thought' rather than 'logic' that enables humans to experience a sense of meaning and purpose.

Narrative as an organising principle

Attempts to organise experiences and insights to resemble a life story are evident from early childhood (McAdams, 2008). Bruner (1990) cites this as evidence of an innate ability in children to comprehend and make use of grammar in order to assimilate and transmit meaning. The incorporation of personal meaning and intentionality supports the reconstruction of past experience and the construction of an imagined future which appears feasible and coherent (McAdams, 2008). According to social constructionism such stories not only describe individuals but directly influence human behaviour (White, 2007). With age and maturity personal narratives become increasingly complex, incorporating new experiences, values, understanding and insights about self and the world (McAdams, 2003). Identity becomes multi-storied in order to incorporate different subject positioning and social roles that have occurred at different stages of a person's life.

The role of narrative in organising and giving meaning to experience is gaining increasing recognition from scientific studies. Pennebaker and colleagues have repeatedly found that expressive writing supports health-related outcomes for a range of populations (Pennebaker & Beall, 1986). This evidence suggests that narrative may have a role in organising and giving new meaning to experience that may otherwise have been associated with distress. The incorporation of narrative structure as part of the writing task has been found to facilitate metacognitive reflection, emotional processing and cognitive restructuring (Pennebaker & Seagal, 1999). A focus on narrative has also been applied to support psychological interventions for complex trauma (Bichescu et al., 2007). In Narrative Exposure Therapy (NET) intervention aims to assist torture victims to incorporate traumatic memories into a more hopeful and future-focussed account of the person's life story (Schauer *et al.*, 2011). Further evidence is evolving from research into psychosis that has identified an association between personal narratives that lack self-descriptions and higher levels of negative symptoms, disorganised behaviour, social isolation and withdrawal (Lysaker *et al.*, 2012).

Narrative impoverishment in psychosis

According to Holma and Aaltonen (1998b) schizophrenia represents a chronic disintegration of narrative. The self-narratives of individuals with psychosis have been observed to lack temporal structure, self-reference and coherence (Gallagher, 2003). Lysaker and colleagues suggest that the cognitive capacity for 'thinking about thinking', also referred to as 'metacognition', may be a precondition for narrative coherence (Lysaker *et al.*, 2010). Metacognitive difficulties are widely observed in psychosis (Brune *et al.*, 2011); attempts to account for this have pointed to predisposing problems with emotion recognition, poor affect regulation, theory of mind (ToM) and difficulties with the encoding of episodic autobiographical memory (Dimaggio & Semerari, 2001; Gallagher, 2003; Holma & Aaltonen, 1998a, 1998b; Lysaker *et al.*, 2010, 2012). Given a high incidence of trauma (Mueser *et al.*, 2010) in the same population, the Morrison *et al.* (2003) integrated model suggests that psychotic symptoms may represent misidentified traumatic symptoms resulting either from early trauma or more recent psychotic experiences. Metacognitive difficulties are likely to limit opportunities for the construction of coherent narratives following trauma and psychosis resulting in impoverished narrative.

Despite factors which limit the construction of narrative, the will for meaning appears to remain intact during psychosis. Within the context of difficulties with autobiographical memory processing and dissociative experience or incoherent descriptions, confabulations and abstractions in psychotic dialogue may represent attempts to narrate and organise experience (Lysaker & Lysaker, 2006). Implausible stories which appear internally consistent but implausible to others may represent attempts to contextualise and give meaning to intrusive and hallucinatory experiences that are difficult for the individual to make sense of (Lysaker & Lysaker, 2006). Stories of special powers, spiritual significance, telepathy or thought-insertion from spiritual beings, demonstrate that narrative construction and meaning-making remain even during acute psychosis (Roberts, 2000). Whilst psychotic narratives may lack flexibility and plausibility to others, it is possible that they offer meaning for the person and provide an explanation for events and experiences in the person's life.

Dialogical theories of narrative coherence

Dialogical theories in psychology describe metacognitive reflection as being located in dialogical processes by which persons carry out conversations both with others and themselves (Lysaker *et al.*, 2010). Integrative psychotherapy for psychosis, the Open Dialogue approach and Narrative Therapy are all based upon dialogical theories of self (Lysaker *et al.,* 2010; see also Chapter 2 this volume). Lysaker claims that metacognitive deficits limit dialogical process in psychosis leading to a loss of evolving self-experience and diminished self-identity. Lysaker and colleagues have categorised narrative breakdown in psychosis suggesting three differing types: barren, monological or cacophonous (Lysaker & Lysaker, 2006). Barren narratives are those that contain limited accounts of self-agency such that a person's life story is underdeveloped. Descriptions of self are brief and contain historical information with only limited accounts of the future. Consequently, motivation and activity is limited resulting in negative symptoms and social withdrawal (Lysaker & Lysaker, 2006). The monological narrative is relevant for individuals who present with rigid delusional beliefs. Narratives appear internally consistent but resistant from external influences. Such beliefs may offer an explanation for events which seems plausible to the person; however, a lack of contextual information prevents meaning from being understood by others (Lysaker & Lysaker, 2006). Finally, a cacophonous narrative is hypothesised to develop when all hierarchy has been abandoned leading to a 'dizzying-array' of self-positions which lack order or reference to each other. The presentations of these narratives with multiple contradictions do not appear to follow logic or reason due to a lack of temporal sequence (Lysaker & Lysaker, 2006).

Lysaker *et al.* (2010) have argued that reliance on these three narrative forms limits dialogue with others, restricting the incorporation of new information from the social world. In order to address this, narrative therapies aim to support the development of a more coherent and flexible narrative about self and psychosis which appears plausible to others, gives meaning to past experiences and enables opportunities for dialogue with others (Lysaker *et al.*, 2010).

Narrative approaches and interventions

Many have argued that psychotherapy itself is a narrative enterprise and that all talking therapies can be seen as working with the stories that people tell about their lives (McLeod, 1997). Whilst this is a common feature in all therapies, narrative approaches can be distinguished by their use of key interventions, principles and techniques which aim to encourage narrative coherence through the renegotiation and re-authoring of experience and associated meanings. White's (2007) Narrative Therapy, Narrative CBT (Rhodes & Jakes, 2009), the Open Dialogue approach (see Chapter 2) and Lysaker's approach to integrative psychotherapy are all consistent with this description. Narrative Therapy however does not require a committed network to attend therapeutic sessions. This is particularly useful when relationships with family members and care teams have become conflictual, leading the person to withdraw and resist contact. A focus on re-authorship rather than the uncovering of an old version of self aims to supports the person to overcome social isolation, powerlessness and inaction.

Narrative Therapy for psychosis

White's (2007) Narrative Therapy is interested in observing the limiting effects of 'problem stories' on the accounts individuals tell about themselves (e.g. self as weak, failure, a bad person). 'Problem stories' are narratives which dominate a person's identity and lead to alternative understandings about the person to be subordinated. Personal narratives are unable to encapsulate all of our life experiences and rarely present the whole or only story. In psychosis, distressing intrusions and threatening experiences that have led a person to feel frightened and mistrustful lead personal narratives to become dominated by this theme and by the stories told about the person within this context (such as persecution, vulnerability, helplessness, insanity). Other experiences that may speak of insight, personal achievement, agency and resilience are obscured or discounted as not fitting with the person's storied identity (White, 2007). For individuals labelled as having a 'mental illness', discrimination and marginalisation further exacerbates the problem with stigmatising social stories forming a part of the person's storied identity (Wahl, 1999). In White's Narrative Therapy the therapeutic approach aims to deconstruct 'problem stories' and social stigma in order to make way for multi-storied accounts of self-identity that include self-agency and hope (White & Epston, 1990).

When working with psychosis, Narrative Therapy remains open to conversations that focus on the idiosyncratic meaning and interpretation of psychotic experience. The aim is not to challenge the client's understanding but to restore dialogue about the person's experiences leading to the development of richer and more coherent narratives. This approach is in direct contrast to traditional medical perspectives where the view that psychotic narratives are nonsensical symptoms results in the closing down of opportunities for dialogue. Open Dialogue supports the client to narrate their experience of psychosis. The focus is on deconstructing 'problem stories' which limit social participation and recovery and authoring alternatives that might counter them. In some instances, particularly where self-blame has been internalised, relocating the origins of problems in historical and contextual experiences can support the deconstruction of negativistic self-scripts. Where the client is unable to tolerate this, re-authorship remains focussed on the here and now. The therapeutic process could be described as a joint narration of experience in order to improve consistency and self-agency. Whilst White (2007) does not view coherence as a central aim in the general therapeutic approach, the adaptation for working with psychosis requires a longer period of open dialogue or narration aimed at improving consistency.

Aims, stages, strategies and techniques

Therapeutic aims are case specific and based upon a 'client-centred' approach. The therapist resists the temptation to impose their own interpretation of the client's story, focussing instead upon creating a space for dialogue about troubling problems. Difficulties with low mood, confidence and social isolation are often viewed as a priority to clients rather than psychosis and its symptoms. It is these problems that become the focus of intervention. If psychotic intrusions and beliefs are the focus, then the development of a common language is a first step towards the re-authoring of the client's relationship with psychotic experience.

Stage 1: Assessment and engagement

The first stage involves the development of alliance that supports Open Dialogue regarding the client's personal narrative. Other tasks include the assessment of narrative content and form, negotiation of power and control, contracting arrangements for session arrangements and managing expectations about therapy. Clients who have been treated or detained against their will may have learnt to hold back details of unusual or psychotic experiences due to fears of hospitalisation. They may fear that therapy will be too much for them to cope with and the therapist will need to demonstrate a commitment to sharing control and moving at the client's pace.

Further assessment of the client's narrative is guided by client-centred principles. The therapist maintains a curious, non-expert and open stance requiring that pre-existing theories and psychological models are put aside. A focus on the client's storied experience empowers them to be an active participant in therapy. Open Dialogue in this first stage provides the opportunity for clients to narrate their own experience (see also Chapter 2). Descriptions of experiences which appear delusional or implausible are accepted as being meaningful for the client. Where narratives appear impoverished or incoherent an analysis of the narrative structure and form can be beneficial (e.g. barren, monological, cacophonous). Those presenting with cacophonous or monological narratives may benefit from a longer period of open dialogue which focuses on developing shared meaning before the nature of the 'problem story' can be identified with the client (Seikkula et al., 2001). When the client is able to identify and explore a 'problem story' or a focus for change, then therapeutic work can move on to the next stage.

Narrative therapists often resist using psychometric assessments that locate problems in persons rather than within the wider social context. When working with 'hard to engage' clients, it is important that a full range of health and social care needs are assessed in order that appropriate intervention is put in place (e.g. medical problems, housing and social problems, psychiatric medication, violence and aggression, problematic substance use, risk). Where the client is not ready to address these needs, or the development of alliance is sensitive, comprehensive assessment work incorporating structured or psychometric assessment can be completed by an alternative practitioner or multi-disciplinary colleague.

Stage 2: Externalising the problem and mapping its effects

The aim of the second stage is to establish the exact nature of the problem story and the client's position for or against its effects. Key techniques include externalising conversations, the naming of the problem, mutual influence questioning and deconstruction.

Externalising conversations and naming the problem

The diagnostic labels and narratives of psychiatry have been accused of problematising persons and closing down opportunities for insight and meaning to develop (Roe *et al.*, 2008; Tranulis *et al.*, 2009). Carey and Russell (2004: 2) suggest that in Narrative Therapy 'the person is not the problem, the problem is the problem'. Externalising conversations challenge internalising discourses and encourage the client to narrate their own story. The technique aims to assist people to view their problems as separate from themselves. Subtle changes in grammar have the effect of reversing internalised descriptions ("I am a schizophrenic"). The use of nouns in place of adjectives (e.g. "how long has 'this schizophrenia' been influencing your life?") highlights the relationship between persons and the problems that influence their lives. During externalising conversations the client is encouraged to make use of metaphor in order to select a name which fits their lived experience of the problem. This is then described as being external to the person. Asking the client to name and externalise the problem story assists them to see it as separate from their own identity and sense of self. The therapist can approach this directly asking the client how he or she would like the problem to be referred to or the therapist could make a suggestion based upon language that the client has already used. Common problem stories in psychosis include experiences of persecution, anxiety or difficulties with confidence and self-esteem. The name selected should fit with the client's lived experience of the problem; this name is not fixed, and can be adapted to incorporate new understandings developed in therapy. White (2007) is well known for developing playful metaphors that describe the problems as though there were fictional creatures or monsters that possess qualities and intentions of their own (e.g. 'the worry monster').

An externalising approach to working with voices and intrusive experience rejects the view that experiences must be accepted and owned by the individual as representing part of the self (White, 1995). The narrative approach shares the position taken in Cognitive Behavioural Therapy; that is that the client can choose to revise their relationship with the voice in the present without locating origins in the past (Chadwick *et al.*, 1996; Chadwick, 2006). Questions to support externalising conversations in psychosis are:

"How long has this schizophrenia/problem been bothering you?"
"What does the problem tell you about yourself?"
"If the problem were a person/character/object what qualities would it/they have?"
"If this schizophrenia was an animal what would it look like?"
"What kind of creature/animal would you say it was?"

"What name would you give to this problem?"

"The persecutors, what sort of qualities do they have?"

"What intentions does the problem have for your life?"

"When does this persecutor usually visit you?"

"What do you make of the voices – do you think they have anything valuable to say?"

Mutual influence questioning

After the problem has been named and externalised, mutual influence questions encourage the person to describe their problem in terms of its influence on them ("how does the problem influence your work/relationships/interests?"). Useful questions highlight the relationship with the problem rather than the problem itself. A similar line of questioning can be used to explore the influence of the person on the problem (e.g. "tell me about a time you have been able to overthrow the problem/get the upper hand"). These questions highlight opportunities for self-agency and empowerment and provide the beginnings of alternative stories that might support a multi-storied self. Mutual influence questioning leads to a discussion about the client's position on the problem in which the therapist invites the client to state their position for or against its effects.

Deconstructing problem stories

Deconstruction refers to interventions that draw attention to procedures that subvert taken-for-granted realities (White, 2007). Where contextual circumstances have included unbalanced practices of power, Narrative Therapy seeks to highlight this. Deconstructive questions explore how the person was first recruited into totalising descriptions of themselves (e.g. failure, worthless, not good enough, to blame). The aim is to draw connections with past experiences of a person's power being restricted through social marginalisation, racism or experiences of emotional and physical abuse. Questions focus upon the history and social context of such ideas. For example: "who told you that men should always be fearless?", "When was it that you first came to know that persecution was something you should be afraid of?". In some instances, clients may resist this line of questioning which draws attention to past experiences of adversity and harm and that may be too difficult for them to tolerate.

Stage 3: Re-authoring alternative and preferred accounts

The third and final stage of therapy is focussed on re-authorship. Interventions aim to author and thicken preferred stories about the person which may assist them to move forward from the problem. Interventions focus on building stories that support the person's own values and intentions and this is approached through the identification of 'unique outcomes'. Other techniques used in this stage include the naming and thickening of the preferred story, outsider witness practices and therapeutic documents.

Unique outcomes and exceptions

'Unique outcome' is a term, initially used by White (2007) which refers to actions and events when the person has been able to resist the influence of the problem. Highlighting 'unique outcomes' provides a starting point for the development of alternative plots, themes and story lines in people's lives. Actions which have been perceived as helpful are linked with a person's intentions and values, offering a richer description of the person's preferred identity (e.g. "so you ignored the voice when it ordered you to jump, what does that say about your intentions in life?"). Continued discussions regarding 'unique outcomes' aim to support the development of a 'preferred story', which is connected to the person's own desires for their future. This can lead to the development of goals and behavioural interventions that support the client to develop the preferred story outside of therapy. Questions to help draw attention to 'unique outcomes' are:

"Tell me about a time when the problem nearly got you to act upon its orders but you somehow managed to refuse it?"
"Have you ever managed to get the upper hand on the hopelessness?"
"How did you manage to overcome the evil machines in this way?"
"Tell me about a time that you have been able to distance yourself from 'the schizophrenia'?"
"What did it take for you to get ready for this step?"
"What personal qualities were you relying on to organize yourself for this?"
"When you took action against the problem what intentions/desires/values did that speak of?"
"What experiences have told you that this situation needs to change?"
"Equipped with this new knowledge about yourself, how might you move forward in the coming days/weeks?"

Naming and thickening of the preferred story

The naming of a preferred story highlights its presence in order that the person might reconnect with other memories, experiences and ideas which fit this preferred account. A name is selected to fit with the person's own description. This is usually a description of values and qualities that the person hopes to build upon (e.g. resilience, 'strong will'). The therapist might ask whether the preferred story has made an appearance at any other times in the client's life. Another useful line of questioning explores whether there are other people in the person's life that are aware of the person's qualities. This can lead to further examples of actions observed from the perspective of this person.

Outsider witness practices

Outsider witnesses such as family members, carers or support workers can be brought into a session in order to strengthen preferred social stories that are told about the person. Outsiders are invited to witness the client's story and therapeutic journey and to comment upon the positive qualities that they witness in the person. Within multi-disciplinary teams this intervention can be used to challenge problem-saturated perceptions and blaming attitudes which position the person as the problem. This also provides an opportunity to introduce the principles of externalising to staff, enabling them to be united with the client in a joint endeavour to overcome the 'problem'.

Therapeutic documents as shared formulation

The narrative approach views formulation as an evolving process rather than a static account of the problem (Harper & Spellman, 2006). Therapeutic documents, letters, documents of knowledge and certificates which detail the workings of the problem story along with alternative stories worked on in therapy are considered to be tools for both shared formulation and intervention (Fox, 2006; Harper & Spellman, 2006; White & Epston, 1990). Fox (2006) has provided a useful summary regarding the types of documents frequently employed. Documents shared with the client, support network and MDT aim to support a process of re-authorship regarding the client's account. A therapeutic letter or document which describes the problem as external to the person and identifies some unique outcomes and alternative knowledges can be usefully employed to support an alternative story about the person.

Assessing outcome

Key therapy outcomes include richer descriptions of psychotic experience that include accounts of self-agency in addition to those that explain psychosis. Lysaker *et al.* (2003) have argued that narrative transformation may involve increasing levels of narrative 'complexity, dynamism and subtlety'. As such, accounts of psychosis become more flexible and are perhaps more understandable to others. This can contribute to improvements in social functioning and increased activity. Lysaker and colleagues have developed a number of outcome measures to support the use of a narrative approach (Lysaker *et al.*, 2003). The Narrative Coherence Rating Scale (NCRS) looks at dimensions of logical connections, richness of details and plausibility whilst the Scale To Assess Narrative Development (STAND) focuses upon narrative complexity and examines changes on dimensions of social worth, social alienation, personal agency and illness conception/awareness (Lysaker *et al.*, 2002, 2003).

Case illustration: Adam

Adam is a 38-year-old man who reported hearing voices in his late 20s following the loss of his job. Despite numerous medication trials and hospital admissions the voices continued to trouble him several times a day. Prior to being admitted to hospital Adam had refused to leave his father's home for 18 months.

Assessment and engagement issues

During the initial assessment, Adam reported that his main problem was being stuck in a hospital against his will. He was angry that others referred to him as being unwell when he himself could see no evidence of this. He explained that his family had put him in hospital without cause. Adam denied experiencing voices or suffering from any psychological difficulties other than anger at his care team. Adam was initially ambivalent about therapy; in his view no good had ever come from talking to professionals. Initial sessions focussed on the communication of empathy and support focussed on the challenges of being in hospital. Adam was quiet and appeared unmotivated and shared only limited descriptions suggestive of storied identity and self-agency. Adam eventually acknowledged that he believed he was being persecuted and often heard the voice of prison inmates. The therapist adopted Adam's language and referred to the voices as 'The Persecutors'. The voices would comment upon his actions throughout the day and had done so for most of his life. At times they would say horrible things about him and tell him to take their advice to get ahead. Adam was happy to meet and discuss his experience, but he was clear that in his view he was not unwell. He believed that 'The Persecutors' were real people that were sending him messages.

Adam's narrative about the world was punctuated with themes regarding mistrust. He stated that he had adopted the position in his own life that people were not to be trusted. In his description of himself, accounts of self-agency or hope for the future appeared limited. Adam had few hobbies or interests and when at home he spent his time watching television.

Identifying a problem story

When asked about the main problems in his life Adam spoke about a conspiracy taking place between his family and staff which was designed to keep him 'out of the way'. He was often very angry about this and would regularly shout at staff and visitors. He did not believe that there was anything that talking could do to change the situation and accepted that he would remain in hospital until his family were ready to have him home. Adam could not see any value in discussing this problem but he did agree that it would be useful to distance himself from the voices of the prison inmates somehow. The therapist asked Adam to suggest a name for this problem. He confirmed that 'The Persecutors' was a good fit.

Naming the experience enabled externalisation and mutual influence questions to examine the effect on Adam's life.

Externalising conversations and mutual influence questioning

Questions focussed upon the influence of 'The Persecutors' on his life and relationships with others. For example, I asked Adam if 'The Persecutors' had been getting in the way at college. He remarked that he often felt distracted and unsure of himself because 'The Persecutors' would comment upon what he was doing. Other questions were about what 'The Persecutors' got him thinking about himself and what their plans were for him in life. 'The Persecutors' had contributed to him believing that he was a 'waste of space' that he was 'stupid' and 'pathetic'. He would spend time mostly on his own and made no attempt to develop relationships with others. 'The Persecutors' would tell him that he did not deserve to be happy and that he should be in prison or in hospital where he would cause no harm, and this was their plan for Adam. He was able to identify that he was not happy with the ways that 'The Persecutors' spoke to him. Nor was he happy with how angry and ashamed they would make him feel. He believed that he was weak and inferior to 'The Persecutors' and that he must have done something wrong in the past.

Thickening alternative stories – the multi-storied self

Outsmarting 'The Persecutors'

Exploration and attention to unique outcomes revealed that there were times when 'The Persecutors' did not leave Adam feeling so angry and helpless. He noticed that when he was able to get involved with an activity 'The Persecutors' would leave him alone. Adam concluded that if he did not give them his attention they would eventually get bored. Adam attempted to put this solution into practice with mixed success: attempting to participate in activities on the ward seemed to anger 'The Persecutors' who continued to comment upon his actions ("you're rubbish at that", "you don't know what you're doing", "stop wasting your time"). In therapy sessions we remained curious about other solutions that had worked for Adam in the past. These included listening to loud music and shouting back at the voices – both of which had mixed success. Adam also noticed that these techniques would only work if he was feeling 'energised' and 'relaxed'; when he was tired towards the end of the day it did not seem to have the same effect. Adam also noticed that these techniques were more effective when he was focussed on an activity that he was more confident in. Adam began to recognise that perhaps he was not 'weak' as he had worked out that 'The Persecutors' were not on his side and was able to ignore their comments. This 'unique outcome' was labelled as 'strength of mind'.

Strength of mind

Further questioning focussed on any other times that Adam had exercised this 'strength of mind' in order to overcome persecuting experiences. To support the thickening of Adam's preferred story we agreed to trace it back throughout his life with the use of a time-line exercise. The time-line was an evolving document which recorded Adam's preferred story. Unique outcomes were explored in terms of the intentions, hopes, desires and values that he viewed as important in life. Adam recalled that as younger man he had spoken up and challenged bullying that he had witnessed at work. When asked about the values and intentions in doing this Adam stated that it had always been important to him to be fair, honest and not to let others come to harm. 'The Persecutors' had restricted opportunities for him to live out these values by suggesting that he was a criminal and encouraging him to stay at home where he could do no harm. However, 'unique outcome' questioning identified situations when Adam had supported other patients on the ward by asking others to help them when they were distressed. Adam recognised that others were unwell and in need of care despite behaviours that were distracting and unpleasant at times (e.g. shouting, violence). Re-authoring conversations explored the metaphor of 'strength of mind' to explore ways in which this might be exercised and developed further. Adam began to read psychoeducation materials based upon confidence and self-esteem and was more open to therapeutic group programmes available on the ward.

Shared formulation

Therapeutic documents were shared with others involved in Adam's care, with his agreement. Adam's sister and keyworker were given copies of Adam's time-line. Therapy was documented through therapeutic letters that summarised our conversations. Over time other professionals began to refer to Adam's voices as 'The Persecutors', enabling them to collaborate with him. Adam's keyworker assisted in the development of this by supporting him to join in with other activities when he appeared distracted. When observed talking back to 'The Persecutors' staff would offer activities to divert Adam's attention elsewhere. Over time Adam developed therapeutic relationships with the staff team who he now felt understood his situation.

Reclaiming recovery and hope

Although 'The Persecutors' remained in his life, Adam reported that he felt more confident in keeping them in check. He began to involve himself with group activities and developed relationships with the staff team. Adam also began to question some of the paranoid beliefs he experienced about family and staff. Whilst he remained cautious about developing new relationships Adam requested additional help to build confidence in forming friendships with others. The use of unique outcome questioning had increased Adam's awareness of times that he had supported others by asking for help for them.

Progress and outcomes

Following twenty sessions of one-to-one therapy, Adam continued to hear 'The Persecutors', but accepted that this experience was normal for him. 'The Persecutors' would occasionally make negative comments about him but he would ignore them and remind himself of his achievements. Adam developed a range of interests and in turn his own self-narrative involved a richer description of hopes and intentions. He developed a goal to begin voluntary work with a dog-walking service for older adults with dogs. This helped him to stay connected with his own values about helping others and gave him more purpose in his life. Adam's relationships with staff improved; following their acceptance of his problem story they were able to work together in order to overcome 'The Persecutors' and Adam began to question the idea that they had been involved and viewed them as supporters and allies. This was a positive outcome for the staff who felt more able to collaborate with Adam to discuss his needs and plan his care.

Conclusions and implications

In Narrative Therapy a more flexible approach to meaning and sense-making supports the development of alliance and the negotiation of narrative meaning. This position is ideal for clients who feel that other people's meanings – whether formulations or diagnostic categories – do not fit with their own lives. Narrative Therapy enables meaning to be shared, opening up space for collaboration within therapy. For some clients, the opening up discourse through the use of a narrative approach can make way for the inclusion of other evidence-based techniques and strategies that might support the development of a preferred story.

Obstacles to adopting a narrative approach: Deconstructing problem stories within the team

Social constructionism reminds us that problem stories exist beyond individuals and have their origins in social systems. When working within the context of teams, the stories shared about clients directly influence their own narratives. By involving teams in narrative work, 'problem stories' are deconstructed and alternatives disseminated. Those involved in supporting the person can then be invited to see themselves as a support team for the person and to play a role in encouraging and identifying unique outcomes.

Making the case for the narrative approach

Unlike other models, Narrative Therapy does not require the client to accept biological or psychological explanations for their difficulties. This means that intervention remains feasible even when insight is considered as a barrier to participation – something that can preclude the use of other models. Accepting the person's narrative, rather than applying an alternative label, increases the likelihood of therapeutic engagement, and also makes it possible to use narrative interventions when psychotic experiences persist. A focus on revising the client's relationship with symptoms mirrors evidence-based interventions and research into cognitive behavioural models (e.g. Chadwick, 2006). Indeed, Narrative Therapy has been adapted to incorporate cognitive behavioural formulations and interventions (Rhodes & Jakes, 2009), suggesting that it need not be a standalone intervention and can be integrated with other models and approaches used within mental health teams.

References

Bargenquast, R. & Schweitzer, R. (2013). Metacognitive narrative psychotherapy for people diagnosed with schizophrenia: An outline of principle-based treatment manual. *Psychosis, 1*, 1–11.

Bichescu, D., Neuner, F., Schauer, M. & Elbert, T. (2007). Narrative exposure therapy for political imprisonment-related chronic posttraumatic stress disorder and depression. *Behaviour Research and Therapy, 45*(9), 2212–2220.

Brune, M., Dimaggio, G. & Lysaker, P. H. (2011). Metacognition and social functioning in schizophrenia: Evidence, mechanisms of influence and treatment implications. *Current Psychiatry Reviews, 7*(3), 239–247.

Bruner, J. (1990). *Acts of meaning.* London: Harvard University Press.

Burr, V. (1995). *An introduction to social constructionism.* London: Routledge.

Burr, V. (2003). *Social constructionism.* London: Routledge.

Carey, M. & Russell, S (2004). *Narrative Therapy: Responding to your questions.* Adelaide, Australia: Dulwich Centre Publications.

Chadwick, P. (2006). *Person-based cognitive therapy for distressing psychosis.* Chichester, Sussex: John Wiley & Sons.

Chadwick, P. D., Birchwood, M. J. & Trower, P. (1996). *Cognitive therapy for delusions, voices and paranoia.* Chichester, Sussex: John Wiley & Sons.

Dimaggio, G. & Semerari, A. (2001). Psychopathological narrative forms. *Journal of Constructivist Psychotherapy, 14*, 1–23.

Fox, H. (2006). Using therapeutic documents – a review. *International Journal of Narrative Therapy & Community Work, 4*, 26–35.

Gallagher, S. (2003). Self narrative in schizophrenia. In T. Kircher & A. David (eds), *The self in neuroscience and psychiatry* (pp. 336–360). Cambridge: Cambridge University Press.

Gergen, K. J. (1992). *The saturated self: Dilemmas of identity in contemporary life.* New York: Basic Books.

Harper, D. & Spellman, D. (2006). Social constructionist formulation. In N. L. Johnston & R. Dallos (eds), *Formulation in psychology and psychotherapy: Making sense of people's problems* (pp. 98–125). London: Routledge.

Holma, J. & Aaltonen, J. (1998a). The experience of time in acute psychosis and schizophrenia. *Contemporary Family Therapy, 20*, 265–276.

Holma, J. & Aaltonen, J. (1998b). Narrative understanding in acute psychosis. *Contemporary Family Therapy, 20*, 253–263.

Lysaker, P. H., Clements, C. A., Plascak-Hallberg, C. D., Knipscheer, S. J. & Wright, D. E. (2002). Insight and personal narratives of illness in schizophrenia. *Psychiatry: Interpersonal and Biological Processes, 65*(3), 197–206.

Lysaker, P. H., Wickett, A. M., Campbell, K. & Buck, K. D. (2003). Movement towards coherence in the psychotherapy of schizophrenia: A method for assessing narrative transformation. *The Journal of Nervous and Mental Disease, 191*(8), 538–541.

Lysaker, P. H. & Lysaker, J. T. (2006). A typology of narrative impoverishment in schizophrenia: Implications for understanding the processes of establishing and sustaining dialogue in individual psychotherapy. *Counselling Psychology Quarterly, 19*(1), 57–68.

Lysaker, P. H., Glynn, S. M., Wilkniss, S. M. & Silverstein, S. M. (2010). Psychotherapy and recovery from schizophrenia: A review of potential applications and need for future study. *Psychological Services, 7*(2), 75–91.

Lysaker, P. H., Erikson, M., Macapagal, K. R., Tunze, C., Gilmore, E. & Ringer, J. M. (2012). Development of personal narratives as a mediator of the impact of deficits in social cognition and social withdrawal on negative symptoms in schizophrenia. *The Journal of Nervous and Mental Disease, 200*(4), 290–295.

McAdams, D. P. (2008). Personal narratives and the life story. In O. John, R. Robins & L. A. Pervin (eds), *Handbook of personality: Theory and research* (pp. 241–261). New York: Guilford Press.

McLeod, J. (1997). *Narrative and psychotherapy*. London: Sage.

Morrison, A. P., Frame, L. & Larkin, W. (2003). Relationships between trauma and psychosis: A review and integration. *British Journal of Clinical Psychology, 42*(4), 331–353.

Mueser, K. T., Lu, W., Rosenberg, S. D. & Wolfe, R. (2010). The trauma of psychosis: Posttraumatic stress disorder and recent onset psychosis. *Schizophrenia Research, 116*(2), 217–227.

Pennebaker, J. W. & Beall, S. K. (1986). Confronting a traumatic event: Toward an understanding of inhibition and disease. *Journal of Abnormal Psychology, 95*(3), 274–281.

Pennebaker, J. & Seagal, J. D. (1999). Forming a story: The health benefits of narrative. *Journal of Clinical Psychology, 55*(10), 1243–1254.

Polkinghorne, D. (1988). *Narrative knowing and the human sciences*. New York: New York University Press.

Prasko, J., Diveky, T., Grambal, A., Kamaradova, D., Latalova, L., Mainerova, B., & Vrbova, K. Trcova, A. (2010). Narrative Cognitive Behaviour Therapy for psychosis. *Activitas Nervosa Superior Rediviva, 52*, 135–146.

Rhodes, J. & Jakes, S. (2009). *Narrative CBT for psychosis*. London: Routledge.

Roberts, G. A. (2000). Narrative and severe mental illness: What place do stories have in an evidence-based world? *Advances in Psychiatric Treatment, 6*(6), 432–441.

Roe, D., Hasson-Ohayon, I., Kravetz, S., Yanos, P. T. & Lysaker, P. H. (2008). Call it a monster for lack of anything else: Narrative insight in psychosis. *The Journal of Nervous and Mental Disease, 196*(12), 859–865.

Sarbin, T. (ed.) (1986). *Narrative psychology: The storied nature of human conduct*. New York: Praeger.

Schauer, M., Neuner, F. & Elbert, T. (2011). *Narrative exposure therapy. A short-term treatment for traumatic stress disorders.* Göttingen: Hogrefe & Huber.

Seikkula, J., Alakare, B. & Aaltonen, J. (2001). Open Dialogue in psychosis I: An introduction and case illustration. *Journal of Constructivist Psychology, 14,* 247–265.

Wahl, O. F. (1999). Mental health consumers' experience of stigma. *Schizophrenia Bulletin, 25*(3), 467–478.

White, M. (1995). *Re-authoring lives: Interviews and essays.* Adelaide, Australia: Dulwich Centre Publications.

White, M. (2007). *Maps of narrative practice.* London: W.W Norton and Co.

White, M. & Epston, D. (1990). *Narrative means to therapeutic ends.* London: W. W. Norton & Co.

Part III

Innovations in group and whole team interventions

Chapter 11

Group Rational Emotive Behaviour Therapy for paranoia

Richard Bennett and Louise Pearson

Introduction

Rational Emotive Behaviour Therapy (REBT) is perhaps less well known compared with Beck's Cognitive Therapy (CT), despite the fact that the philosophical and conceptual foundations of Cognitive Behavioural Therapy (CBT) were first laid down by Albert Ellis, the originator of REBT, in the late 1950s. We suggest that REBT may better placed than other CBT models to work with the particular problem of paranoia with hard to reach groups by virtue of its transdiagnostic emphasis and its particular focus on evaluative thinking. The latter allows individuals to retain their appraisal of events without the concern that the therapist will challenge them or not believe them, which has benefits in terms of promoting engagement. This chapter describes the development of an REBT group therapy programme within a medium secure hospital setting, aimed at reducing distress related to individual experiences of paranoia within forensic mental care.

Theoretical background and development of *Safe*

Ellis's seminal work, "Reason and Emotion in Psychotherapy" presented his ABC model (Ellis, 1962) of human distress and behaviour; although its roots are described earlier (Ellis, 1957). Ellis was heavily influenced by ancient Greek and Eastern philosophy and was the first to apply the central tenet of the cognitive model to psychotherapy; namely, that an individual's psychological disturbance is not wholly determined by events, but rather it is heavily influenced by the beliefs that people hold about those events. Ellis conceptualised this fundamental principle in terms of an ABC model, now common to many therapies under the CBT umbrella (see Figure 11.1). Here cognitions are seen as central in determining the range of responses one might have to any given event. These activating events (A) may be real or imagined, internal or external phenomena, and may be located in the individual's past, present or future. Within the model, A consists of the stimulus plus the inference made about the stimulus. Contiguant to an activating event, an individual often experiences cognitive, emotional, physiological and behavioural consequences. Because these follow the event it is often assumed that these consequences (C) are caused by the A. Indeed, it is common in everyday parlance to hear A–C language, such as "She makes me so angry" or "Big crowds of people frighten me". However, the ABC model postulates that this is not a direct relationship, and the nature of a person's response at C is determined by the content of their evaluative beliefs (B) about A. Thus, in REBT, inferences are not seen as responsible for emotional or behavioural consequences. For example, one might observe the behaviour of others and infer, "No-one likes me". Whilst this might rightly be viewed as a 'negative automatic thought', the ABC model would argue that this is not enough to cause distress. It is only the process of evaluating this inference negatively that will do that. To continue the example, believing that people *should* like me or that I am somehow *less of a person* if they do not, may well lead to depression and withdrawal. REBT distinguishes between inferences (A) and evaluative beliefs (B) for this reason. Inferences are not challenged, whereas evaluative beliefs are, where they lead to unhealthy consequences such as depression and withdrawal.

Healthy or adaptive consequences are determined by rational beliefs, whereas unhealthy or maladaptive consequences are determined by irrational beliefs. Rational beliefs are those that are flexible, pragmatic (in the sense that they facilitate outcomes that are consistent with an individual's goals), logical and consistent with reality. In contrast, irrational beliefs tend to be rigid, self-defeating, logically incoherent and inconsistent with reality (Dryden, 2008; Ellis *et al.*, 2010). The model suggests that, even if a person encounters a significantly adverse event, this is not sufficient to cause an unhealthy emotional response and that if such a response does indeed develop, it will have more to do with holding irrational beliefs about the adversity than with the adversity itself.

REBT helps individuals to recognise the role of beliefs in shaping their response to the adversities they experience and how irrational beliefs sit at the heart of

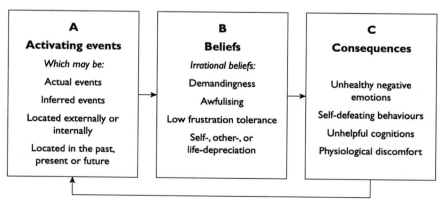

Figure 11.1 The ABC model of psychological distress

emotional disturbance. Ellis identified four types of irrational belief: demandingness, awfulising, low frustration tolerance and depreciation (Dryden, 2008). REBT theory proposes that demandingness is the primary irrational belief implicated in the development of psychopathology, and that the others are derivative beliefs that are similarly extreme in nature. Awfulising is the process of evaluating an activating event as being the worst that it could possibly be. Low frustration tolerance refers to the belief that one is incapable of tolerating the conditions presented by the adversity. Depreciation beliefs are global, negative evaluations that are either applied to oneself, another person, present conditions or life in general. The combination of demandingness and its derivative beliefs about an activating event is largely responsible for the cognitive, behavioural, physiological and emotional problems that are associated with a variety of forms of psychopathology. The organisation of the components within REBT theory has received empirical support through the use of factor and meditation analysis (Fulop, 2007; DiLorenzo et al., 2007).

Given the interest within mainstream CBT for isolating its active ingredients in pursuit of a transdiagnostic model (Harvey et al., 2004; Ellard et al., 2010), it is useful to be reminded that Ellis' original cognitive model was certainly transdiagnostic in its utility and we would argue that it can even be considered as pan- or non-diagnostic. Thus, REBT offers a robust theoretical understanding of emotional function and dysfunction that can readily be applied in a range of contexts. However, relatively little has been written about REBT in relation to paranoia or psychosis, despite its flexibility as a model that can explain and ameliorate distress irrespective of diagnosis.

REBT and other cognitive approaches to the problem of paranoia

REBT and CBT have many similarities in both theory and practice, although there are some key points of divergence (see Hyland & Boduszek, 2012). In addition, when the underlying predictions of the different theoretical models have been examined using structural equation modelling, greater support has been found for REBT theory and the primary role of demandingness beliefs in the development of distress symptoms (Hyland et al., 2014).

Despite the apparent dominance of CBT for psychosis, effect sizes are modest (Hepworth et al., 2013) and there are methodological issues that make it difficult to reach definitive conclusions about efficacy. CBT approaches have also been less successful in addressing paranoid beliefs (Freeman, 2011; Jones et al., 2012). Many CBT models emphasise cognitive restructuring as the cornerstone of their active intervention (e.g. Freeman et al., 2006; Turkington et al., 2009). Whilst much literature has focussed on the process by which paranoid individuals make *inferences* about the causes of events (e.g. Bentall et al., 1994), REBT shifts the emphasis toward the *evaluative* beliefs that the individual holds about the inferences they have made.

To illustrate the difference between the approaches, let us consider how paranoia might be addressed in forms of CBT where the focus is on inferential change. Smith *et al.* (2003: 69) offer the following example of the experience of 'Mavis', expressed in ABC terms:

A. Saw treating psychiatrist in the corridor at the hospital – he greeted me but didn't smile.
B. He doesn't want to see me again.
C. Anxious.

Here, the focus in CBT would be on challenging the inference that the psychiatrist doesn't want to see Mavis again, and working toward developing an alternative explanation of the psychiatrist's behaviour using empirical challenges (e.g. "Where's the evidence that he doesn't want to see you again?").

From the perspective of REBT theory, there are a number of potential limitations to this approach when dealing with paranoid individuals. Firstly, one might argue that this is a sophisticated means of denying the person's experience and that challenging this interpretation of events may pose a potential threat to the therapeutic relationship. The empirical approach appears to imply that there is a truth and that the 'delusional' or paranoid interpretation of events is not it, which might provoke shame and resistance. Thus, the therapist and service user can become distanced in their understanding, and, in a worst case scenario, the service user sees the empirical challenge as evidence that the therapist is not interested in seeing things from their point of view, and may even be 'part of the plot'. Secondly, without addressing the beliefs about the inference that the psychiatrist does not want see her again (which are absent in the above example), Mavis may not generalise any gains that are made from working on the inference alone. Inferential change may be unstable, meaning that when she makes similar inferences about other people, or even the same person in a different situation, she remains anxious. Thirdly, the inference may be true – the psychiatrist may not want to see her again, or, Mavis may cling to this view unswervingly, whether it is true or not. In both circumstances, empirical challenges may be weak and ineffective, as, try as the therapist might, Mavis will produce more and more evidence for her interpretation of events.

The latter issue is of particular relevance within a forensic mental health population as there are frequently valid and adaptive reasons why service users present with a paranoid disposition or characteristic mistrust of others, albeit that this may sometimes move into a psychotic realm of functioning. Such individuals may have been socialised into an environment where an excessive mistrust of others was protective. For example, those with long histories of engagement in criminal behaviour have learned to 'watch their backs' as a means of protecting themselves from criminal associates or the attention of the authorities. In addition, within a secure unit setting, such individuals are detained against their will, closely observed around the clock by people they do not know well and in an environment characterised by unusual behaviour exhibited by others as a function of psychotic illness. In short, they may have good reason for making paranoid inferences and attempting to challenge these can be at best ineffective, and at worst, potentially damaging.

The CBT approach to working with Mavis in REBT terms is an example of A–C reasoning. An REBT therapist would seek to reformulate Mavis's experience in ABC terms in order to elicit what evaluative beliefs she holds that are relevant to this situation:

A. Situation: Saw treating psychiatrist in the corridor at the hospital – he greeted me but didn't smile. Inference: He doesn't want to see me again.
B. Demand: I want to be seen and therefore I need him to see me right now. Low Frustration Tolerance: I can't stand it if he doesn't.
C. Emotion: Anxious. Behaviour: Avoidance or excessive reassurance-seeking.

Here Mavis's distress is a function of the way that she evaluates her inference that the psychiatrist doesn't want to see her. Her preference for receiving intervention is established, but this is escalated into a demand. She also believes that she cannot tolerate the experience of not being seen. In REBT these beliefs would be seen as unhelpful in the sense that they promote the unhealthy negative emotion of anxiety and its action tendency of excessively seeking reassurance, which is likely to form a maintaining cycle. Such a formulation allows Mavis to retain her interpretation of events without challenge whilst allowing the therapeutic work to focus on increasing her ability to tolerate the perceived adversity, which may be better able to generalise to other situations in which she perceives criticism or rejection. We believe this is a more functional position than challenging the inference. It promotes the mutual acceptance of the idea that there is no absolute truth, consistent with a constructivist view of the world. REBT allows the service user to maintain the same initial interpretation of the threat whilst identifying an alternative means of evaluation aimed at producing a more adaptive emotional and behavioural response.

In working therapeutically using REBT the therapist would first elicit a more functional goal, defined by its emotional, behavioural, and cognitive components. Mavis would be encouraged to think about what alternative beliefs would be likely to facilitate such a goal, as opposed to the currently held beliefs, which are leading to unhelpful consequences. This is illustrated in Figure 11.2 using the ABC form that is the central means by which our therapists and service users collaborate on reaching a formulation of their experience of distress related to paranoid inferences.

Following the collaborative ABC formulation process, the focus of REBT intervention shifts to establishing an understanding of the B–C connection. This involves developing the insight that unhelpful beliefs about paranoid inferences (e.g. that the events described by them must not be, or are truly awful) tend to lead to unhelpful consequences, whereby rational beliefs about the same situation tend

A – Activating Event	
Situation: Saw treating psychiatrist in the corridor at the hospital – he greeted me but didn't smile.	
Inference: He doesn't want to see me again.	
iB – Irrational/Unhelpful Beliefs	**rB – Rational/Helpful Alternative Beliefs**
Demand: I want to be seen and therefore I need him to see me right now.	**Preference:** I want to be seen but I don't have to be seen right now.
Low Frustration Tolerance: I can't stand it if he doesn't.	**High Frustration Tolerance:** It's difficult not getting what I want but I can stand it.
uC – Unhelpful Consequences	**hC – Helpful Consequences**
Emotion: Anxious.	**Emotion:** Healthy concern.
Behaviour: Avoidance or excessive reassurance-seeking.	**Behaviour:** Approach the psychiatrist to talk about my thoughts and feelings.

Figure 11.2 An ABC form illustrated with Mavis's example

to have more functional outcomes. Once established, this helps the individual to make a decision about whether or not they wish to translate these more functional outcomes into goals of therapy. If they decide to pursue these alternatives as emotional and behavioural goals, commitment is sought regarding working toward changing beliefs about paranoid inferences, rather than changing the inferences themselves. The view expressed within REBT is that attempting to change any aspect of the A (e.g. the situation or the inferences about it), if done at all, is best achieved after distress has reduced and the person is less disturbed about it (Dryden, 2006). For example, it is difficult to become more accepting of the reality that health professionals will talk about you in your absence if you are still making yourself angry about the fact. Thus, the focus is on facilitating evaluative belief change through a process known as disputing.

Disputing focuses on the evaluative content at B and the inferences at A are not challenged. In practice, this has the advantage of allowing the individual to hold their appraisal of events in place without the concern that the therapist will challenge them. That is not to say that the therapist needs to publicly agree with paranoid inferences that they privately may not share, rather that the service user's view in this regard is accepted as being valid and is not a matter for debate. In our experience this assists the therapeutic alliance and the development of trust between service user and therapist. Assuming that the currently held interpretation is correct also facilitates the identification of the beliefs that pertain to their experience and that are central to understanding their disturbance (Dryden, 2008).

Disputing is the most active phase of intervention and involves the individual subjecting their irrational beliefs and the more rational alternatives to the same scrutiny in order to establish which is the most workable, logical and consistent with what is known about how the world works. The process is guided by the therapist and offers a range of options for promoting belief change beyond the empirical challenges employed within CBT. The three aforementioned elements of disputing can be distilled as facilitating a process of enquiry that asks the individual to consider the irrational and rational beliefs that have been identified and asking, "Which of these is (1) the most helpful, (2) makes the most sense, and (3) is true?" A full account of the disputing process is beyond the scope of this chapter, although DiGiuseppe *et al.* (2013) provide a comprehensive description of how REBT makes use of these cognitive techniques, alongside a range of other imaginal and behavioural interventions to effect change.

Trower (2003) argued that REBT can provide a powerful intervention for addressing a range of cognitive, emotional and behavioural problems associated with the diagnosis of schizophrenia; both when conceptualised as an adverse life event in itself, and at the level of individual positive and negative symptoms. Early support for applying the ABC model to psychosis comes from studies which have found that beliefs about psychotic phenomena (e.g. voices) mediate an individual's emotional and behavioural response (Chadwick & Birchwood, 1994; Birchwood & Chadwick, 1997) and that changes in these beliefs (e.g. about the power of a voice) are key to reducing distress and behaviour (Trower *et al.*, 2004).

The challenges of medium secure care

Service users in forensic secure care are automatically faced with the juxtaposition of living within a care environment that needs to balance mental health needs with that of risk management. Whilst there is a growing recognition that it is possible to reduce risk of re-offending whilst building richer lives, the sense that articulating one's emotional distress when it has usually been linked to offending behaviour remains a challenge (Drennan & Alred, 2012). Paranoid ideas and beliefs will often have been associated with offending behaviour and there is an expectation that they should be treated for risk reduction purposes. However, service users themselves are often hesitant to reveal such beliefs in case they are seen as evidence of deterioration, thereby potentially increasing restrictions and jeopardising their recovery. Encouraging service users to speak about them requires careful facilitation within the context of a supportive therapeutic relationship.

It is important for any model that is chosen to inform intervention in this area to be able to explain the relationship between paranoia and distress. Persecutory beliefs have a strong association with distress, and, with regard to concerns relevant within forensic mental health care, distress has a strong association with risk (Douglas *et al.*, 2003). Accordingly we wanted the intervention to be aimed at distress reduction, rather than the more usual target of symptom reduction. All too often within forensic mental health care it seems that a psychiatric diagnosis is promoted as being the causal factor in offending, which, in Ellis' terms represents an A–C model of thinking and formulating, in that the symptoms lead directly to a behavioural consequence. Indeed the CT literature is often characterised by many of the same assumptions, concerning itself with a disease model in which the cognitive processes of 'patients with schizophrenia' are 'inadequate' (Beck *et al.*, 2009: 86). Our desire was to apply a collaborative ABC model as described earlier to the issue of paranoia, in which an individual's beliefs about their experiences are seen as the driver for the behaviour that follows.

Developing the Safe programme

The majority of medium secure patients have a diagnosis of paranoid schizophrenia (Rutherford & Duggan, 2008) indicating a clinical need for therapies to address otherwise treatment resistant symptoms. A key consideration for us was how to address the needs of our service users distressed by their paranoid views and how to create a 'Safe' and effective intervention. Whilst delivery of the intervention in a group format allowed for important considerations such as efficiency and normalisation to be addressed, the programme was also made available on a 1:1 basis for those service users for whom working in a group was not possible for a range of clinical reasons.

Aims, stages, strategies and techniques

The main aims of the programme were to enable individuals to develop an understanding of the nature of their paranoid beliefs and their role in the experience of psychological distress, and to facilitate the development of psychological strategies for alleviating such distress. On completion of the programme, it was hoped that group members would have:

- Shared their experiences of the impact of paranoid beliefs in a group situation;
- Developed a theoretical understanding of the nature and function of paranoid beliefs and their impact upon psychological wellbeing;
- Developed skills for reducing the distress associated with paranoid beliefs;
- Learned maintenance strategies for managing their distress in the longer term.

The name of the group was an important factor in designing an intervention that services users would wish to participate in. 'Safe' was chosen to convey the link between paranoia and the distress of feeling un-'Safe' in the world. It was hoped that the aspiration of understanding one's paranoia and subsequently leading a less distressing life would be a selling point for service users who might otherwise be resistant for the reasons discussed above.

Selection for the groups and setting considerations

The focus was on distress reduction and the primary inclusion criteria were for service users to have a desire to reduce their distress associated with their experience of paranoia; regardless of its etiology. There was also an expectation that service users would commit to attending the group regularly and be capable of participating in group-based discussion around their emotional experiences. Some degree of 'psychological mindedness' is required to understand some of the material and concepts of REBT, although we did not want to impose strict limitations in this regard. In our experience, there is a normalising benefit to hear that one's experiences are shared by others, even if some of the theoretical concepts may be more difficult to grasp for some. Self-referrals are actively encouraged as well as from more traditional sources. As the group was held in a therapy centre, which was away from the residential units within the secure perimeter, it was problematic to facilitate service users requiring high levels of escort (2:1 or above) attending the group. A further exclusion criterion was when service users were experiencing substantive and overwhelming active symptoms of psychosis. Close liaison with the clinical team and unit staff as well as dynamic risk assessment is standard good practice in the setting and helped to inform appropriate attendance.

If a service user opted into the group, clinical teams were consulted as to their opinions on the appropriateness of the self-referral and where it fitted into their recovery pathway and associated rehabilitation goals. If a clinical team referred a service user, the semi-structured pre-group assessment ascertained the service user's view on the team referral for work around their paranoia. In most incidences, good practice ensured that all psychological group referrals had been collaboratively discussed as part of the care management process and the service users acknowledged that they had this particular clinical need. Service users who did not think that they had this need were excluded.

In our experience, the group runs best with two experienced clinicians as lead facilitators and at least one co-facilitator, who might be a non-qualified member of staff. All facilitators should be skilled at group delivery, with the two lead facilitators being trained to advanced level in REBT. A multi-professional mix of facilitators works well and is encouraged with a minimum of three regular staff to secure the stability of group dynamics.

Stages

The Safe programme is delivered with reference to a clear manualised protocol (Bennett *et al.*, 2007). The group can be considered as consisting of three discrete phases or stages:

Assessment

Assessment is carried out of the individual's experience of distress as it relates to their paranoia. This involves the completion of two psychometric tests within a semi-structured interview: the Evaluative Beliefs Scale (EBS; Chadwick *et al.*, 1999) and the Outcome Questionnaire (OQ-45; Lambert *et al.*, 1996). The EBS comprises 18 negative person evaluation statements defined as stable, global and total condemnations of an entire person, either oneself or another. It measures six evaluative themes characteristic of either attachment to others or self-definition. Negative person evaluations may be expressed in three directions, depending on who is evaluating whom. The OQ-45 is a 45-item questionnaire designed to measure a service user's progress in therapy. It has the advantage of being valid for frequent use to routinely and effectively monitor outcome within clinical practice. Responses yield three subscale scores (symptom distress, interpersonal relationships and social role performance) and a total score. It is sensitive to change over short periods of time while maintaining high levels of reliability and validity.

Active intervention

Twelve sessions each lasting 75 minutes are delivered. This stage has four discrete phases. The first two sessions introduce the group aims and content.

SESSIONS 3–7

The REBT model of psychological disturbance and its application to paranoia enables group members to develop an understanding of both helpful and unhelpful beliefs underpinning their appraisal of the paranoid inferences they have made, or might make, in a range of situations. The ABC framework provides a mechanism to facilitate this and helps to promote the reduction of associated distress.

SESSIONS 8–11

The focus here is on facilitating change of unhelpful beliefs through the process of disputation. This process helps to weaken the conviction in these beliefs and assist in the development of alternative helpful beliefs that are associated with more adaptive emotional and behavioural consequences.

SESSION 12

Session 12 is held a month after the first 11 weekly sessions and focusses on reviewing members' experience of the group and their use of the ABC model in practice.

Strategies and techniques

A number of REBT strategies and techniques are used alongside general principles over the course of the 12 week group:

a) Weakening beliefs that lead to distress and/or unhelpful behavioural consequences;
b) Members are encouraged to develop their own formulations about their paranoia;
c) Members use cognitive strategies to forcefully dispute their beliefs about situations in which they have made paranoid inferences;
d) Members help other group members to dispute their beliefs;
e) Didactic teaching methods are employed involving the use of mini-lectures, analogies and parables;
f) Practical exercises;
g) Group disclosure;
h) Group discussions.

Evaluation

Group members are re-assessed using the initial measures. An independent evaluator also interviews each group member to encourage the individual group member to provide a summary of their experience of the group, including measuring therapeutic factors and satisfaction with Safe.

Case illustration: John

John was 22 years old when he was legally detained in medium secure care. The offence for which he was detained was 'wounding with intent', relating to an incident in which John stabbed a police officer in the neck. John had been approached by two officers in the town centre when he was in a distressed state, responding to unseen stimuli and brandishing a knife. When they tried to arrest him, John struck out with the knife, stabbing and seriously injuring one of the officers.

John was the younger of two brothers from a working class background and he had no previous convictions. His parents separated acrimoniously when he was 12, and when his 18-year-old brother was away at university. He reportedly found the fragmentation of the family very difficult and he became withdrawn and anxious to the extent that this was noticed at school where he had previously been academic and diligent. John's mother developed anxiety and depression and he was supported by his grandmother, with whom he spent increasing amounts of time despite intense separation anxiety from his mother. John's grandmother eventually moved into the family home, which afforded some stability, and once again John began to attain academically, eventually securing a place reading medicine at a London university.

He settled well into both academic and social life at university. He dated a fellow student for nine months until she ended the relationship. This was John's first intimate relationship and he described feeling 'devastated' when it ended. He later stated that although they had been 'inseparable', he had never felt good enough for her, and doubted her fidelity without having the assertiveness to confront her. He took her ending the relationship as proof that she was seeing someone else, despite the absence of any objective evidence.

On the advice of his mother, John saw his GP and was referred for counselling, as well as being prescribed anti-depressant medication. John started the medication, but did not follow up the counselling referral, and over the following months he became increasingly distressed, experiencing increasingly paranoid ideas. By this time he was living in shared accommodation and had begun using alcohol and cannabis on a regular basis.

He began to struggle with the academic demands of the course and would ruminate over his perceived shortcomings following his 'abandonment' by his girlfriend. He also came to see himself as responsible for the break-up of his parents' marriage. He also experienced an increasing sense of isolation and detachment from his housemates at this time, which he referred to as "feeling like a square peg in a round hole". John began to perceive his housemates' behaviour as being intentionally aimed at highlighting that he was 'different' to them because he came from a 'broken home' and a working class background. He inferred that they thought he did not deserve to be in their company or be studying at the university. Eventually, John stopped attending college, compounding his sense of failure. Isolating himself in his room more and more, he continued to abuse cannabis and alcohol and became increasingly paranoid. He remained in the house alone during the vacation and it was at this point that John began to experience derogatory, persecutory and omnipotent voices. Feeling angry and under threat, John equipped himself with a knife for protection, eventually setting out to find those responsible for the conspiracy against him and put an end to it at all costs.

Assessment and engagement

John had already established a good therapeutic relationship with his team psychologist when he was approached about undertaking the Safe group in addition to the 1:1 intervention he was already receiving. John had made good progress since admission, responding well to antipsychotic medication and the therapeutic milieu of the unit. He had begun to develop a psychological understanding of the development of his difficulties leading up to the offence. However, this understanding was in its early stages, with him recognising that he had been paranoid at the time of the offence, but of the view that this particular symptom of his illness (A) had directly caused his offending as a behavioural consequence (C).

His current distress related to his perception that others within the unit had negative views about him because of his offence and were talking about him in a derogatory way. At the time of referral to the Safe group, John's rehabilitative progress was being impeded because he struggled to go to the dining room to eat, or leave the unit for therapeutic activity.

Initially within the group, John was a quiet member who did not offer spontaneous contributions. This was expected due to his on-going beliefs that peers perceived him negatively due to the nature of his offence. John developed the ability to work on his own emotional material by utilising parallel examples that held less direct relevance for him. For example, he developed an ABC formulation around joining a university seminar group for the first time. This afforded John the opportunity to build his understanding of the model, without feeling too threatened to be able to work through his most sensitive offence-related issues within the group, and without being blocked by associated shame.

John later reported that he found hearing others' similar experiences of paranoia hugely normalising. He had not realised that his distressing emotional experiences had commonalities with those of his peers, or that they too had felt the need to carry weapons. This was of relevance to John because as his mental state and insight improved, so too did the sense that he had made 'the wrong decisions' when unwell. This is consistent with the REBT philosophy that individuals always retain an element of choice and self-determinism, even in the face of significant adversity. He began to suggest how he might have responded differently to the adverse experience of paranoid ideation, even if he might not have been able to change the experience itself. John's developing ability to hear the paranoia-related distressing experiences of others facilitated the development of his acceptance of others. He became more able to understand difficult circumstances around his peers' paranoia without making global negative appraisals about them. As a consequence, John developed the confidence to take the risk to share some of his own experience within the group and developed the ability to tolerate the uncertainty of how others might view him and his offending behaviour.

As previously discussed, both John and the clinical team felt that his rehabilitation was being impeded because he avoided communal areas, particularly the dining room, due to anxiety about how others viewed him. With support John was able to generate the following ABC formulation of this particular situation.

He practised the process of disputation within the sessions with peer support, successfully weakening his conviction in the unhelpful and irrational beliefs, whilst strengthening the more helpful and rational ones. This translated into John

Situation Going to the dining room. Adversity People are talking about me and my offence. They think bad things about me.	
Irrational Beliefs I don't want people to talk about me in a negative way and therefore they should not. I can't stand this – I've got to get away before I punch someone! They are bad people and must be punished if they keep talking about me.	**Rational Beliefs** I don't want people to talk about me in a negative way but they don't have to do what I want. It's really hard and it's uncomfortable but I can stand it. It might be worth trying and tolerating difficult things could make me stronger. Even if they are talking about me, it does not make them bad people. Like the rest of us, they are capable of good, bad and neutral thoughts and acts.
Unhelpful Consequences Anxious Struggling with the discomfort Agitated Leave the dining room and refuse to go again. Avoid the people 'involved'.	**Helpful Consequences** Concerned Tolerating the discomfort Calm Stay in the dining room and so demonstrate I can manage my distress to the clinical team.

Figure 11.3 John's ABC

successfully being able to engage in exposure, whereby he attended the dining room whilst practising disputation. He learned that he was able to tolerate being there for increased periods of time, to the point that he was able to order food and eat communally.

Regarding change in pre- and post-group measures, John demonstrated improvement on all subscales of the OQ-45. We note, however, that the improvements in John's self-efficacy and emotional wellbeing may not have been truly captured, as the demonstrable change in his confidence and behaviour did not appear to entirely correlate with his self-report.

At the time of writing, John has been conditionally discharged from hospital under the social supervision of his clinical team. He lives in his own flat, attends college, and has a positive social network around him.

Conclusions and implications

When working with paranoid individuals in a forensic mental health setting there is a need for an approach that addresses distress reduction rather symptomatic change. REBT offers such an approach and is accepting of an individual's own experience. It allows both parties to construct explanations of paranoia-related distress and offending that are non-stigmatising, acceptable, accessible, and that draw from common experience outside of psychosis. Using a trandiagnostic model of therapy has the advantage of promoting philosophical change, which may be more likely to generalise to other areas of function. Indeed, the flexibility of the model has led to other group REBT interventions, notably addressing voices, anger, and self-acceptance. This enables service users to bring their expertise of applying the model in one group programme to other aspects of their recovery and rehabilitation.

The relatively small numbers of service users that move through a medium secure unit, and the relatively static nature of the inpatient population, means that the collection of a meaningful sample of outcome data is in its early stages. Pre- and post-data from our initial groups are encouraging and have demonstrated small improvements on the measures we have adopted in terms of symptom related distress, interpersonal functioning and social role. By the very nature of the group our clients are often reluctant to complete formal measures. We are currently in the process of identifying outcome measures that have the best ecological validity for use with the particular population with whom we work. In addition, the collection of follow-up data regarding the on-going rehabilitation of group members, with particular regard to avoiding readmission or reoffending, remain a work in progress. Qualitative evaluations of the programme by service users suggest that the Safe programme is an acceptable and useful intervention that has contributed to increased knowledge about their experience of paranoia and the development of effective strategies for managing distress. Whilst Safe has been developed for a forensic population within a medium secure setting, we believe its principles are broadly applicable to all individuals with paranoid beliefs and experiences.

References

Beck, A. T., Rector, N. A., Stolar, N. & Grant, P. (2009). *Schizophrenia: Cognitive theory, research, and therapy.* New York: The Guilford Press.

Bennett, R., Churchman, C., Khan, S., Pearson, L & Johnson, R. (2007). *SAFE: A group for service users distressed by paranoia. Therapist manual.* Unpublished.

Bentall, R. P., Kinderman, P. & Kaney, S. (1994). Cognitive process and delusional beliefs: Attributions and the self. *Behaviour Research and Therapy, 32,* 331–341.

Birchwood, M. J. & Chadwick, P. D. J. (1997). The omnipotence of voices: Testing the validity of the cognitive model. *Psychological Medicine, 27,* 1345–1353.

Chadwick, P. D. J. & Birchwood, M. J. (1994). The omnipotence of voices: A cognitive approach to auditory hallucinations. *British Journal of Psychiatry, 164,* 190–201.

Chadwick, P. D. J., Trower, P. & Dagnan, D. (1999). Measuring negative person evaluations: The Evaluative Beliefs Scale. *Cognitive Therapy and Research*, 23(5), 549–559.

DiGiuseppe, R. A., Doyle, K. A., Dryden, W. & Backx, W. (2013). *A practitioner's guide to rational emotive behaviour therapy* (3rd edn). New York: Oxford University Press.

DiLorenzo, T. A., David, D. & Montgomery, G. H. (2007). The interrelations between irrational cognitive processes and distress in stressful academic settings. *Personality and Individual Differences*, 42, 765–777.

Douglas, K. S., Hart, S. D, Webster, C. D. & Belfrage, H. (2013). *HCR-20v3: Assessing risk for violence*. Burnaby, BC, Canada: Mental Health, Law and Policy Institute, Simon Fraser University.

Drennan, G. & Alred, D. (eds.). (2012). *Secure recovery: Approaches to recovery in forensic mental health settings*. Hove, E. Sussex: Routledge.

Dryden, W. (2006). *Helping yourself with REBT: First steps for clients*. New York: Albert Ellis Institute.

Dryden, W. (2008). *Rational emotive behaviour therapy: Distinctive features*. Hove, E. Sussex: Routledge.

Ellard, K. K., Fairholme, C. P., Boisseau, C. L., Farchione, T. & Barlow, D. H. (2010). Unified protocol for the transdiagnostic treatment of emotional disorders: Protocol development and initial outcome data. *Cognitive and Behavioral Practice*, 17, 88–101.

Ellis, A. (1957). Rational psychotherapy and individual psychology. *Journal of Individual Psychology*, 13, 38–44.

Ellis, A. (1962). *Reason and emotion in psychotherapy*. New York: Lyle Stuart.

Ellis, A., David, D. & Lynn, S. J. (2010). A historical and conceptual perspective. In D. David, S. J. Lynn & A. Ellis (eds), *Rational and irrational beliefs: Research, theory, and clinical practice* (pp. 3–22). Oxford: Oxford University Press.

Freeman, D. (2011). Improving cognitive treatments for delusions. *Schizophrenia Research*, 132, 135–139.

Freeman, D., Freeman, J. & Garety, P. (2006). *Overcoming paranoid and suspicious thoughts*. London: Constable & Robinson.

Freeman, D., Garety, P. A., Bebbington, P., Smith, B., Rowlingson, R., Fowler, D. . . . Dunn, G. (2005). Psychological investigation of the structure of paranoia in a non-clinical population. *British Journal of Psychiatry*, 186, 427–435.

Fulop, I. E. (2007). A confirmatory factor analysis of the attitude and belief scale 2. *Journal of Cognitive and Behavioral Psychotherapies*, 7, 159–170.

Harvey, A., Watkins, E., Mansell, W. & Shafran, R. (2004). *Cognitive behavioural processes across psychological disorders: A transdiagnostic approach to research and treatment*. Oxford: Oxford University Press.

Hepworth, C., Startup, H. & Freeman, D. (2013). Emotional processing and metacognitive awareness for persecutory delusions. In E. M. J. Morris, L. C. Johns & J. E. Oliver (eds), *Acceptance and commitment therapy and mindfulness for psychosis* (pp. 33–46). Chichester, Sussex: John Wiley & Sons.

Hyland, P. & Boduszek, D. (2012). Resolving a difference between cognitive therapy and rational emotive behaviour therapy: Towards the development of an integrated CBT model of psychopathology. *Mental Health Review Journal*, 17, 104–116.

Hyland, P., Shevlin, M., Adamson, G. & Boduszek, D. (2014). The organisation of irrational beliefs in posttraumatic stress symptomology: Testing the predictions of REBT theory using structural equation modelling. *Journal of Clinical Psychology*, 70, 48–59. doi: 10.1002/jclp.22009.

Jones, C., Hacker, D., Cormac, I., Meaden, A. & Irving, C. B. (2012). Cognitive behaviour therapy versus other psychosocial treatments for schizophrenia. *Cochrane Database of Systematic Reviews*, Issue 4, Art No.: CD0087.12. doi:10.1002/14651858.CD008712. pub2.

Lambert, M. J., Hanse, N. B., Umphress, V., Lunnen, K., Okiishi, J., Burlingame, G. . . . Reisinger, C.W. (1996). *Administration and scoring manual for the Outcome Questionnaire (OQ 45.2)*. Wilmington, DE: American Professional Credentialing Services.

Rutherford, M. & Duggan, S. (2008). Forensic mental health services: Facts and figures on current provision. *The British Journal of Forensic Practice*, *10*, 4–10.

Smith, L., Nathan, L., Juniper, P., Kingsep, P. & Lim, L. (2003). *Cognitive behavioural therapy for psychotic symptoms: A therapist's manual*. Perth: Centre for Clinical Interventions.

Trower, P. (2003). Theoretical developments in REBT as applied to schizophrenia. In W. Dryden (ed.), *Rational Emotive Behaviour Therapy: Theoretical developments*. Hove: Brunner-Routledge.

Trower, P., Birchwood, M., Meaden, A., Byrne, S., Nelson, A. & Ross, K. (2004). Cognitive therapy for command hallucinations: A randomised controlled trial. *British Journal of Psychiatry*, *184*, 312–320.

Turkington, D., Kingdon, D., Rathod, S., Wilcock, S. K. J., Brabban, A., Cromarty, P. . . . Weiden, P. (2009). *Back to life, back to normality: Cognitive therapy, recovery and psychosis*. Cambridge: Cambridge University Press.

Turkington, D., Wright, N. & Tai, S. (2013). Advances in CBTp. *International Journal of Cognitive Therapy*, *6*, 150–170.

Chapter 12

Team-Based Cognitive Therapy for distress and problematic behaviour associated with positive symptoms

Alan Meaden, Andrew Fox and David Hacker

Introduction

Cognitive Behavioural Therapy (CBT) for psychosis is now well established as part of standard evidence-based practice and in some settings is the only psychological therapy that is supported. Disappointing reviews and recent trials (Jones *et al.*, 2012; Lynch *et al.*, 2010; Wykes *et al.*, 2007) have led to a recent reappraisal of its aims (Birchwood & Trower, 2006; Birchwood *et al.*, 2014), emphasising reduction in distress and behaviour as primary outcomes rather than alleviation of symptoms and preventing relapses. However, despite this renewed focus, many people experiencing psychotic symptoms appear not to benefit from these interventions and require on-going care. We may define this group as having complex mental health and behavioural needs. For this group we may usefully borrow a metaphor. Here individual sessional CBT may be viewed as placing a drop of ink in a pond of water that quickly dissipates and whose impact is soon lost. Care for such individuals largely takes place in multidisciplinary settings. We argue for an approach that mobilises the resources of the team to enable recovery for this hard to treat and hard to reach group and outline it in this chapter.

Theoretical background and development: Team-Based Cognitive Therapy

In a previous work (Meaden & Hacker, 2010) we described our solution to working with this treatment resistant group as part of a broader framework: Team-Based Cognitive Therapy (TBCT). A number of key assumptions underpin our rationale for TBCT:

1. ABC formulations are the core model (and interlink the team's beliefs and behaviour with that of the clients). Here A is the activating event, B the Beliefs or appraisals for these events and C the emotional and behavioural Consequences of these beliefs (Chadwick *et al.*, 1996).
2. Beliefs can be categorised into two broad types, '*Pan-situational beliefs*' which are ever present across a range of situations and include beliefs about

the person, others and the world and include psychotic beliefs. These are the usual targets of CBT but often show a poor response. Pan-situational beliefs give rise to specific interpretations in specific situations.

3. Pan-situational beliefs are present all or most of the time but the client is not always distressed or engaging in behaviour related to them. Rather it is we propose '*In-situation*' beliefs which then mediate distress and behaviour. These constitute inferences about what is happening and may include so-called cognitive biases such as Jumping to Conclusions (e.g. Moritz & Woodward, 2005). These are the targets of TBCT.

4. A clear focus on behaviour and distress rather than pan-situational belief change.

5. Client behaviours are the activating events (the A in our model) for the team's beliefs about the client and their behaviour (its assumed function): "*they are doing this to gain attention/because they are manipulative*".

6. The team's beliefs are legitimate targets for intervention since they lead to unhelpful care responses or behaviours which mitigate against delivering consistent effective and recovery focused interventions.

7. Disputation (the D in our cognitive therapy model) is best delivered in the situations in which distress and behaviour present.

8. Targeting of the client's beliefs is more effective in the presence of early warning signs (which behaviourally indicate that triggers or As are present).

Our TBCT model can be represented diagrammatically as follows (see figure 12.1):

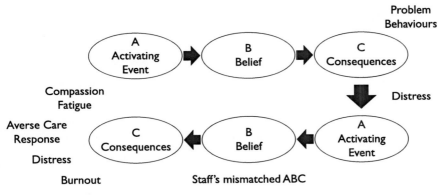

Figure 12.1 ABC mismatch

In our subsequent application of TBCT we have made some further refinements. We now see a set of evident parallels between the components of TBCT for the client and their care team (see Table 12.1):

Table 12.1 TBCT A to H Relevance to Clients and Teams

Model Component	Client Relevance	Team Relevance
A (activating event)	The trigger for the client's beliefs (usually a combination of distal and proximal events)	The trigger for the team's beliefs (usually the clients behaviour – distally and proximally)
B (Pan-situation)	Beliefs operating across a wide variety of situations and contexts	Team beliefs about care and the nature of mental health difficulties and personality
B (In-situation)	The immediate driver of distress and (risk/problem) behaviour	The immediate driver of distress and (care) behaviour
Ce (emotional consequence)	The client's fear, anger, anxiety etc	Team fear, anger, anxiety etc
Cb (behavioural consequence)	Problem behaviour: avoidance, self harm, assault	Team behaviour: avoidance, exclusion, restraint
D (Disputation)	The in-situational challenge – weighing alternatives – antidote to biases (e.g. Jumping to conclusions)	The alternative perspective offered by the shared formulation
E (Experiment) **E** (Evidence)	A test of the client's belief (in the form of a behavioural experiment) – evidence for validity of the alternative belief	Evidence that the formulation is correct when behavioural change occurs and/or distress is reduced, through changed care responses – constituting advanced disputation of team beliefs
F (Disputation)	Formulation in ABC terms of specific distress and behaviour	Disputation of the staff's beliefs about the client
G (Goal)	Intervention is focussed on working towards shared recovery goals	Goals are SMART: **S**mall, **M**easurable, **A**chievable, **R**elevant, (to the clients recovery goals), **T**imely
H (Hope)	Having hope held – barriers to a valued life will be lifted	Holding hope – change is possible – positive risk taking

Table 12.2 Client and Team Parallel Processes

Client Processes	Team Processes
Establishing a working alliance is key before attempting to reframe and dispute clients' beliefs	Establishing a working alliance with the team is key before attempting to engage them in TBCT
Clients need to be socialised into the ABC model	Teams need to be socialised into the TBCT model
Clients' beliefs need to be formulated	Team beliefs need to be formulated
Clients are hard to reach and treat	Teams are hard to reach and treat

These parallel processes are useful to consider when formulating and planning care and targeting intervention efforts: when embarking upon TBCT. We have noted further parallels between the client and the team in terms of the process involved in introducing TBCT. Clinicians may usefully consider these when introducing TBCT in order to lessen resistance and set realistic expectations for change.

Formulating the team in this way allows the clinician to establish what needs to be in put in place first and what obstacles are likely to be faced. On the basis of this formulation clinicians may decide that broader level organisational or team initiatives are required such as training for the team, or working with organisational change managers. Just as CBT is not effective for everyone, TBCT will not be effective for all teams.

Aims, stages, strategies and techniques

Our initial aim is to realign the client's and staff ABC, thus relocating the problem to the client's A–B (the client's appraisal of an event) rather than the team's C–B explanation (their functional explanation of the client's distress and behaviour). This is illustrated in Figure 12.2.

By relocating the problem, our intention is shift the focus of intervention for problematic or risk behaviour away from often negatively impacting responses following the occurrence of the behaviour to one that addresses its true function. Problem behaviours act as barriers (e.g. continued detention under the Mental Health Act) to leading as valued a life as possible.

Understanding the function of the behaviour enables the team to address each of the factors which drive the client's distress and behaviour. In terms of the contribution of TBCT to this process, the aim is to target the in-situation belief rather than the more usual CBT target of the client's pan-situational beliefs. In doing so all interactions with the client provide the opportunity to incorporate CBT principles when signs are evident that the in-situation belief will be triggered, thereby making the CBT live and feel less abstract.

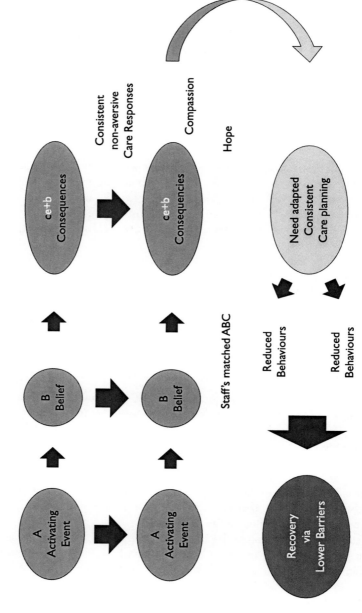

Client's ABC

A
Activating
Event

B
Belief

ce+b
Consequences

Consistent
non-aversive
Care Responses

A
Activating
Event

B
Belief

ce+b
Consequencies

Compassion

Hope

Staff's matched ABC

Need adapted
Consistent
Care planning

Reduced
Behaviours

Reduced
Behaviours

Recovery
via
Lower Barriers

Figure 12.2 Shared formulation aims

Stages

In keeping with our theme of parallel processes we outline the key stages for both clients and teams for developing a shared TBCT care plan. The ABC framework is used to elicit the actual A, from the client's point of view. Eliciting the A clarifies whether or not the behaviour is being driven by objectively understandable triggers or whether the behaviour is being driven by psychotic interpretations of innocuous events (aligned with pan-situational beliefs). Care team members often struggle to understand behaviour that is not clearly driven by obvious external events. It is vital therefore to understand the client's internal world and how this interacts with the external world as shared by others. The assessment and initial formulation process places the C at the beginning. Each problem behaviour potentially has its own specific in-situation belief/s. Consequently clarifying the behaviour as the starting point is important if the intervention is to be accurately targeted. The same CAB framework can be used to elicit both immediate and distant triggers, but this requires separating out the As further. Our process for indetifying the client's ABC is as follows:

1. Agree a specific event to examine. A recent event where the client was distressed and/or engaged in a behaviour which everyone (including ideally the client) saw as problematic;
2. Clarify the behaviour (Cb); this usually elicits the client's B–C explanation (belief and behaviour);
3. If the emotional consequence is not clear, clarify it (obtain the Ce);
4. Enquire about the actual A which led to the interpretation or belief;
5. Establish the A–B link by offering a clarifying question: "*So A happened and you took that to mean B?*"
6. Reflect back the information from this process as an A–B–C chain: "So A happened and you took that to mean B and you felt/did C?" This step begins the process of socialising the client into the model, making them more receptive to TBCT;
7. Identify and examine similar incidents over a relevant recent period in order to clarify if the in-situation belief is part of a consistent pattern.

Clinicians should be mindful that with hard to reach clients this process may involve several sessions. It is also possible, indeed likely, that such clients will not engage in this process; locating the problem firmly at A in cognitive therapy terms "X did this to me," (they are the problem). In these cases the team and facilitating clinician will need to hypothesise from observation what Bs may be present or likely. Challenging such hypothetical Bs as part of the team's subsequent disputation process will need to be even more sensitively approached.

Eliciting the team's ABC is the next stage. We often begin by bringing together the key members of the team most involved with the client and their care (what we term the Case Formulations Team or CFT). The resulting formulation simultaneously begins the process of disputing team members' beliefs about the client and their behaviour. Potentially carers too can be involved in this process.

1. The ABC model is introduced by agreeing the behaviour and distress (Ce and Cb) to be targeted. Some time may need to be taken at this stage in arriving at a consensus regarding which behaviour is most usefully targeted and team members will likely have differing views on this. It is helpful to consider which behaviour might be most amenable to change, which is most frequent (providing the opportunity to intervene) and which creates the most barriers to recovery.

2. The notion is introduced that the aim is to reduce distress and behaviour and not to eliminate symptoms or the associated pan-situational beliefs but rather the ones more directly or immediately responsible for the behaviour.

3. Team members are then encouraged to express their own views about the causes or reasons for the client's behaviour (team members' A–B) without challenging them directly. Rather it is emphasised that all views are valued.

4. Information gathering (fairly examining the evidence) involves each member of the team seeking out and collating evidence to support and test different hypotheses. This may involve direct observation, interviewing the client (when calm) after any incidents of problematic behaviour, reviewing the case notes and reports, administering relevant measures. Useful cognitive therapy measures to help elicit pan-situational and in-situation psychotic beliefs include: the Beliefs About Voices Questionnaire–Revised (Chadwick et al., 2000); Cognitive Assessment of Voices (Chadwick & Birchwood, 1995); and the Beliefs and Convictions Scale (Brett-Jones et al., 1987). The Psychotic Symptom Rating Scales or PSYRATS (Haddock et al., 1999) is also useful for providing a measure of belief related distress; its frequency and severity. We also find the Safety Behaviour Scale (Hacker et al., 2008; Freeman et al., 2001), a useful semi-structured interview for assessing the ways in which people may act on their delusional beliefs or voices as well as the type of threat they perceive (social or physical threat). The Antecedent and Coping Interview (Tarrier, 1992) is a useful schedule for identifying antecedents and modifiers for psychotic symptoms and the efficacy of any coping strategies.

5. A review of the information gathered provides an opportunity to complete a formulation of the both the client's and the team's ABCs alongside a formulation of all of the factors resulting in and maintaining the client's distress and behaviour.

For risk or problem behaviours we have developed (see Meaden & Hacker, 2010) a formulation model we call CARM (Cognitive Approach to Risk Management). It is in essence a functional interactional cognitive and behavioural model which is designed to enable staff to have a better understanding of how cognitive and behavioural factors interact and result in problematic behaviours, illustrating both the client's perspective and the broader interpersonal care context. The CARM formulation hinges around a specific problem behaviour which should be clearly and operationally defined, helping the team to move away from fuzzy descriptions such as 'aggression 'or 'manipulative' which imply function and lack objectivity. Vulnerability factors are included in the template capturing the client's psychological dispositions which are most relevant to the problem behaviour. These might include developmental factors, personal beliefs and attitudes, poor problem solving skills, as well as pan-situational beliefs associated with psychotic symptoms. Exacerbations of these vulnerability factors we argue constitute setting events. Setting events or distant triggers are factors which may make the behaviour in question more likely to occur but are still distal in time from the occurrence of the behaviour; they represent the build up to the behaviour in question. We conceptualise setting events as both external in nature (e.g. having an argument earlier in the day with a friend) or internal (e.g. persistent, derogatory voices, having a poor night's sleep). Early Warning Signs of Risk (EWS-R) are a particularly useful aspect of the CARM model and constitute the external observable signs of internal setting events, combined with external setting events. These observable characteristics of the client's presentation prior to previous occurrences of the behaviour can be operationally defined and crucially serve as a guide to the team about when to intervene with cognitive techniques. Immediate triggers may follow. These are the internal or external events which lead immediately (or almost) to the occurrence of the behaviour. They again can be both external (e.g. an insult from another person) or internal (e.g. a voice command). Often they will be an interaction of the two: a delusional misinterpretation of a real-world event. The final aspect of the CARM formulation concerns those areas which are traditionally the focus of applied behavioural conceptualisations. Reinforcers are a consequence which follow the behaviour and as a result make the behaviour more likely to occur in the future, or maintain its future occurrence. Positive reinforcers are where a consequence is added as a result of the behaviour occurring (e.g. the person gains attention). Negative reinforcers on the other hand involve removing something following an occurrence of the behaviour (e.g. reduced distress through substance use). More usually reinforcers are viewed in external terms: shouting at team members to avoid medication (negative reinforcement). Reinforcers we also conceptualise as internal processes: smoking cannabis to dampen down or remove voices or to reduce stress (internal negative reinforcement) or punching a member of staff thus increasing one's status (internal positive reinforcement).

Internal processes are often harder for team members to understand, recognise and acknowledge their contribution. This aspect of the CARM formulation is therefore a key aspect of our Disputation process.

6. Sharing and revising the template with the broader multidisciplinary team (or MDT) is the next stage. Depending on the team processes, type and organisation this can be done through calling a case conference, case busting, at handover meetings etc. The completed formulation is subsequently shared with the whole MDT (since most of the client's TBCT is aimed at promoting

consistent care from a team that operates a team-based approach), and views elicited. Any changes can then be made before agreeing a final formulation.
7.   Planning the intervention is the next stage. Here the client's in-situation beliefs (hypothesised or directly elicited) are targeted when early warning signs are present.

The strategies and techniques of TBCT

In order to enlist team members as co-cognitive and behavioural therapists the formulation process will need to effectively address any unhelpful team beliefs about the client and their behaviour. Systemic techniques involving circular questioning can be helpful in examining the team's beliefs in the light of the emerging formulation. Evidence from case notes, direct observations and interview with the client can aid the process of clarifying and agreeing the various components of the CARM formulation template. The strategy here is to realign the team ABC to the client's ABC.

Where consensus cannot be reached the facilitating clinician will need to suggest that not all competing theories can be resolved at this stage. The effectiveness of interventions is the strategy at this point, with any subsequent change in the client's behaviour providing evidence (E) that the new understanding is correct; thus acting as an experiment and consequent disputation (D) for the team's beliefs.

Opportunities for team members to act as co-therapists are sought within day-to-day interactions with the team. Guidance for these interventions is developed with the team with the aim of diffusing specific in-situation delusional interpretations of events to reduce both the client's distress and the need for them to engage in the problem behaviour.

Team members are taught basic techniques for eliciting beliefs, and empathising with the client's emotional responses using reflection, paraphrasing and suspension of disbelief. They are then taught how to identify the actual A when they observe any EWS-R. Typical questions may include:

"What did [x] do to indicate that they were doing this (e.g. persecuting you)?"
"How did you figure this out?" (avoiding words like 'think' or 'believe', which discredit the client's experience.)

This enables the team to clarify the actual A and feed this back as an ABC: the real event (A), the client's interpretation of it (B) and their subsequent feelings and behaviour (Ce and Cb). Subsequent possible alternative explanations or interpretations of the A can then be elicited or suggested. This re-interpretation of the A utilises traditional cognitive therapy procedures:

1.   Eliciting supporting evidence and weighing it – fairly examining the evidence;

2.   Examining alternatives;
3.   Exploring logical inconsistencies;
4.   Testing out beliefs.

These stages, strategies and techniques are illustrated in our case study of Matthew described below. Meaden and Hacker (2010) have previously described in detail the process for implementing TBCT. In our case study we illustrate how we have evolved our practice of TBCT further to take into account clinical presentation, our formulation of the team and the setting. In Matthew's case the team at the Unit are well versed in our work and the team processes described in Table 12.2 have been addressed. This enables us to move quickly to formulating the case in the CARM model and removes the need to more formally formulate and address the team's unhelpful beliefs. We can focus instead on better understanding Matthew's behaviour, the reason for it and targeting the team's interactions utilising CBT principles to address it. In line with developments in cognitive therapy for command hallucinations (Birchwood *et al.*, 2014) we have also incorporated the notion of social rank theory into appropriate TBCT cases such as Matthew.

Case illustration: Matthew

Matthew is a 45-year-old man who has been admitted to an inpatient unit in the last month following the breakdown of a previous placement. He has a diagnosis of schizophrenia and takes anti-psychotic medication to manage this with support of the nursing staff. Matthew hears voices that he converses with much of the time. Several times a week he will shout very loudly at the voices, arguing with them, and becomes overtly distressed; however, he has declined to talk about this with the psychologist.

In conversation with staff Matthew has explained that he feels he is being monitored at the Unit with people watching him all the time. He has also made several comments that he feels the Unit is a 'women's unit'; he is reluctant to engage in many of the activities offered on the Unit but likes to watch films in his room. Matthew has made requests to be allowed off the Unit to take part in activities, as he says this helps him feel better about himself – Unit activities are for 'old men' not 'virile' men of 45 years old. Recently, Matthew has been making verbal threats to staff who ask him to keep his shouting down (e.g. "I'm going to stab you"). On two occasions he has also been physically aggressive towards staff: when asked to stop shouting at the voices he ran at a female member of staff who managed to duck out of the way; when asked to clear up after making his dinner he threw an object at a female member of staff.

Team Meeting

At his initial care review it was agreed to discuss formulation for problematic behaviours – particularly regarding Matthew's shouting at the voices and his aggression towards staff. An initial Team Meeting identified that many (but not all) of the staff felt anxious when approaching Matthew – when around Matthew (A) they thought his behaviour was unpredictable, and he might be physically aggressive towards them (B), which led to feelings of anxiety (Ce) and avoidance (Cb). However, this was problematic as staff tended to leave Matthew alone for most of day, and would not engage with him except to ask him to stop shouting at the voices. Usually, by this time Matthew was very agitated towards the voices, shouting and pacing up and down and more likely to displace his feelings of anger onto others around him. It was agreed that it would be helpful to work on three goals with the team:

1. Early warning signs of distress at the voices, so staff would have the opportunity to intervene before Matthew became excessively agitated;
2. Develop an understanding of Matthew's relationship with the voices;
3. Develop a formulation of Matthew's verbal aggression towards the staff (i.e. a CARM formulation).

In terms of data collection for the formulations the team were able to generate ideas regarding Matthew's behaviour from ongoing observations, the Unit's assessment tools and case notes. This information sharing quickly enabled them to feel less anxious around Matthew as they had started to develop an under-standing of his relationship towards the voices and they believed this made his behaviour more predictable (i.e. the staff belief had been modified). They explained that they noted he had a changeable relationship with the voices, often joking and laughing with them. However, sometimes Matthew would become defensive, start calling the voices names and shout at them to stop talking about 'political bullshit'; at these times it sounded as though the voices might be being critical of Matthew.

To collect more information regarding Matthew's experience of voices, the Unit psychologist spent time in communal areas with Matthew. Several conversa-tions were struck up with Matthew regarding his interest in films and this was used to develop relationship-building. Matthew agreed that he did not mind if the psychologist joined him for some of his pacing around the Unit, and regular pacing sessions were tentatively scheduled each week, where Matthew would talk about whatever was on his mind, which quickly revealed information about his relationship to the voices.

Assessment of the voices

Matthew explained that the voices were characters from films he has seen that he talks with to keep himself occupied. He described the voices as a creation of his own imagination that would talk back to him when he spoke to them. He described himself as keeping to himself, as he did not want to get into fights with some of the 'bigger ones' (other residents); he described this as a pattern he had followed most of his life while in hospital so as to stay 'out of trouble'. Matthew described how he felt 'trapped' in his psychosis, but he only experienced this at night in his dreams – during the day he was not (in his view) psychotic, and the voices were his own creation. Much of the time the voices would say positive or benign things and they kept Matthew occupied. However, sometimes they would start talking about things he did not want to hear about, such as the local elections, and events happening in the news. At these times he would tell the voices to 'shut up', but they would then start to say unpleasant or derogatory things to him which made him feel angry. He would then start shouting at them, and they would continue with their criticism of him, and he would continue shouting at them to 'put them in their place'.

Matthew acknowledged that he felt regret at aggressive outbursts towards the staff, but described how he would 'suddenly snap' following 'all their nagging, like a mothers' meeting'. Matthew agreed he could understand the issues with shouting at staff and voices (e.g. complaints from neighbours, upsetting others and delaying his discharge) and that he would like to be able to respond differently when asked by staff not to shout so loudly.

Development of CARM formulation

A further review of Matthew's notes and discussion with him identified a critical incident had been his father's suicide. Around this time, aged 21, Matthew had been experimenting with alcohol and illicit substances, and had gone into hospital. While in hospital his father had died. Matthew described himself as coming from a large family, with his mother as the head of the family, and father absent (at work). Much of Matthew's talk was of the hierarchy in the family, and that, after his father died, Matthew had been expected to 'step up' and take his place in the family. Matthew would talk about childhood events, such as playing football on the local street, and how roles and responsibilities were divided between the local children based on hierarchy. It was also noted that Matthew would often refer to perceived hierarchies on Unit – for example. when describing his difficulties with his 'dream psychosis', he referred to the 'nurse level' was when he was unwell, the 'psychologist level' when slightly better and the 'doctor level' when he had no difficulties.

It was felt by Matthew's named nurse that he was particularly sensitive to social rank. Many of the staff who felt less anxious around Matthew were older members of staff, and Matthew explained that he saw them as 'mums and dads' and that one should 'respect your elders'. Both staff who had been targets of aggression were younger female members of staff. Recent advances in cognitive therapy for voices were incorporated into the CARM formulation, including that of social rank theory for voices (Birchwood et al., 2000, 2004), as not only had Matthew demonstrated awareness of social rank or hierarchy on the Unit, but he had also described sensitivities to this in his past. It was hypothesised that if Matthew was in an interpersonal relationship with the voices, then at times when they criticised him he was feeling as though the voices were trying to subordinate him. At these times (when he felt his rank was threatened by the voices) he would attempt to retain his social rank by shouting at the voices to 'put them in their place'. When staff would approach Matthew to ask him to quieten, they were asking Matthew to comply with a request – which implies that they are in a more powerful position than Matthew, and that he should obey their requests. As he was already feeling intimidated and subordinated by the voices, this additional threat to his place in the 'pecking order' at the Unit led to him shouting at or threatening the staff member to 'to put them in their place' and reduce the social rank threat. Matthew would be more likely to use shouting with people he perceived as able (or acceptable) to subdue or dominate, such as young or female staff. It was suggested that physical violence (e.g. throwing objects) represented an escalation of aggression when repeated shouting (at voices and staff) had not reduced the feeling of social rank threat.

Intervention

The CARM formulation (Figure 12.3) was used as the basis for the team's understanding of Matthew's relationship with his voices to formulate his verbal aggression towards staff. This also included identification of early warning signs for verbal aggression, and staff were able to use this to intervene with Matthew before his behaviour escalated. The way for staff to intervene safely came from Matthew: he designed a 'warning card' for staff to hold up to him as a prompt to go to his room to shout at the voices or lower his voice. He described this as less intrusive than a person coming to verbally ask him to lower his voice.

Time was also spent with Matthew discussing his relationship to the voices and how this might be modified through responding mindfully to these experiences (Chadwick, 2006). Matthew declined formal practice sessions but agreed to practise mindfulness from a CD in his room, and to continue to meet the psychologist for 'film chats'. Matthew expressed a continuing desire to engage with his voices, and continued to spend time in conversation with them.

Outcome

Using early warning signs, staff could identify when Matthew was starting to become agitated by the voices and intervene early (such as engaging Matthew in conversation) before he became too distressed. When the card was used to prompt him regarding his shouting, Matthew was able to respond by lowering his voice or going to his room to continue to talk to the voices. This simple intervention reduced aggressive incidents (shouting, verbal threats) to almost zero. Matthew continued to engage with his voices and reported that he found the practice of mindfulness helpful. He was more receptive to conversations about the voices though he continued to decline formal therapy.

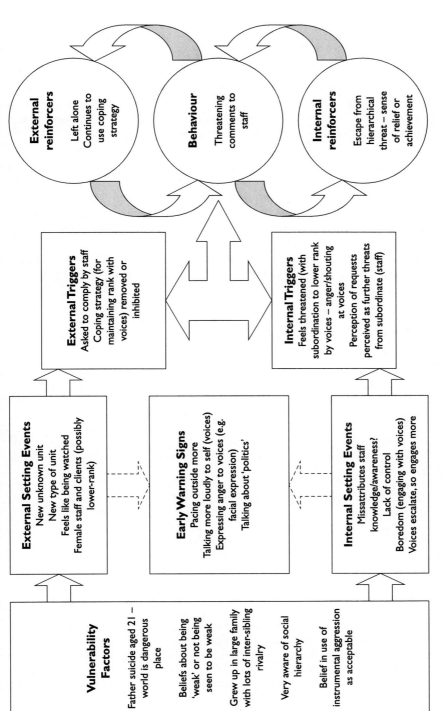

Figure 12.3 CARM formulation of Matthew's aggression towards staff

Conclusions and implications

Our approach to TBCT is continually evolving. It is a ready vehicle for incorporating new developments in CBT and as we show here can be utilised effectively by focussing on different components. Sometimes the interventions generated are quite simple but are always based upon a shared understanding that facilitates a consistent, hopeful and compassionate team approach.

Evaluating TBCT more formally is a next stage, and we remain interested primarily in our work with teams working with those who are hard to reach and have complex mental health and behavioural needs. It is difficult to disentangle the impact of TBCT from the efforts of the wider care team; however, we have started to use qualitative methodologies to evaluate their experiences of the approach and their perception of the value of TBCT. We are also using similar methodologies in an effort to evaluate service user experiences of teams where the approach is used. It is hoped that this will facilitate further development and refinement of TBCT, increase the effectiveness of the approach and, in turn, further support service users in their recovery.

References

Birchwood, M. & Trower, P. (2006). The future of cognitive–behavioural therapy for psychosis: Not a quasi-neuroleptic. *The British Journal of Psychiatry, 188,* 107–108.

Birchwood, M., Michail, M., Meaden, M., Tarrier, N., Lewis, S., Wykes, T. . . . Peters, E. (2014). Cognitive behaviour therapy to prevent harmful compliance with command hallucinations (COMMAND): A randomised controlled trial. *Lancet Psychiatry, 1,* 23–33.

Birchwood, M., Meaden, A., Trower, P., Gilbert, P. & Plaistow, J. (2000). The power and omnipotence of voices: Subordination and entrapment by voices and significant others. *Psychological Medicine, 30,* 337–344.

Birchwood, M., Gilbert, P., Gilbert, J., Trower, P., Meaden, A., Hay, J. . . . Miles, J. N. (2004). Interpersonal and role-related schema influence the relationship with the dominant 'voice' in schizophrenia: A comparison of three models. *Psychological Medicine, 34*(8), 1571–1580.

Brett-Jones, J., Garety, P. & Hemsley, D. (1987). Measuring delusional experiences: A method and its application. *British Journal of Clinical Psychology, 26,* 257–265.

Chadwick, P. (2006). *Person-based cognitive therapy for distressing psychosis.* Chichester, Sussex: John Wiley & Sons.

Chadwick, P. & Birchwood, M. (1995). The omnipotence of voices II: The Beliefs About Voices Questionnaire. *British Journal of Psychiatry, 166,* 773–776.

Chadwick, P., Birchwood, M. & Trower, P. (1996). *Cognitive therapy for delusions, voices and paranoia.* Chichester, Sussex: John Wiley & Sons.

Chadwick, P., Lees, S. & Birchwood, M. (2000). The Revised Beliefs About Voices Questionnaire (BAVQ-R). *British Journal of Psychiatry, 177,* 229–232.

Freeman, D., Garety, P. A. & Kuipers, E. (2001). Persecutory delusions: Developing the understanding of belief maintenance and emotional distress. *Psychological Medicine, 31,* 1293–1306.

Hacker, D. A., Birchwood, M., Tudway, J., Meaden, A. T. & Amphlett, C. (2008). Acting on voices: Omnipotence, sources of threat and safety-seeking behaviours. *British Journal of Clinical Psychology*, *47*(2), 201–203.

Haddock, G., McCarron, J., Tarrier, N. & Faragher, E. B. (1999). Scales to measure dimensions of hallucinations and delusions: The psychotic symptom rating scales (PSYRATS). *Psychological Medicine*, *29*, 879–889.

Jones, C., Hacker, D., Cormac, I., Meaden, A. & Irving, C. B. (2012). Cognitive behaviour therapy versus other psychosocial treatments for schizophrenia. *Cochrane Database of Systematic Reviews*, Issue 4. Art. No.: CD008712. doi: 10.1002/14651858.CD008712. pub2.

Lynch, D., Laws, K. R. & McKenna, P. J. (2010). Cognitive behavioural therapy for major psychiatric disorder: Does it really work? A meta-analytical review of well controlled trials. *Psychological Medicine*, *4*, 9–24.

Meaden, A. & Hacker, D. (2010) *Problematic and risk behaviours in psychosis: A shared formulation approach.* London: Brunner-Routledge.

Moritz, S. & Woodward, T. S. (2005). Jumping to conclusions in delusional and non-delusional schizophrenic patients. *British Journal of Clinical Psychology*, *44*, 193–207.

Tarrier, N. (1992). Management and modification of residual positive symptoms. In M. Birchwood & N. Tarrier (eds), *Innovations in the psychological management of schizophrenia* (pp. 147–171). Chichester, Sussex: John Wiley & Sons.

Wykes, T., Steel, C., Everitt, B. & Tarrier, N. (2007). Cognitive Behavior Therapy for schizophrenia: Effect sizes, clinical models, and methodological rigor. *Schizophrenia Bulletin* 25 October [online].

Chapter 13

Long-Term Supportive Psychotherapy as a team-based therapy

Alan Meaden and Helen Hewson

Introduction

Despite the best efforts of researchers and clinicians in supporting the routine delivery of psychosocial interventions, the long-term impact of these evidence-based treatments has not been clearly demonstrated, with initial reported benefits being lost to follow-up at 18 months (Jones *et al.*, 2004) or being quickly lost once treatment has ended (Yung, 2012). Clearly for some individuals longer term treatment is required. The provision of long-term therapy is now unfashionable, especially in an era of cost efficiency. However, the cost of longer term therapy must be balanced against the continued use of hospital, staff burnout and poor quality of life experienced by those who both give and require on-going care. In this chapter we describe an approach to working with teams who work with this group of high need service users.

Theoretical background and development: A review of the literature on supportive psychotherapy

Supportive therapy is not a well-defined or unique intervention and has no overall unifying theory. It is commonly used as an umbrella term to describe a range of interventions from 'befriending' to more formal psychotherapy (Buckley & Pettit, 2007) and has sometimes been viewed as 'the Cinderella of psychotherapies' (P. R. Sullivan, 1971: 119). Supportive approaches overlap with counselling and most embrace concepts from Rogerian counselling: empathic listening and warmth. Early definitions saw supportive psychotherapy quite narrowly as a body of techniques, primarily involving advice, exhortation and encouragement and used to treat severely impaired patients (Dewald, 1964, 1971); reflecting its use by often inexperienced therapists to treat the majority of patients seen in psychiatric clinics and mental health centres (Werman, 1984). More formal supportive therapy approaches have presented an integrative framework combining psychodynamic, Cognitive Behavioural and interpersonal models and techniques (Winston *et al.*, 2004). They tend to be flexibly delivered in terms of frequency and regularity of sessions and time frame. The focus is on reinforcing healthy patterns of thought and behaviour and to promote an adaptive approach to on-going disability and symptoms. Hogarty *et al.* (2004) describe their approach to supportive therapy with schizophrenia as fostering illness management through applied coping strategies and education. Therapists may offer advice, support and reassurance with the aim of encouraging adaptation (Crown, 1998). Unlike in psychoanalysis, in which the analyst acts as a 'blank canvas' for transference purposes, in supportive therapy the therapist engages in encouraging and containing and offers a supportive relationship which fosters the growth of healthy defence mechanisms.

The concept of supportive psychotherapy was developed in the early part of the twentieth century to describe a treatment approach with objectives which were more limited than those of psychoanalysis. In part the approach evolved to address the long-term difficulties of patients with so-called chronic diseases and complaints (Fenton, 2000). Perhaps surprisingly it has also been cited as the individual psychotherapy of choice for most patients with schizophrenia (Lamberti & Herz, 1995) and has been used as a condition in CBT trials to control for the effects of the therapeutic relationship. Some of these trials have unexpectedly demonstrated similar benefits for supportive therapy to the 'active' therapy (against which supportive therapy was intended to serve as a control) (Jones *et al.*, 2012). The Danish Schizophrenia Project (DNS) compared a two-year supportive psychotherapy and treatment as usual for first-episode patients and found observed positive changes for both the Positive and Negative Syndrome Scale (PANSS) and the Global Assessment of Functioning Scale (GAF) (Rosenbaum *et al.*, 2012). Interestingly this change at the symptomatic level has not been demonstrated by CBT approaches (Jones *et al.*, 2012). Elements of supportive psychotherapy such as enhancing coping strategies have been adopted as part of routine best practice psychosocial interventions (Jones & Meaden, 2010). The approach has also been found to have positive though modest effects on cognitive deficits (Hogarty *et al.*, 2004). More generally, Fenton *et al.* (1997) report that a patient's feeling of being listened to and understood is a strong predictor of medication compliance and associated with good outcomes in mainstream psychiatric care (McCabe, 2004).

Whilst the number of empirical studies validating the effectiveness of supportive psychotherapy remains small, an increasing interest in the approach is demonstrated by case studies (Lysaker *et al.*, 2007) and other papers that attempt to describe the therapeutic strategies and techniques (Bedi & Vassiliadis, 2010; Penn *et al.*, 2004). Supportive psychotherapy has also been put forward as a model that could enhance everyday psychiatric practice if provided by psychiatric care staff alongside routine care (Bedi & Vassiliadis, 2010). Unlike other more active therapies such as CBT, intervention is not necessarily focussed upon change. However, it has been argued that an integrative approach to working with psychosis can adopt a recovery focus (Lysaker *et al.*, 2010; Seikkula *et al.*, 2006). Drawing upon constructionist philosophy and systemic psychotherapy, diaological theory has argued that psychosis represents a breakdown of intra-psychic and interpersonal dialogue. Lysaker *et al.* (2010) cite narrative incoherence, poor metacognitive functioning and limited self-identity as core problems in schizophrenia that limit dialogue within and between people. Supportive psychotherapy provides a holding relationship that could support the development of dialogue about life and about psychosis. According to Lysaker *et al.* (2010) this relationship can support the development of metacognitive functioning enabling the client to sustain open dialogue, reflect upon experiences and develop coherent stories about self, other and the world. Rather than the recovery of an old or pre-morbid self or the achievement of a symptom-free presentation, recovery as facilitated by supportive interventions involves the development of resilience and self-identity such that the individual is more able to cope with the pressures of life.

Long-Term Supportive Psychotherapy (Meaden & Van Marle, 2008; LTSP) has attempted to build on these developments and applications to psychosis but with a specific focus on those with long-term complex mental health and behavioural needs who are hard to reach. Its principles have previously been outlined for working with personality disorders (Van Marle & Holmes, 2002) and usefully summarised for rehabilitation populations by Davenport (2006). These authors place particular emphasis on achieving a psychodynamic understanding of the person and their difficulties as well as giving consideration to the more practical tasks of assessment and management. They stress the importance of developing a long-term therapeutic relationship with service users, providing support over different phases of recovery and relapse and offering consultancy, support and supervision to others most closely involved in the person's care.

LTSP is a psychodynamically informed approach aimed at supporting high quality comprehensive routine care for those with the most complex difficulties. In common with supportive psychotherapy approaches in general it also incorporates Cognitive Behavioural techniques as well as systemic elements. In this sense it may best be described as a pragmatic therapy offering a flexible need-adapted framework responsive to the changing and case-specific needs of the individual with complex long-term needs. Since most such individuals (who have a diagnosis of psychosis) are cared for by MDTs, it is helpful to think about how LTSP can be enhanced to support a team-based approach. Team formulations (Meaden & Hacker, 2010; Whomsley, 2010) are steadily emerging as a helpful means of promoting a consistent approach to care, installing psychological mindedness and addressing unhelpful team dynamics (Davenport, 2006), attitudes and behaviours (Meaden & Hacker, 2010). This approach is particularly relevant for those for whom current psychosocial interventions have proven ineffective or where individuals cannot engage in more structured interventions for a variety of reasons.

LTSP might also be considered as a helpful framework for working with teams who, for a variety of reasons, are unable to embrace more active modes of treatment. When people do not recover clinically and continue to present with high levels of long-term need teams can become frustrated, lose their perspective on what the aims of the care provided are or should be and may focus only on crises neglecting the overall needs of the client. We have developed our use of LTSP to help teams work more therapeutically with such individuals. LTSP has adopted a multi-axial formulation framework (Meaden & Van Marle, 2008) derived from the diagnostic categories of the American Diagnostic and Statistical Manual of the American Psychiatric Association IV (DSM-IV). We have found that this tool supports MDTs to move beyond a narrow framework of diagnostics whilst recognising their role in the current health economy. The framework highlights the importance of other factors and how these interact to perpetuate difficulties and impede recovery. Relationships, personality traits and disorders, co-morbid mood and substance misuse problems, environmental destabilisers and other health and social care needs can be understood within a framework accepted and understood by our MDT colleagues. Following the development of DSM-V we have incorporated a dimensional perspective to assessment and formulation which supports teams to observe the ways in which personality can directly influence distress and engagement in treatment by people experiencing psychosis. A focus on the notion of their being a personality continuum facilitates an introduction to psychodynamic principles. On-going shared formulation work with both the MDT and the client supports the incorporation of person level and narrative formulations focusing more explicitly upon psychological vulnerabilities, client narratives and psychodynamic processes.

Aims, stages, strategies and techniques

As an integrative psychotherapy many of the strategies and techniques of LTSP are adopted from other approaches. Psychodynamically informed principles are however especially important when addressing patient-related dynamics which may prove particularly disruptive to providing good quality care. Cognitive Behavioural principles may be most useful in more active phases of the therapy when there is a more stable period of functioning and the client is most able to make use of them. In LTSP these interventions are also applied to the team in order to assist them to make sense and cope with the complex dynamics being enacted.

Therapeutic aims are adapted to the individual's case-specific and changing needs, a philosophy of care we have taken from the Need Adapted Treatment approach (Alanen, 1997) as it helpfully captures the way in which interventions are offered flexibly according to periods of relapse and recovery. The longer duration of therapy offered by LTSP affords the opportunity for interventions to be tailored to changing needs and allows the person to grow and adapt at a pace they can sustain. LTSP aims may be summarised as:

1. Establish and maintain a therapeutic alliance; considering psychological and practical barriers to engagement – with a frequency and length of therapeutic contact that is sustainable for the client and the team (reducing burnout).

2.   Promote awareness of transference issues.
3.   Hold and contain the client and the team.
4.   Facilitate the maturation of defences.
5.   Promote adjustment and adaptation through improving coping.
6.   Reduce relapses and the inappropriate use of services.

Stages

In our tiered approach to formulation we continue to see the value in adopting the DSM-IV Multi Axial framework which is our starting point for summarising difficulties and exploring the way in which these interact. To this we have added what we have termed a Person Level shared formulation which constitutes a broad psychological understanding of the person including development factors. Several templates are available which support this process (e.g. Meaden & Hacker, 2010; Dudley & Kuyken, 2014). We have adopted the 5Ps (Dudley & Kuyken, 2014) as this most readily incorporates personality based problems. The 5Ps may be summarised as the Presenting difficulty, Predisposing factors, Perpetuating factors, Precipitating factors and Protective factors. To these we have added a sixth P, representing Plan or care plan. LTSP principles both inform this process and also guide how the formulation is translated into routine care planning and management.

Stage 1: Assessment and formulation with the client and the team

The principles and aims of LTSP are introduced to the team through a discussion of the client's difficulties and needs, reviewing what has been offered (ensuring that other evidence-based interventions have been offered or at least considered); which will usually necessitate some pre-meeting work (e.g. reviewing case notes). This is often a time to stop and think. This is also an acknowledgement that the current care plan is not working and something else must be tried. The LTSP practitioner may usefully ask: "*how is this approach working for you?*" LTSP can be suggested as one possible way forward. Team members will likely have differing views on the best way forward and the LTSP practitioner's role is to support the team to step back and reconsider the nature of the client's difficulties in light of review findings.

Initial formulation meetings with the team take place outside of therapeutic contact with the client. We have found that this approach enables unhelpful beliefs and attributions of the staff about the client to be identified at the earliest stage. This is particularly valuable, for teams who are faced with behaviours experienced as challenging or problematic that staff do not associate with an 'illness' model (usually attributed to personal characteristics: Markham & Trower, 2003). Whilst staff empathise with service user experiences of delusions and hallucinations, they often feel frustrated and powerless when confronted with patterns of behaviour that appear maladaptive, 'anti-social' or 'attention seeking' (Meaden &

Hacker, 2010). Negative feelings about clients have important implications for therapeutic alliance. In the absence of appropriate support negative transference relationships can lead to a reduction in job satisfaction and a sense of 'burnout' for front-line staff. As demonstrated by previous research (Summers, 2006) shared formulation which incorporates an explanation of transference patterns and the roots of these in developmental experience, common stress triggers and a functional analysis of 'problem behaviours', can support staff understanding and promote greater confidence when working with clients to address behavioural problems. Accordingly team members are supported to share information and knowledge to complete a multi-axial formulation:

Axis I   Diagnostic Category
Axis II   Personality Traits, Disorders & Developmental Factors (including attachment patterns and possible defences: denial, projection, omnipotence, splitting, passive-aggression)
Axis III Physical & Constitutional Factors
Axis IV   Environmental Factors (past & present)
Axis V   Current Level of Functioning Summary.

The formulation serves to educate team members about the client's developmental history and attachment patterns together with likely maintaining and perpetuating factors. Meetings are often supported with the use of structured assessments designed to explore personality traits and disorders, executive functioning and co-morbid presentations which might be suitable treatment targets. Where possible client rated assessments of personality and psychosis can be informative; however, these are only used when they can be acceptably introduced to and tolerated by the client (see Meaden, 2010 and Meaden & Hacker, 2010 for a summary of useful assessment tools). At this early stage, the focus is often upon noting interactions between staff members or staff members and the client, what is said and how each behaves, along with what this may indicate regarding transference. Contrary to Freud's notion that patients with schizophrenia could not develop transference (Gabbard, 2000), H. S. Sullivan (1962), who spent his life's work with this group of patients, saw the importance of early interpersonal difficulties. As Davenport (2006) has noted, difficult dynamics are often played out in current relationships with staff. Such observation and reports along with any clinician rated tools are used to support a psychological understanding of the client. The supportive psychotherapy practitioner begins to develop a tentative formulation regarding psychodynamic processes relevant for the client's presenting problems. The aim is to achieve an understanding about what the client can be expected to tolerate and cope with in the context of therapeutic work.

Alongside meetings with the team, initial contact with the client provides an opportunity to explore their understanding of current problems and to introduce aspects of the formulation that are relevant to coping in the 'here and now'.

Sessions are carried out jointly with team members focussing primarily on alliance, assessment, a review of current support and collaborative formulation at the person level. The LTSP practitioner draws upon a 'scaffolding approach' incorporating prompts, cues and questions that invoke curiosity in order to facilitate the development of new understandings. The extent of what can be shared depends to some extent upon the client's mental state, emotional stability and metacognitive functioning. We have found the use of person level formulations particularly useful when working directly with the client. These constitute a broad psychological understanding of the client and typically include development, maintenance factors as well as those which serve to exacerbate difficulties and those which promote stability. Formulations can be adopted to reflect the client's perspectives which may differ from the descriptions provided by the team. This is an opportunity to negotiate meaning and develop new understandings about the client's problems that 'make sense' for both the client and for the team. At the assessment stage, formulations are brief and tentative; comprehensive formulation including developmental factors and maintaining processes is more feasible within the context of on-going work when a therapeutic alliance has had sufficient time to develop. Throughout assessment, engagement and ongoing LTSP contacts, insights and understandings offered by the client are incorporated into a re-working of the formulation which continues to develop throughout the on-going therapeutic work. The idea is to support curiosity about the client and their difficulties which can often be lost when working with such hard to reach clients. It is also about supporting a reflective practice approach for the team and underpinning the notion that we never fully know a person; thus the importance of avoiding making assumptions – particularly negative ones.

Following initial assessment and formulation the decision to offer LTSP should be made in collaboration with both the client and the team. Factors for consideration include the client's views on psychotherapeutic contact, motivation to engage, suitability of other evidence-based therapies and the team's commitment to long-term work. One factor which might be viewed as a precondition is the ability for the client to develop an alliance through which empathy, warmth and compassion can successfully be communicated and received. Unlike other approaches the identification of specific goals is not necessary as a precursor to therapeutic work, achieving stability is considered an appropriate aim. It is not uncommon for other healthcare staff to provide a supportive psychotherapy approach (Bedi & Vassiliadis, 2010). Where clients are ambivalent about engaging with psychologists or psychotherapists it is sometimes appropriate to provide supervision for multidisciplinary team members who have already developed a therapeutic alliance.

Stage 2: Supportive psychotherapy with the client

In LTSP the therapeutic relationship is the most important component. The therapeutic style adopted by the LTSP practitioner is characterised by emphatic validation, praise, advice giving and gentle confrontation. As well as focussing on therapeutic process the therapist aims to improve self-awareness (e.g. of defences) by the client and team members; in the latter case through supervision and reflective team meetings. For the duration of therapy, interventions with the client aim to maintain a collaborative alliance which allows them to feel safe and supported. Key principles and strategies that support this are documented elsewhere (beginning with the Boston Psychotherapy study, Gunderson *et al.*, 1984). The use of advanced empathy and therapeutic challenge is balanced against the need to provide containment. Whilst the expression of emotion is at times encouraged and can bring relief, therapy does not aim to uncover repressed material. Anxiety and affective experience is managed and contained rather than exposed and challenged. In contrast with active versions of psychodynamic therapy, the practitioner avoids long periods of silence that will likely contribute to anxiety for this client group.

In LTSP maintenance of a flexible approach aims to respond to the changing needs of clients within the context of both environmental and internal stressors, different phases of psychosis and recovery (Fenton, 2000). In order to respond appropriately, the therapist uses a variety of interventions and strategies. Fenton (2000) has highlighted the importance of therapist capacity to 'shift gears' and change roles during therapy. In the early stages of LTSP sessions are primarily focussed on the development of alliance and the achievement of stability. The management of and recovery from emotional crises, stressful life events and psychotic relapse often emerges as an important part of the work. In these periods interventions are adapted to focus on the most relevant biological, psychological and social needs. Maslow's hierarchy of needs provides a useful model to guide decisions about the most valuable interventions at any stage. For example, when faced with life events and social difficulties that challenge the person's problem solving abilities (e.g. housing issues, debt, victimisation) a joint problem solving approach may be necessary to limit the destabilising effect of such stressors. In a post-acute phase it may become possible to introduce cognitive behavioural interventions that aim to enhance coping strategies (Tarrier, 1993), and identify early signs such that the likelihood of future admissions is reduced. These interventions may set the scene for Cognitive Behavioural interventions focussing more explicitly on disputing beliefs about psychotic experiences, capacity to cope, the need for reassurance or other negative inferences about self, the world and others.

The presence and continued support of the therapist throughout periods of relapse and stability aims to support the development of a secure base. Some dependence upon the therapist is accepted as this can support the developing alliance. However, the long-term aim is to support the client in accessing resources, coping more effectively, developing mature defences and meeting needs independently. Throughout the work, the therapist supports the client to build healthy defence mechanisms and in some instances those that are harmful are challenged. The incorporation of psychodynamic principles is often subtle.

The psychodynamic formulation assists the therapist to manage countertransference responses and foster positive transference in the client in order to sustain supportive contact. Attempts to offer interpretations may be appropriate but only when the client achieves a level of stability that allows these to be received.

Stage 3: Supportive psychotherapy with the team

Therapists working with both personality disorder and psychosis have been found to experience less satisfaction from their role (Bourke & Grenyer, 2010; Jackson, 2001). According to Jackson (2001) therapists and those trying to help psychotic clients are required to tolerate confusing countertransference; this requires the capacity to follow multiple, and often paradoxical threads of communication simultaneously. Multidisciplinary teams may benefit from a supportive psychotherapy framework which focusses upon supporting staff. In achieving this, the supportive psychotherapy practitioner needs to be aware of powerful transference processes played out within the team. These can lead multidisciplinary staff to appear unwilling to deliver care and resistant to reflective processing regarding their emotional experience of the client. Just as we may meet resistance and reluctance in our clients when we attempt to encourage reflection upon emotional meaning teams may also resist such input. We have understood this to be both a parallel process that mirrors the emotional experience of the client and a functional defence required by the team when confronted by powerful countertransference reactions and projections that provoke strong feelings of anger, anxiety and fear. LTSP provides a useful framework through which staff can be supported to acknowledge and cope with such experiences through a similar supportive relationship, to that which is offered to the client. This is routinely offered through consultation meetings, informal discussions and team meetings. As well as working with the broad care team, LTSP requires a supportive team (Meaden & Van Marle, 2008) to be in place. Members of this team will be most closely and routinely involved in working with the client. Membership will need to be carefully negotiated. Considerations include:

- Who can sustain the client's difficult transference issues and slow progress (if any)?
- Who should provide practical support?
- What should be the frequency of contact?

Other chapters in this book (see Chapters 12 & 14) describing team-based approaches highlight how staff themselves may also be conceptualised as being treatment resistant even to being socialised into these new team-based approaches. In such cases LTSP may provide a useful framework. Within MDTs the interpretation of transference can increase awareness of transference reactions and may improve staff engagement and commitment to helping through the development of empathy and alliance. However, this work can be challenging and is also associated with an increased awareness of personal conflicts and institutional challenges that impinge upon the practitioners' own values and approach to care. We have found that the adoption of a supportive stance can facilitate the development of mature defence mechanisms and emotional awareness. Here the LTSP practitioner applies a supportive approach to the team, containing their emotions, surviving alongside them and not necessarily challenging their assumptions. In the early stages of such work, we allow staff to keep their defences intact, intervention focuses on acknowledging the challenges faced when attempting to maintain contact with this client group. Over time we view it as our role to encourage them to acknowledge these defences and work through them in order that reactions and communications directed back to the client are experienced by the client as being helpful and containing. As teams begin to accept and utilise reflective space it becomes possible to share further knowledge regarding relevant psychodynamic theory. At this stage we have found Klein's (1948) object relations theory to be a useful model which provides a language to explain unpleasant emotional responses experienced by the team.

Therapeutic strategies provided with the client and the team

Psychoeducation

Psychoeducation (of the person and the team) is an intrinsic part of developing and progressively sharing the multi-axial formulation, and emphasises understanding of current difficulties in a development context. Broader psychoeducation goals with the person may involve education about diagnostic issues and the biopsychosocial stress-vulnerability model (Nuechterlein & Dawson, 1984); learning to minimise stress and preventing and managing relapses. This may involve work on Early Warning Signs of relapse and/or risk which can be carried out with the client or with the team (Meaden & Hacker, 2010).

Coping/adaptive strategies

These aim to promote a sense of agency, control and self-management. These strategies emphasise the refocussing of coping skills in order to remediate symptoms; adopting a long-term approach where on-going efforts are made to promote coping. Members of the supporting team or MDT more generally may usefully support the client to utilise these at appropriate times.

Environmental interventions

This is a helpful component of LTSP that explicitly acknowledges the value of developing a meaningful routine and healthy lifestyle. Based on the multi-axial shared formulation the therapist can work with other team members to support appropriate health promotion, accessing of community resources and supports. This may involve encouraging the use of creative activities or social interventions such as increasing contact with voluntary organisations or members of the support network. Other environmental interventions may focus on intervening to address exacerbating factors which the person is not ready to deal with.

Dealing with transference and team holding

As Davenport (2006) has noted psychotic clients and those with abuse histories will often display difficult to manage interpersonal behaviours and dynamics which are likely to negatively influence engagement. Team members may inadvertently re-enact early patterns of abuse and become enmeshed in unhealthy, destructive interactions (e.g. splitting, projective identification). Positive transference is actively nurtured but not interpreted; though the therapist remains mindful of potential idealisation (van Marle & Holmes, 2002). Clients are encouraged to understand the reasons for their unhelpful interactions and modify them. Cognitive techniques such as clarifying and challenging dysfunctional assumptions and identifying their triggers may also be employed when they are judged as likely to be of most benefit.

Attention to transference issues may also provide further insight into the client's interpersonal difficulties. This can be used to contribute towards both the team's and the therapist's understanding of the client's ways of relating and their key vulnerabilities. An important LTSP principle is to promote survival alongside the client weathering the storm of sometimes frequent relapses, crises and other stressful episodes.

The LTSP principle of team holding can be used to help minimise such interactions and negative attitudes and help to reduce the potential for staff burnout. Providing supervision and on-going support for the supporting team are key.

Reformulation, review and recovery

For this group of clients the concept and expectation of a full 'recovery' can be misleading both for the client and teams. More often, a recovery focus involves developing skills and knowledge that the client's developmental experiences prevented them from achieving. This requires a long-term approach to intervention and outcome; for most a positive outcome involves increasing stability, self-awareness and participation in the social world rather than the elimination of symptoms or a return to full functioning. Within this context reformulation and review both with the client and the team aims to encourage reflection on interventions and coping strategies that have been successful. Taking the time to step back and notice the progress achieved provides a supportive function for staff who often feel frustrated by the lack of progress that can be made. Given that LTSP is often provided over several years rather than weeks or months it can be incorporated routinely into care reviews. These should provide an opportunity to reflect on the work, share any new information or understanding more formally with the team, client and others involved in their care and highlight any progress. The incorporation of any outcome measures can provide a useful adjunct to this process.

Case Illustration: Liam

Liam is in his early 40s with a 20-year-old history of schizoaffective disorder including 18 admissions to psychiatric hospital, each lasting an average of 3 months. Liam's previous treatment had been provided by a community mental health team who offered out-patient appointments with a psychiatrist and regular support from a Community Psychiatric Nurse (CPN). He had been prescribed various antipsychotics with mixed compliance. Engagement with services was poor and he frequently presented in crisis. Liam's family supported him to continue living at home. However, frequent conflicts led them to withdraw and ask for Liam to leave the family home. He was referred to an Assertive Outreach Team (AOT) in the hope of reducing hospital admissions and assisting him to achieve stability and consistent engagement with psychiatric services.

Liam was born and brought up in Glasgow. When he was seven years old his family moved to Birmingham leaving Liam in the care of his grandparents. During this time he was sexually assaulted by his paternal uncle. When he reached 11 years he joined the family in Birmingham. At home, Liam and his three brothers would fight playfully. At times this would escalate to violence and Liam recalls being injured. He went on to university to study Sociology. Whilst there he invested money in a business venture with a friend who intended to open a retail outlet. The venture failed and he lost all his money, which ended the friendship. Liam felt angry and let down. This was the start of his mental health problems. He withdrew from university and relationships. Liam went on to experience a number of losses in his life, the death of his mother and breakdown of a romantic relationship were precipitants for further relapses.

The AOT gradually established an alliance with Liam but attempts to engage him in standard best practice psychosocial interventions failed. At times his presentation would appear uncharacteristic and bizarre. Liam would discuss tangential issues and fantasies at length that appeared to lack relevance to current problems that were readily apparent. He would refer to himself in the third person and by a different name, dress in bizarre clothing and misidentify staff. When challenged about this he would become frustrated and angry with staff refusing to engage in suggested interventions or withdrawing contact. He would rarely engage with discussions about mental health difficulties or acknowledge his own limitations and difficulties but would frequently demand support from the team stating that he felt unable to cope (e.g. to clean his flat, sort out debts, etc); difficulties at Axis V. Staff became frustrated with his fluctuating mood, demands and aggressive behaviours, leading to regular changes in team members who were willing to work with him. Following the breakdown of the alliance with Liam's CPN the MDT made a referral for psychological therapy.

Initial intervention focussed on assessment and engagement with key team members and also with Liam. During meetings with Liam's CPN and Support Worker a multi-axial formulation was developed (see Table 13.1); this highlighted the presence of personality difficulties and an ambivalent attachment style (Axis II) alongside his well-established diagnosis of schizoaffective disorder (Axis I). Early life experiences were discussed including Liam's experience of sexual abuse, limited parental care and boundary setting at home. Connections were drawn with current problems that were acting as barriers to recovery and engagement within the AOT. Liam appeared to lack a meaningful daily routine or structure to the day and a supportive social network was absent. Attempts by the team to put this in place routinely ended following outbursts of aggression and other inappropriate or bizarre behaviours (walking into the local accident and emergency with a knife saying that he wanted to rescue all unborn children, walking naked back from a casino – having been thrown out for demanding free drinks) that had led to Liam being excluded from college and banned from community groups and many other places. Liam struggled to cope with any attempt by the team to explore the meaning of these behaviours or form a more psychotherapeutic relationship. Contacts would often end when staff felt unable to make sense of his communications and behaviours. This presentation appeared consistent and was often apparent in the absence of any observed evidence of active psychosis. Liam's presentation would fluctuate and during some visits he would present as an articulate and grounded man. This incongruence confused team members and led to them concluding that he was manipulating them somehow.

Following an initial meeting with the team joint visits to Liam with the LTSP practitioner focussed on reviewing the benefits of relationships with team members and previous therapists. From this review it became apparent that Liam would rely upon others and feared being left to cope on his own. He stated that people always let him down in the end and that he was unsure about whether he should trust the therapist as they would probably let him down or leave. During the engagement phase he would often present with tangential speech and bizarre behaviour which detracted from discussions leaving us feeling confused. He would regularly talk in the third person using a language which he appeared to have made up. When challenged his behaviour became increasingly bizarre to include impersonations of mythological characters. It was quickly apparent that he was unable to comprehend responsibility for change. When explaining his difficulties he located the source of them in others who he felt had abandoned him by leaving him to cope on his own.

Developing shared understandings

Further to meeting with Liam the LTSP practitioner reviewed Liam's case notes and talked with all members of the team who had been involved with Liam over

Table 13.1 Multi-axial Formulation Framework for Liam

Axis I	Clinical disorders Other conditions that may be a focus of clinical attention	Diagnostic Category Schizoaffective Disorder
Axis II	Personality traits and disorders	Schizotypal, Borderline and Dependant Personality Traits Attachment Style: insecure–predominantly anxious Defences: fantasy, dissociation derealisation and splitting
Axis III	General medical conditions	Diabetes, high blood pressure
Axis IV	Psychosocial and environmental problems (past and present)	Previously disclosed experience of childhood sexual abuse Ex Partner's financial abuse and abandonment Relationship with current partner remains insecure leading to attachment anxiety and regular arguments Lack of meaningful role in the family due to strained relationships, family no longer happy to support him to live at their home Mother died in 2012 Limited range of meaningful roles and goals Unemployment Housing conditions poor
Axis V	Global assessment of functioning	Poor social functioning 18 past admissions 2 informal admissions in past 3 years
Summary	Liam's early life was unstable. He has disclosed an experience of childhood sexual abuse but has been unwilling to share any further information. When he was 7 years old his parents and siblings moved to the Midlands leaving him in Glasgow under the care of his grandmother. Moved to England at 11. Father returned to Glasgow after marital breakdown. Current relationships with family are strained. Interpersonal conflicts within romantic relationships precipitate instability of mood and behaviour. Need to be treated as special, demands Insecure attachment pattern Unstable sense of self Autistic cognitive style Reliance on immature defences: fantasy, dissociation, acting out, splitting	

several years in some cases. Their frustrations, difficulties and ideas about him were discussed. The multi-axial formulation template was then shared with a core group of staff currently most closely involved in Liam's care. These were his psychiatrist and a CPN. Ideas were shared and the template populated with the aim of facilitating deeper understanding regarding the nature of Liam's difficulties. When the team became stuck the LTSP practitioner offered ideas as well as using the meeting to further explore transference issues. This enabled the team to stand back from their interactions and recognise important transference issues. In addition it helped them to identify more realistic therapeutic aims that could guide their on-going work with him.

Therapeutic aims and interventions

It was clear from this initial multi-axial formulation that Liam was likely to require on-going supportive interventions and that an attempt to promote change through time-limited 'manualised' interventions would not be likely to be of benefit. If anything these treatment attempts were likely to reinforce Liam's perception that he was being abandoned and left to cope alone since they placed more responsibility on him and staff were likely to disengage when they did not work.

Therapeutic work was refocused on achieving the level of support necessary to reduce relapse whilst minimising stress and burnout within the supporting team. This involved support focussed on containment, such that he would be more able to tolerate difficult emotions relating to previous losses, relationship difficulties, internal conflicts and destabilising life events. In light of Liam's difficulty tolerating the therapeutic alliance, a focus on activities and achievements was initially prioritised. Support was offered for Liam to attend social activities and to develop a more meaningful routine. Of necessity this involved other members of the team (e.g. a support worker). The effect of this was that Liam appeared more able to tolerate contact with the team and consequently staff reported that contact had been more positive and constructive with fewer sessions being aborted due to staff feeling confused and overwhelmed. This work was subsequently developed to include occupational therapy interventions aimed at increasing the meaningful activity within Liam's life. Whilst this approach appeared to enhance therapeutic contact with the team Liam continued to experience flash points in response to particular environmental and internal triggers. These included perceived rejection by family, difficulties managing bills and housing issues, conflicts with friends and neighbours and memories of past events that had been difficult for him to cope with.

Whilst there were improvements in the team's relationship with Liam they continued to be confronted with telephone contacts in which Liam demanded acknowledgement of his specialness (e.g. reporting that he had predicted a crime or had cured a disease). This was followed by paranoid and persecutory thoughts accusing the team of disbelieving him and letting him down. At these times he would appear verbally aggressive and would make frequent threats of harm to himself and others. These reactions were formulated as defensive strategies and accepted as Liam's usual pattern of relating and coping with the world.

When faced with tangential and metaphorical asides staff were encouraged to focus on here and now problems that had triggered this response. Therapy sessions would focus on emotional support and containment of emotions which overwhelmed him as well as positive experiences in the here and now. This encouraged a more positive transference focussed on Liam's skills and abilities rather than deficits which he continued to project onto others. This allowed the introduction of new coping skills and fostered an alliance which countered Liam's paranoid beliefs.

Prior to LTSP, work with Liam had focussed on identifying coping strategies that he could implement when signs of relapse were present. The team's response involved increased contact and medical review of behaviour and crisis; interpreted as a loss of insight and psychotic relapse. In some instances this led to hospital admission. After the multiaxial formulation had been shared intervention shifted to focus on supporting Liam to acknowledge psychological distress and to identify relevant triggers. This communicated to him that the team were taking him seriously and taught him more appropriate strategies for expressing his thoughts and feelings. This approach increased Liam's self-confidence and faith in the team. During stable periods aspects of the formulation could be shared and alternative coping strategies introduced. Over time it became possible to reformulate Liam's understanding of his mental health difficulties in order to incorporate a longitudinal perspective. The person level 6Ps formulation served to provide an alternative to the diagnosis of schizoaffective disorder which had not made sense to him in the past. The development of this alternative discourse provided another language through which Liam could seek care. Liam's Presenting difficulties were named as being connected with an unstable self-image, emotional instability and relationship difficulties (Perpetuating factors). These were linked with early life experiences (Predisposing factors) that had contributed to core conflicts concerning trust vulnerability. Following this reformulation Liam began to acknowledge events that had triggered periods of instability (Precipitating factors) enabling the team to maintain empathy and sustain their attempts to care (previous lacking Protective factors).

How do the team respond differently?

Following the introduction of the person level shared formulation, consultation and joint working, the team were able to adopt a more consistent approach to working with Liam (the care Plan or sixth P). Tangential speech and uncharacteristic behaviour was formulated as a defence (Protective factor) which functioned to distance Liam from intolerable emotions about reality. This enabled increased empathy and understanding and the team were able to tolerate the confusion and uncertainty that contact with Liam led them to experience.

Increased contact and reflection enabled work to begin to focus more clearly on identifying and increasing awareness of further Precipitating factors which triggered periods of distress and problematic behaviour. The team valued this work as it enabled them to intervene and support Liam to overcome problems and reduce relapses. Whilst Liam continued to experience flash points and periods of crisis these were no longer met with a purely medical response focussing on increased medication or hospital admission. A focus on containing and making sense of distress by the team enabled further learning regarding positive coping and self-care.

Conclusions and implications

Our development of LTSP incorporating different levels of formulation provides a framework for establishing realistic team care plans, reducing burnout and promoting compassion and empathy. These are the most treatment resistant group of all the service users we work with. Research targets should be focussed over the long term to better establish the ability of LTSP to reduce service utilisation and burnout and promote more psychologically informed care. This framework also offers clinicians attempting to support teams who themselves, for various reasons, may find delivering more proactive interventions difficult, a means of managing their own frustrations and setting more realistic expectations and goals.

References

Alanen, Y. (1997). *Schizophrenia: Its origins and need-adapted treatment.* London: Karnac Books.

Bedi, N. & Vassiliadis, H. (2010). Supervised case experience in supportive psychotherapy: Suggestions for trainers. *Advances in Psychiatric Treatment, 16*(3), 184–192.

Bourke, M. E. & Grenyer, B. F. (2010). Psychotherapists' response to borderline personality disorder: A core conflictual relationship theme analysis. *Psychotherapy Research, 20*(6), 680–691.

Buckley, L. & Pettit, T. (2007). Supportive therapy for schizophrenia. *Schizophrenia Bulletin, 33*(4), 859–860.

Crown, S. (1998). Supportive psychotherapy: A contradiction in terms? *British Journal of Psychiatry, 152,* 266–269.

Davenport, S. (2006). Psychodynamic considerations in rehabilitation. In G. Roberts, S. Davenport, F. Holloway & T. Tattan (eds), *Enabling recovery: The principles and practice of rehabilitation psychiatry* (pp. 187–199). London: Gaskell.

Dewald, P. A. (1964). *The strategy of the therapeutic process in psychotherapy: A dynamic approach.* New York: Basic Books.

Dewald, P. A. (1971). *Psychotherapy: A dynamic approach.* New York: Basic Books.

Dudley, R. & Kuyken, W. (2014). Case formulation in cognitive behavioural therapy: A principle-driven approach. In L. Johnstone & R. Dallos (eds), *Formulation in psychology and psychotherapy: Making sense of people's problems* (pp. 18–44). London: Routledge.

Fenton, W. S. (2000). Evolving perspectives on individual psychotherapy for schizophrenia. *Schizophrenia Bulletin, 26*(1), 47–72.

Fenton, W. S., Blyler, C. R. & Heinssen, R. K. (1997). Determinants of medication compliance in schizophrenia: Empirical and clinical findings. *Schizophrenia Bulletin, 23*(4), 637–651.

Gabbard, G. O. (2000). *Psychodynamic psychiatry in clinical practice* (3rd edn). Washington, DC: American Psychiatric Press.

Gunderson, J. G., Frank, A. F., Katz, H. M., Vannicelli, M. L., Frosch, J. P. & Knapp, P. H. (1984). Effects of psychotherapy in schizophrenia: II. Comparative outcome of two forms of treatment. *Schizophrenia Bulletin, 10*(4), 564–598.

Hogarty, G. E., Flesher, S., Ulrich, R., Carter, M., Greenwald, D., Pogue-Geile, M. . . . Zoretich, R. (2004). Cognitive enhancement therapy for schizophrenia: Effects of a 2-year randomized trial on cognition and behaviour. *Archives of General Psychiatry, 61*, 866–876.

Jackson, M. (2001). *Weathering the storms: Psychotherapy for psychosis*. London: Karnac Books.

Jones, C., Cormac, I., Silveira da Mota Neto, J. I. & Campbell, C. (2004). Cognitive behaviour therapy for schizophrenia. *The Cochrane Database of Systematic Reviews*, Issue 4, Art. No.: CD000524.

Jones, C., Hacker, D., Cormac, I., Meaden, A. & Irving, C. B. (2012). Cognitive behaviour therapy versus other psychosocial treatments for schizophrenia. *Cochrane Database of Systematic Reviews*, Issue 4, Art. No.: CD008712. doi: 10.1002/14651858.CD008712.pub2.

Jones, C. & Meaden, A. (2012). *Schizophrenia*. In P. Sturmey & M. Hersen (eds), *Handbook of evidence-based practice in clinical psychology* (Vol. 2, pp. 221–242). Chichester, Sussex: John Wiley & Sons.

Klein, M. (1948). *Contributions to psychoanalysis, 1921–1945*. London: Hogarth Press.

Lamberti, J. S. & Herz, M. I. (1995). Psychotherapy, social skills training, and vocational rehabilitation in schizophrenia. In C. L. Shriqui & H. A. Nasrallah (eds), *Contemporary issues in the treatment of schizophrenia* (pp. 713–734). Washington, DC: American Psychiatric Press.

Lysaker, P. H., Davis, L. W., Jones, A. M., Strasburger, A. M. & Beattie, N. L. (2007). Relationship and technique in the long-term integrative psychotherapy of schizophrenia: A single case study. *Counselling and Psychotherapy Research, 7*(2), 79–85.

Lysaker, P. H., Glynn, S. M., Wilkniss, S. M. & Silverstein, S. M. (2010) Psychotherapy and recovery from schizophrenia: A review of potential applications and need for future study. *Psychological Services, 7*(2), 75–91.

McCabe, C. (2004). Nurse–patient communication: An exploration of patients' experiences. *Journal of Clinical Nursing, 13*, 41–49.

Markham, D. & Trower, P. (2003). The effects of the psychiatric label 'borderline personality disorder' on nursing staff's perceptions and causal attributions for challenging behaviours. *British Journal of Clinical Psychology, 42*, 243–256.

Maslow, A. H. (1943). A theory of human motivation. *Psychological Review, 50*(4), 370–396.

Meaden, A. (2010). Making assessment and outcomes meaningful. In C. Cupitt (ed.), *Reaching out: The psychology of assertive outreach* (pp. 64–94). London: Routledge.

Meaden, A. & Hacker, D. (2010). *Problematic and risk behaviours in psychosis: A shared formulation approach*. London: Routledge.

Meaden, A. & Van Marle, S. (2008). When the going gets tougher: The importance of long-term supportive psychotherapy in psychosis. *Advances in Psychiatric Treatment*, *14*(1), 42–49.

Nuechterlein, K. H. & Dawson, M. E. (1984). A heuristic vulnerability/stress model of schizophrenic episodes. *Schizophrenia Bulletin*, *10*(2), 300–312.

Penn, D. L., Mueser, K. T., Tarrier, N., Gloege, A., Cather, C., Serrano, D. & Otto, M. W. (2004). Supportive therapy for schizophrenia: Possible mechanisms and implications for adjunctive psychosocial treatments. *Schizophrenia Bulletin*, *30*, 101–112.

Rosenbaum, B., Harder, S., Knudsen, P., Køster, A., Lindhardt, A., Lajer, M. & Winther, G. (2012). Supportive psychodynamic psychotherapy versus treatment as usual for first-episode psychosis: Two-year outcome. *Psychiatry: Interpersonal & Biological Processes*, *75*(4), 331–341.

Seikkula, J., Aaltonen, J., Alakare, B., Haarakangas, K., Keränen, J. & Lehtinen, K. (2006). Five-year experience of first-episode nonaffective psychosis in open-dialogue approach: Treatment principles, follow-up outcomes, and two case studies. *Psychotherapy Research*, *16*(2), 214–228.

Sullivan, H. S. (1962). *Schizophrenia as a human process*. New York: W. W. Norton.

Sullivan, P. R. (1971). Learning theories and supportive psychotherapy. *American Journal of Psychiatry*, *128*, 119–122.

Summers, A. (2006). Psychological formulations in psychiatric care: Staff views on their impact. *Psychiatric Bulletin*, *30*(9), 341–343.

Tarrier, N., Beckett, R., Harwood, S., Baker, A., Yusupoff, L. & Ugarteburu, I. (1993). A trial of two cognitive-behavioural methods of treating drug-resistant residual psychotic symptoms in schizophrenic patients: I. Outcome. *The British Journal of Psychiatry*, *162*(4), 524–532.

Van Marle, S. & Holmes, J. (2002). Supportive psychotherapy as an integrative psychotherapy. In J. E. Holmes & A. E. Bateman (eds), *Integration in psychotherapy: Models and methods* (pp. 175–195). Oxford: Oxford University Press.

Werman, D. S. (1984). *The practice of supportive psychotherapy*. New York: Brunner-Mazel.

Whomsley, S. (2010). Team case formulation. In. C. Culpitt (ed.), *Reaching out: The psychology of assertive outreach* (pp. 95–118). London: Routledge.

Winston, A., Rosenthal, R. N. & Pinsker, H. (2004). *Introduction to supportive psychotherapy*. Washington, DC: American Psychiatric Publishing.

Yung, A. R. (2012). Early intervention in psychosis: Evidence gaps, criticism, and confusion. *Australian and New Zealand Journal of Psychiatry*, *46*, 7–9.

Chapter 14

Team-Based Cognitive Therapy for problematic behaviour associated with negative symptoms

Andrew Fox and Alan Meaden

Introduction

Psychosocial interventions have been identified as accepted methods of treating symptoms of schizophrenia (National Institute for Health and Care Excellence, 2014). However, mostly these interventions have focussed on positive symptoms (e.g. delusions and voices) as their primary target, with psychosocial interventions for negative symptoms receiving much less attention in research and developments in clinical practice (Elis *et al.*, 2013) – especially for those who are hardest to reach. In this chapter we describe further developments in the application of the Shared Assessment Formulation and Education (SAFE; Meaden & Hacker, 2010) approach to working with people with negative symptoms of schizophrenia, paying particular attention to Team-Based Cognitive Therapy elements.

Theoretical background and development: Psychosocial interventions for negative symptoms

Negative symptoms of schizophrenia can be defined as blunted affect, poverty of speech, social withdrawal, avolition and anhedonia (Andreasen, 1982). There has been renewed interest in these experiences of psychosis in recent times, as outlined, for example, by Foussias and Remington (2010). These authors point out that while treatments of positive symptoms (such as voices, delusions and paranoia) have had much success in symptom reduction, this has not translated into long-term functional outcomes (Robinson *et al.*, 2004). Part of the reason may be that it is often negative symptoms that are most closely linked to functional outcomes (Milev *et al.*, 2005). A recent review of outcomes for psychosocial treatments of negative symptoms in schizophrenia suggested that, although Cognitive Behavioural Therapy shows some promise in this area, further investigation is required (Elis *et al.*, 2013) with the need for better models to more fully explain the role of psychosocial interventions in mediating change in negative symptoms and their functional correlates.

Recent developments in understanding negative symptoms

Foussias and Remington (2010) advocate a return to the view of negative symptoms as being fundamentally underpinned by avolition – an inability to initiate and maintain goal-directed behaviour. They argue that the different domains through which negative symptoms can be experienced are fundamentally linked to a reduction in the appetitive drive (or 'wanting'). Without this drive, individuals are no longer motivated to engage in goal-directed behaviour, even though the consummatory drive (i.e. 'liking') is still intact (Foussias & Remington, 2010). This begs the question: if individuals can still enjoy activities, why do they not want to engage in them? One possible answer lies in the work exploring dysfunctional thinking biases regarding performance expectancy in people with psychosis.

Recent research has examined the cognitive content regarding behavioural performance in people with psychosis (Grant & Beck, 2009). Aaron Beck and colleagues have been instrumental in outlining a theoretical cognitive framework for negative symptoms structured around negative beliefs about the self and others. They argue that negative symptoms are an extreme version of premorbid personality traits (particularly schizoid and schizotypal traits), and, as such, negative symptoms can be divided into those that are 'secondary' and those that are 'primary' (Beck & Rector, 2005; Rector et al., 2005). Secondary negative symptoms are those that emerge in response to positive symptoms. Particular beliefs (such as hopelessness, etc.) result in particular behavioural responses (e.g. social withdrawal) when faced with positive symptoms such as voices and delusions. Primary negative symptoms, on the other hand, are those that arise independently of positive symptoms of psychosis. These often reflect generally low expectations of pleasure, achievement and acceptance by others (Beck & Rector, 2005). Rector et al. (2005) outline four types of cognitive expectancy: low expectancies for pleasure; low expectancies for success; low expectancies for acceptance; perception of limited resources. These expectancies can influence each other; for example, the belief that one has low ability in an area (perception of limited resources) will influence the expectation of success and the expectation that others will accept you. Furthermore, as negative symptoms worsen, negative expectancy appraisals are reinforced. These beliefs may be proposed as critical targets for CBT for negative symptoms. A developing evidence base has emerged supporting the targeting of CBT interventions towards these appraisals (see Elis et al., 2013 for a review). However, it is also important to consider the role of reduced cognitive resources in the maintenance of negative symptoms; in particular the role of cognitive deficits in schizophrenia.

Cognitive deficits

There is now a large body of literature that suggests differences in the processing of information between people with a diagnosis of some form of psychosis and healthy controls (e.g. Bora *et al.*, 2010). Indeed, although there appears to be much heterogeneity in the types of cognitive deficits experienced (Palmer *et al.*, 2009) it is now acknowledged that these are important targets for intervention (Pfammatter *et al.*, 2011). A large meta-analysis identified that a range of cognitive domains appear to be associated with functional outcome (functioning in the community) in people with psychosis, including both neuro-cognitive (e.g. learning, memory and processing speed) and social-cognitive (e.g. theory of mind, social perception) factors (Fett *et al.*, 2011). The strongest association was between theory of mind deficits and community functioning (i.e. social-cognitive deficits; Fett *et al.*, 2011).

Considering interventions for people with negative symptoms, it appears that there is evidence of a broad range of reduced cognitive processing abilities in people with psychosis. As such, if interventions are to be targeted at low self-efficacy beliefs and negative outcome expectancies, it would be pertinent to consider offering them in combination with strategies aimed at remediation of cognitive difficulties. Reduced abilities to process information would not only serve to provide fertile ground for reinforcing negative outcome expectancies (e.g. through failed tasks due to limited cognitive resources), but they could also reduce the chances of people being able to effectively engage in Cognitive Behavioural therapeutic work (for example, through difficulties achieving homework tasks requiring social interaction where social-cognitive deficits would impair functional performance).

Both cognitive remediation (Wykes *et al.*, 2011) and social-cognitive training therapies (Kurtz & Richardson, 2012) have shown promise (see also Chapter 9 in this volume for an integrative framework for enhancing social functioning). However, in isolation these interventions appear to have limited effects on functional outcomes (e.g. d'Amato *et al.*, 2010), suggesting that further intervention is required to maximise their benefit. Here we argue for additional intervention to translate cognitive improvements further into real-world outcome.

SAFE and the cognitive theory of negative symptoms

So far we have noted how interventions for negative symptoms and associated social-cognitive deficits are promising. However, in order to ensure that research findings are translated into everyday practice, a framework is needed. This is especially the case where individuals are simply not receptive to traditionally delivered psychosocial approaches.

The SAFE approach is an integrative Cognitive Behavioural framework for structuring team-based interventions targeted at the complex needs of service users who present with challenging and risk behaviours (Meaden & Hacker, 2010). We suggest that this model is well placed to incorporate recent theoretical developments in Cognitive Behavioural theory and therapy and make these amenable to team-based intervention (see also Chapter 12). A particular strength of the approach is that the team can apply the shared formulation developed between team members and service users in a broader, more dynamic way, and in more real-world situations than if this were to be delivered through individual therapy. This also increases what we might term the 'dosage' of the CBT being delivered from (most usually) a weekly hour of therapy to daily routine interactions embedded within a formulation which guides the timing and nature of such interventions. To date our work within the SAFE approach has reserved cognitive interventions to more positive symptoms and associated staff beliefs, employing mostly behaviourally derived principles to address behaviours typically associated with negative symptoms. Meaden and Hacker (2010) suggested re-classifying behaviours into excess and deficits to reflect their function for the individual. In the present context behavioural deficits (e.g. failure to perform everyday tasks and activities) relate closely to Beck's proposal of primary negative symptoms (Beck & Rector, 2005; Rector et al., 2005). Cognitive interventions can be usefully applied to support other formulation-driven team interventions to maximise functional outcomes. We outline our framework below and show how the emerging evidence-based strategies can be integrated into an effective treatment approach for those with negative symptoms who respond poorly to standard care.

Aims, stages, strategies and techniques

A key starting point is to understand that formulation needs to occur at multiple levels in order to guide the focus of the team, aid understanding of the person and provide tangible targets for specific problems (defined in behavioural terms) which themselves act as barriers to recovery. The formulation model for understanding behavioural deficits is the Cognitive Approach to Risk Management formulation (CARM; Meaden & Hacker, 2010) – a form of functional analysis. It is the specific component of the broader SAFE framework which we utilise for our TBCT of negative symptoms to integrate developments from the cognitive literature discussed in the preceding sections. In line with the previous chapter, the aim is to target the in-situation belief which means that all interactions with the client provide the opportunity to incorporate CBT principles when signs are evident that expectancy beliefs will be activated.

Using the CARM template to formulate behavioural deficits

When formulating behavioural deficits, it is important to note that these are often present across many situations and are evident at different times. This reduces the ability of teams to identify early warning signs for these behaviours since they may present as continuous or at a very high frequency. For this reason, Early Warning Signs are not included in our formulation to guide TBCT interventions of behavioural deficits. Instead, our focus is on the role of internal mental events that maintain the experience of avolition (or lack of goal-directed behaviour).

The theory of Rector *et al.* (2005) supports at least four broad types of in-situation beliefs relevant to the maintenance of behavioural deficits.

Low expectancies for pleasure

Although clients can experience pleasure (i.e. different to anhedonia), they expect not to. Rector *et al.* (2005) make the distinction between appetitive pleasure (the anticipation of pleasure) and consummatory pleasure (the pleasure experienced from an activity), and provide evidence that people with psychosis report lower appetitive pleasure but similar consummatory pleasure compared with a control group (see also, Gard *et al.*, 2007). As such, clients have little motivation to engage in potentially pleasurable activities as they do not expect to enjoy them.

Low expectancies for success

As well as reduced expectation for pleasure, clients often also report reduced expectation of success from an activity. The cognitive deficits outlined in the previous section may actually make failure at some tasks more likely, so it is important to understand the standards that clients are attempting to meet. Rector *et al.* (2005) point out that clients may be judging their performance in meeting their own expectations and standards as well as other people's expectations and standards. Classical cognitive factors such as hypervigilance to the perception of criticism and memory biases serve to maintain these beliefs.

Low acceptance

The personal impact and stigma of a diagnosis of schizophrenia is profound, with clients often left struggling with feelings of shame and being 'dirty, unacceptable' (Knight *et al.*, 2003: 214). This stigmatising experience is often incorporated in self-appraisals, such that people view themselves as different to others and there being little point in trying to overcome life's challenges. These global beliefs about the self can then reinforce other in-situation beliefs such as expectancies for success ("Why bother, I can't do it because I'm schizophrenic") or lead clients to avoid public activities for fear of being judged negatively (Rector *et al.*, 2005).

Perception of limited resources

Clients often have an awareness of their diminished resources, both in the cognitive domains (as discussed earlier), but also in other areas, such as social support and material domains. However, Rector *et al.* (2005) point out that although these resources are often in some way diminished, the beliefs that clients hold about their resources are often exaggerated and inflexible. When considered alongside low expectations of success and beliefs in likely negative appraisals from others, avoidance of activities can be understood as an attempt to avoid further negative experiences.

Integrating expectancy into the CARM model

It is our experience that, although the beliefs outlined by Beck and colleagues are 'pan-situational' (i.e. global generalised notions about self, world and other, also known as 'core beliefs'), our clients do not act on them all of the time and in all situations; if they did they would simply not function at all and would require high levels of continuing nursed care. According to the CARM model, it is the specific nature of the task faced by the client and their beliefs about this particular task at that particular time that govern their response.

Case illustration: Josh

The staff team were finding it difficult to motivate Josh to get up and take part in Unit activities, such as cooking. He described how he never enjoyed activities (low expectancy of pleasure), and anticipated being judged negatively (expectancy of low acceptance) about his inevitable failure (low expectancy of success); however, he could easily be persuaded to play chess. When asked about this Josh explained that he 'knew' he could usually beat the member of staff at chess (expectancy of success) and he would enjoy (expectancy of pleasure) proving this (expectancy of acceptance).

In Josh's case it is important to formulate the particular behaviour that is the focus of the intervention, and the specific beliefs, events and triggers that are active in maintaining the behavioural deficit (e.g. Unit activity such as not cooking). Often a pan-situational belief may be at the root of the deficit, but it is the in-situation belief that maintains the deficit and is usually the immediate focus of the intervention. Longer term work is typically required to modify the pan-situational belief, often after several formulations of different behaviours have gathered evidence that can be used to create cognitive dissonance in individual CBT sessions. Interventions (in this case TBCT) which successfully target in-situation beliefs may therefore serve to provide evidence against more broadly or deeply held unhelpful beliefs about personal efficacy which can be examined in individual sessions to support more generalisable pan-situational change.

It is also important to remember that other (non-cognitive) internal and external factors may contribute to the expression and maintenance of a behavioural deficit. For Josh it became apparent that he would be more motivated to play chess when he was playing against someone whose skills were limited. This environmental factor (staff skill at chess) combined with Josh's appraisal of outcome expectancy contributed to the expression of the behavioural deficit.

In Figure 14.1 we show our modified CARM formulation for behavioural deficits for the chapter case study of Amanda. Note that although the pan-situational belief(s) may be common across different behavioural deficits, it may be that different expectations are pertinent to different behavioural deficits. So, for example, while a low expectancy of pleasure may be important in explaining a client's low motivation to make themselves lunch, an expectation of both lack of acceptance from others and low expectation of pleasure might better explain a client's low motivation to engage in a trip to the local sports centre. It is important to consider several different examples of behavioural deficits in an effort to fully formulate the different outcome expectancies a client may be experiencing and the pan-situational beliefs behind these. Once the expectations have been identified, work can be targeted on these beliefs, as they are, in effect, predictions or inferences. In some cases it will be identified that these are inaccurate, as is particularly the case in the low expectation of pleasure. In other cases, such as expectation of stigma from others, these predications may be accurate. In this case, work at further cognitive levels may ultimately be needed to examine the meaning derived from such experiences (e.g. at the level of person evaluations – "this means I am a failure/defective as a person"). This constitutes work at the pan-situational level which may be possible following successful TBCT for in-situation beliefs.

Developing the shared team-based formulation

The same process as outlined in Chapter 12 can usefully be followed when working to develop a shared team-based formulation and is outlined here:

1. Utilising the CAB framework to elicit both immediate and distant triggers.
2. Identifying the client's ABC by examining a specific example of not engaging in or performing an activity (emotional consequences may be less readily apparent but are usually there – hopelessness, despair).
3. Identifying and examining similar incidents over a relevant recent period in order to clarify if the in-situation belief is part of a consistent pattern.
4. Eliciting the Case Formulation Team's ABC having agreed the behaviour and distress (Ce and Cb) to be targeted. Staff feelings and beliefs are formulated and then reformulated following the formulation of the client's behavioural deficits. The primary intervention when working with team beliefs is the development of a shared formulation of the client's behavioural deficits; once this has been identified, staff beliefs regarding the cause of the client's behaviours change, leading to feelings of compassion and hope for the future.
5. Eliciting team members' views about the causes or reasons for the client's behaviour (team members' A–B) without challenging them directly.
6. Initiating the process of information gathering to examine the evidence to support and test different hypotheses.

In contrast to TBCT for behavioural excesses, few scales or tools are used. The Challenging Behaviour Checklist for Psychosis (CBC-P; Meaden & Hacker, 2010) is used to identify problem behaviours for intervention and assess its effectiveness. However, behavioural observations are the main method. The skills of Occupational Therapists are particularly helpful in terms of assessing the functional skills and deficits of individuals with behavioural deficits, especially as they relate to activities of daily living.

7.   Sharing and revising the template with the broader multidisciplinary team is the next stage. Depending on the team processes, type and organisation this can be done through calling a case conference, case busting, at handover meetings etc. The completed formulation is subsequently shared with the whole MDT (since TBCT is aimed at supporting a consistent approach to the management of problems behaviours), and views elicited. Any changes can then be made before agreeing a final formulation.

8.   Planning the intervention is the final stage. Here client's in-situation beliefs (hypothesised or directly elicited) are targeted whenever the behaviour is present or an activity is agreed, planned and encouraged.

In following this process it is important to decide carefully upon which behaviour to tackle first. Usually teams will automatically engage in a weighing up of the importance of the behaviour with how easy it will be to generate evidence to modify the in-situation belief. Importance can be partially judged through the life goals that the behavioural deficits prevent the service user from achieving (for example, meeting a romantic partner). The more important the goal is to the service user, the more potential there is for generating emotional 'heat' from cognitive dissonance (i.e. expectation versus outcome) and the greater the likelihood of success. That the consummatory mechanism for pleasure is still intact means that the testing out of expectation (i.e. behavioural experiments) is a critical focus of the intervention.

Identifying potential barriers to engagement

In our experience it is likely that the team may present with various ideas regarding the underlying mechanism behind negative symptoms, and these can be implicit or explicitly held beliefs.

It is 'behaviour'

This typically refers to the belief that the service user is in some way in control of the negative symptoms and that these symptoms are gainful for them. Another related comment is that the behavioural deficit is 'attention seeking' behaviour. TBCT can be used to elicit these beliefs, make them explicit and identify the associated feelings amongst the staff team. Alternative, more helpful, ways of conceptualising the behavioural deficit can then be offered and team beliefs and feelings can be reformulated.

Staff member 1:   It's behaviour, he does it on purpose

Therapist: Okay, assuming you are right what might be the purpose (eliciting ideas regarding the behaviour's function)

Staff member 1:   He does it (stays in bed) because he does not want to do his chores

Therapist: Okay why do you think that might be (e.g. expectancy of a negative outcome)?

They are lazy

This belief is often simply expressed, but when considered through TBCT, it transpires that the concept of 'laziness' is actually quite difficult to define. Laziness is actually a descriptor with little explanatory power – it is another way of describing the behavioural deficits ("he can't be bothered") and equates to a functional explanation rather than a behavioural descriptor. Questions to clarify and define what 'lazy' actually means often reveal the limits of this way of thinking, especially when combined with questions about how to intervene to remediate 'laziness'. In our experience, what staff often mean when they refer to laziness is some concept linked to 'discomfort tolerance'. Discomfort tolerance is an ability of a person to tolerate uncomfortable experiences (such as unpleasant emotions, sensations or thoughts) often for a perceived reward later, and is a common concept in Rational Emotive Behaviour Therapy usually referred to as Low Frustration Tolerance (Dryden, 2003). Tolerance beliefs are usually expressed in several parts: the statement of the unpleasant experience, the low tolerance of this, and the negation of anything good coming out of the experience (e.g. it is unpleasant when staff try to get me out of bed in the morning, I can't stand it, and it's not worth it). Discussing the concept of discomfort tolerance can be a useful place to start with staff in this area, particularly when thinking about the 'worth it' component, as this often links to client's broader recovery goals (e.g. it is worth getting out of bed to practise making lunch so that I can prove that I can live on my own). This can get the team thinking about what motivates them to tolerate discomfort, and whether these factors are present / absent for the client. This necessarily links to the Service Level Formulation, which identifies barriers to valued activity and recovery goals (Meaden & Hacker, 2010). It may be that the team need to support the service user to articulate some recovery goals or valued activity to support the service user to tolerate the short-term discomfort (behavioural experiments) in exchange for long-term comfort (recovery).

Case illustration: Amanda

Amanda is a 35-year-old woman with a diagnosis of schizoaffective disorder. In her early 20s she worked at a local call centre, selling magazine subscriptions to industry. She left her job at the call centre following feelings of anxiety, low mood and worries that her colleagues were talking about her and bullying her.

She lives at home with her mother (her parents divorced when she was a teenager) and has done for the last 10 years. Amanda is supported by a local community mental health team and sees her community psychiatric nurse approximately once a month who visits her at home. She has declined offers of individual psychological therapy and referral to the local day centre and group programme. Amanda's mother reports that she spends most of the day in her room, staying in bed until about midday; she will accompany her mother once a week to the shops to help her to buy groceries. Three months ago Amanda's mother had to go into hospital for an operation. Due to concerns from her family about her ability to look after herself while her mother was in hospital Amanda agreed to enter a residential rehabilitation programme. Amanda's stated recovery goal is to complete an adult education course and to make some more friends.

Amanda has been at the Unit for 3 months and staff report that she spends most mornings in bed, getting up at about 1 pm for her lunch. She will then go back to bed, getting up at about 4 pm for her evening meal. She is overweight, with a BMI of 33. Staff say that they think she is "lazy" and that she "needs to get herself out of bed"; there are also questions among the team about whether she is 'ready' for rehabilitation. Sometimes, with a great deal of staff prompting and assistance, Amanda will attend groups on the Unit, and once or twice has attended the local sports centre where she has been observed to enjoy talking with one or two other residents in particular. Her mother visits her once a week to take her out to the cinema or café; however, Amanda is reluctant to do this with anyone else.

Engagement and assessment

Amanda agreed to meet with psychology for a 'chat' following encouragement from her mother and on condition she could leave whenever she wished. She reported that she knew she had 'low self-esteem' and would consider help with this. Sessions were kept short (less than 20 minutes) and were scheduled at the same time (in the afternoon) and day each week to help Amanda to adopt this into her routine. Amanda was able to identify that getting out of bed was a difficulty she wanted help with and agreed to develop an individual formulation that could be shared with the team. After a number of sessions, Amanda agreed to collaborate in developing a shared formulation focussed around the avoidance of activities due to the anxiety she experienced about completing these activities.

The assessment identified negative outcome expectancies regarding pleasure, success and acceptance, and it was hypothesised that these were pan-situational. The formulation suggested that staying in bed was functional for Amanda in the short-term as it avoids the expectation of failure, negative judgement from others about this failure, and the associated expectation of lack of pleasure. However, in the longer term the lack of activity or progress towards Amanda's recovery goals reinforces the pan-situational beliefs of failure.

Team-based formulation

Amanda agreed that this initial formulation be taken to the team in order to develop a CARM formulation (see Figure 14.1). It was identified that the team could work together to support her to achieve her goal of getting out of bed before lunchtime every day. An initial team supervision session focussed on discussing the formulation and articulating this to the wider team. At the start of the session, staff reported feelings of frustration and annoyance with Amanda, centred on the primary behavioural deficit of staying in bed (the team's A). We identified the feelings among the staff team, which were mainly anger and frustration, and staff explained that they felt she was 'wasting' a bed there, and that her 'lazy attitude' was stopping them from doing their job (see Table 14.1).

We discussed the alternative formulation: that Amanda did not believe that anything would provide her with pleasure, that she would inevitably fail at everything she did and that she believed that others were judging her negatively. This was drawn out as a simple ABC (A = staff asking her to do an activity; B = negative expectancies; Ce = anxiety; Cb = staying in bed). It was pointed out that staff were in a good position to help Amanda to test out these beliefs – some had managed to encourage Amanda to attend a local sports centre, and she had reported 'enjoying' this. We agreed that her attendance at the sports centre would be the initial focus of the formulation. This was critical, in that it allowed staff to collaborate with Amanda on testing out specific negative outcome expectancies (e.g. I am un-coordinated so will be unable to contribute to the cricket game in any way).

The notion of cognitive bias was shared with staff: that mood incongruent information is ignored, so it is likely that Amanda does not recall times when she has contradicted the negative outcome expectancies. Staff identified general ways that they could prompt Amanda to challenge the negative expectations: by recording positive outcomes and reminding her of these, by minimising their expression of social judgement, and by encouraging her to keep a record of 'pleasure and mastery' of each activity she engages in (to be used as evidence against the negative outcome expectancy). Following this formulation staff were encouraged to articulate their feelings again (see Table 14.1). The Key-Worker agreed to articulate this formulation to the rest of the team and co-ordinate the care-planning to ensure a team-based intervention.

Evaluation

The team attempted to target the negative outcome expectancies in the situations that Amanda was faced with. Staff used her pleasure scores to remind her that she sometimes enjoyed these outings and, as the courts at the sports centre were booked for exclusive use by the rehabilitation unit, Amanda was able to attend without feeling that members of the public were judging her negatively. Staff offered her positive feedback focussed around acceptance (e.g. "Everyone seemed

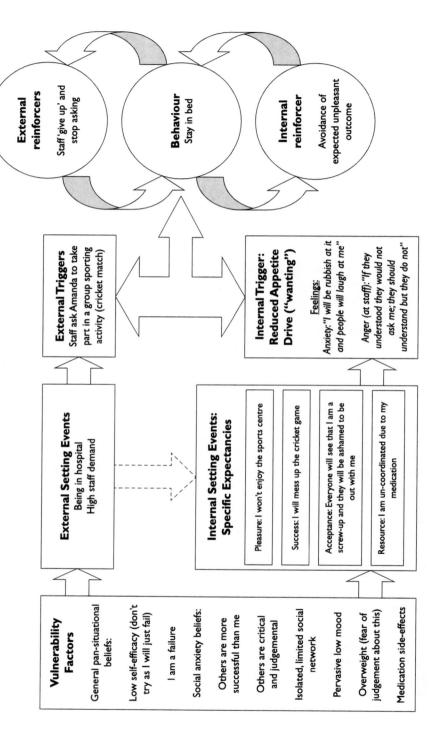

Figure 14.1 CARM formulation of Amanda's specific behavioural deficit

Table 14.1 Staff Attributions Pre- and Post-formulation

Model Component	Pre-formulation	Post-formulation
A (activating event)	Amanda remains in bed until after lunchtime	Amanda remains in bed until after lunchtime
B (In-situation)	She can get up but she is just lazy	This is her way of avoiding pain and distress
	She enjoys the attention	She has lost much in her life
	She is stopping me doing my job	We can help her to learn better ways of coping
	There are other people who could make better use of this rehab placement	
Ce (emotional consequence)	Frustration, anger	Sadness, hope
Cb (behavioural consequence)	Avoidance of Amanda Punitive methods (raising voice, commanding)	Helping behaviours, care providing (verbal encouragement, reminders of past successes)

to have a good time") and feelings (e.g. "You looked like you were enjoying that") and avoided judgments (e.g. avoiding global judgements such as "You are good at cricket"). Staff did, however, offer feedback for specific predictions, particularly around the effects of her medication on her co-ordination, which was not as marked as Amanda expected. Amanda reported that she felt pleased with herself for attending the sessions, and was able to get up before lunchtime for approximately half of the week – usually when she had a specific activity to attend. Activity scheduling was then used to ensure Amanda had activities to focus on during the week, and additional CARM formulations were developed for each of these with Amanda's Key-Worker. Amanda spent time in individual psychology sessions discussing her self-esteem difficulties, and using the various evidence gathered by the team in specific situations to reduce her conviction in the pan-situational beliefs. Specifically, work was focussed on the beliefs in herself as a 'failure' and that others are critical. This individual work moved on to involve the approach discussed in Chapter 9 regarding the recovery of the skills and resources critical in the development of the social self.

Conclusions and implications

There is a developing evidence base for the use of psychosocial interventions in remediating behavioural deficits (or 'negative symptoms'). This can be effectively assimilated into existing models for use with people who have complex needs and are difficult to engage (e.g. SAFE).

Despite the increased research into this area, the efficacy of these interventions is still unclear. In a randomised controlled trial of CBT for negative symptoms that was focussed on the negative outcome expectancies identified by Rector *et al.* (2005), Klingberg *et al.* (2011) observed some improvement in negative symptoms. However, this was not different to the improvement seen in the control group, who were provided with cognitive remediation therapy (Klingberg *et al.*, 2011). The authors speculate that the lack of difference between the groups may have been due to the CBT and cognitive remediation inadvertently acting on the same cognitive factors (i.e. reducing negative outcome expectancies).

Specific research is required to establish whether the cognitive approach to behavioural deficits is any more effective than existing interventions for this hard to reach and hard to treat group. However in this chapter we show the utility of integrating emerging models into the SAFE approach to extend its scope. By definition, people with these needs are less likely to engage in high quality randomised controlled trials, and as such there may be a case of looking to novel methods of evaluating effective and good practice in these areas.

Supporting the team to work with behavioural deficits is critical as experience suggests that teams can experience frustration and other unpleasant emotions when working to support service users. The CARM formulation offers a flexible framework for offering an explanation for behavioural deficits that staff can understand, use to identify treatment targets, and thereby foster hope within the staff team that change is possible. TBCT can then be used to challenge beliefs within the team that act as potential blocks to service user recovery.

References

Andreasen, N. C. (1982). Negative symptoms in schizophrenia. Definition and reliability. *Archives of General Psychiatry, 39,* 784–788.

Beck, A. T. & Rector, N. A. (2005). Cognitive approaches to schizophrenia: Theory and therapy. *Annual Review of Clinical Psychology, 1,* 577–606.

Bora, E., Yucel, M. & Pantelis, C. (2010). Cognitive impairment in schizophrenia and affective psychoses: Implications for DSM-V criteria and beyond. *Schizophrenia Bulletin, 36,* 36–42.

D'Amato, T., Bation, R., Cochet, A., Jalenques, I., Galland, F., Giraud-Baro, E. . . . Brunelin, J. (2010). A randomized, controlled trial of computer-assisted cognitive remediation for schizophrenia. *Schizophrenia Research, 125,* 284–290.

Dryden, W. (2003). 'The cream cake made me eat it': an introduction to the ABC theory of REBT. In W. Dryden (ed.), *Rational Emotive Behaviour Therapy: Theoretical developments* (pp. 1–21). Hove, E. Sussex: Brunner-Routledge.

Elis, O., Caponigro, J. M. & Kring, A. M. (2013). Psychosocial treatments for negative symptoms in schizophrenia: Current practices and future directions. *Clinical Psychology Review, 33,* 914–928.

Fett, A. J., Viechtbauer, W., Dominguez, M., Penn, D. L., van Os, J. & Krabbendam, L. (2011). The relationship between neurocognition and social cognition with functional outcomes in schizophrenia: A meta-analysis. *Neuroscience & Biobehavioral Reviews, 35*, 573–588.

Foussias, G. & Remington, G. (2010). Negative symptoms in schizophrenia: avolition and Occam's razor. *Schizophrenia Bulletin, 36*, 359–369.

Gard, D. E., Kring, A. M., Gard, M. G., Horan, W. P. & Green, M. F. (2007). Anhedonia in schizophrenia: Distinctions between anticipatory and consummatory pleasure. *Schizophrneia Research, 93*, 253–260.

Grant, P. M. & Beck, A. T. (2009). Defeatist beliefs as a mediator of cognitive impairment, negative symptoms, and functioning in schizophrenia. *Schizophrenia Bulletin, 35*, 798–806.

Klingberg, S., Wölwer, W., Engel, C., Wittorf, A., Herrlich, J., Meisner, C. . . . Wiedemann, G. (2011). Negative symptoms of schizophrenia as primary target of cognitive behavioral therapy: Results of the randomized clinical TONES study. *Schizophrenia Bulletin, 37*(S2), S98–S110.

Knight, M. T. D., Wykes, T. & Hayward, P. (2003). 'People don't understand': An investigation of stigma in schizophrenia using Interpretative Phenomenological Analysis (IPA). *Journal of Mental Health, 12*, 209–222.

Kurtz, M. M. & Richardson, C. L. (2012). Social cognitive training for schizophrenia: A meta-analytic investigation of controlled research. *Schizophrenia Bulletin, 38*, 1092–1104.

Meaden, A. & Hacker, D. (2010). *Problematic and risk behaviours in psychosis: A shared formulation approach.* Hove, E. Sussex: Routledge.

Milev, P., Ho, B. C., Arndt, S. & Andreasen, N. C. (2005). Predictive values of neurocognition and negative symptoms on functional outcome in schizophrenia: A longitudinal first-episode study with 7-year follow-up. *American Journal of Psychiatry, 162*, 495–506.

National Institute for Health and Care Excellence (2014). *Psychosis and schizophrenia in adults: Treatment and management. NICE Clinical Guideline 178.* London: National Institute for Health and Care Excellence. Retrieved 25 March 2014 from: http://guidance.nice.org.uk/cg178/

Palmer, B. W., Dawes, S. E. & Heaton, R. K. (2009). What do we know about neuropsychological aspects of schizophrenia? *Neuropsychological Review, 19*, 365–384.

Pfammatter, M., Brenner, H. D., Junghan, U. M. & Tschacher, W. (2011). The importance of cognitive processes for the integrative treatment of persons with schizophrenia. *Schizophrenia Bulletin, 37*, S1–S4.

Rector, N. A., Beck, A. T. & Stolar, N. (2005). The negative symptoms of schizophrenia: A cognitive perspective. *Canadian Journal of Psychiatry, 50*, 247–257.

Robinson, D. G., Woerner, M. G., McMeniman, M., Mendelowitz, A. & Bilder R. M. (2004). Symptomatic and functional recovery from a first episode of schizophrenia or schizoaffective disorder. *American Journal of Psychiatry, 161*, 473–479.

Wykes, T., Huddy, V., Cellard, C., McGurk, S. R. & Czobor, P. (2011). A meta-analysis of cognitive remediation for schizophrenia: Methodology and effect sizes. *American Journal of Psychiatry, 168*, 472–485.

Chapter 15

Concluding remarks

Andrew Fox and Alan Meaden

When psychological approaches began to gain increasing respectability (positioned as they still are as adjuncts to psychiatric interventions) in the early 1990s (e.g. Chadwick & Lowe, 1990), they did so by largely targeting populations who were not responding to standard psychiatric treatment (e.g. medication, rehabilitation). These innovations (CBT, Behavioural Family therapy, coping strategy enhancement, etc.) promised a breakthrough in treatment and were extensively trialled. Clients themselves often preferred these interventions to the side effects of medical treatments. However, over two decades later there clearly remains a substantial group for whom these approaches have not proven to be of benefit (Jones *et al.*, 2012; Meaden & Hacker, 2010) and there remains a need to continue to understand how current practice can be improved.

What emerges from the collection of approaches in this book is that not only is there an increasing range of therapies that can be offered (many with quite different value systems) but that they share many common features. Many strongly advocate the use of formulation – not only at an individual level but also at a team level. This notion of shared formulation encompasses not only the value of ensuring that all of those providing help do so in a consistent manner but also ensures interventions do not contradict each other. Crucially, shared formulations may also be harnessed to address unhelpful team dynamics which can often create barriers to effective care (e.g. Chapters 12 and 14). These principles may usefully be incorporated into existing approaches. A second key lesson is that approaches which offer a different value base, are more person-centred, and pay attention to the person's own strengths and context, tend to support engagement in therapy.

What is also apparent is that the goals of therapy may be usefully reconsidered. In their seminal paper, Birchwood and Trower (2006) argued for the refocussing of goals around distress and behaviour. The approaches collected here echo this sentiment, reinforcing the need for a refocussing of goals onto what troubles the person and is important to them and not on what diagnosis or symptoms the person may or may not have. Sometimes the goals may be quite short-term (e.g. identifying a solution, Chapter 5) or they may need to be quite long-term (Chapter 13). Therapeutic efforts may focus on less usual goals (e.g. gaining a romantic partner, Chapter 9) or different types of belief than those usually targeted in current CBT approaches (Chapters 11 and 14). It seems apparent that an explicit consideration and agreement regarding a collaborative goal for intervention is critical when providing services to those who are difficult to engage.

Although some of the approaches described here are already the focus of research effort, the focus on less traditional goals may make them more difficult to measure in terms of routine outcomes (e.g. symptom reduction) and less amenable to trial-based evaluation. We believe that these outcomes are the most meaningful for the people who (albeit reluctantly) use our services, and it is these goals that increase the chances of positive outcome for service users. In some cases, the interventions' effects may also be difficult to separate from the efforts of others in the team and their input is invaluable in an era of scarce resources. Research that supports the evaluation of these outcomes in routine practice is more likely to fit with such approaches (i.e. practice-based evidence).

How to choose which therapy to offer remains an elusive question. It will in part depend upon the therapist's own values and position, the values of the team and the degree to which the team feel stuck and accepting of available alternatives. Of course, the client remains key, and some discussion, where possible, may usefully be had regarding what the approaches available might involve and which are most acceptable to the person. Some of these approaches may be more readily apparent for certain individuals and difficulties or may be more easily delivered in particular settings (e.g. for people receiving residential care).

It is also apparent that consideration should be given to the systems and contexts involved in providing care for people with complex mental health needs and limited engagement. Often, it can be helpful to understand and formulate the local team or system. Similarly, there is usually a need to engage people within the wider community, and this will depend very much on the communities that people have access to or wish to be part of. Rather than focussing on change within the individual, change needs to happen both from within and around the person, and this should be guided by the formulation. The person (or people) delivering interventions must then be ready and able to target these interventions at the area suggested by the formulation and supported by services in this endeavour, regardless of whether these are considered as traditional treatment targets or not. This may represent a challenge for services where psychosocial interventions are viewed as happening within a rigid set of rules and boundaries, but in order to maximise service user recovery, it is imperative that such presuppositions about the nature and form of intervention do not detract from clinicians' ability to offer and research these.

References

Birchwood, M. & Trower, P. (2006). The future of cognitive–behavioural therapy for psychosis: not a quasi-neuroleptic. *The British Journal of Psychiatry*, *188*(2), 107–108.

Chadwick, P. D. & Lowe, C. F. (1990). Measurement and modification of delusional beliefs. *Journal of Consulting and Clinical Psychology, 58*(2), 225–232.

Jones, C., Hacker, D., Cormac, I., Meaden, A. & Irving, C. B. (2012). Cognitive behaviour therapy versus other psychosocial treatments for schizophrenia. *Cochrane Database of Systematic Reviews,* Issue 4. Art. No.: CD008712. doi: 10.1002/14651858.CD008712. pub2.

Meaden, A. & Hacker, D. (2010). *Problematic and risk behaviours in psychosis: A shared formulation approach.* Hove, E. Sussex: Brunner-Routledge.

Index

shared mental representation, concept of 6
short intervention: aim of 58, 136; stages
of 59–60
single sessions, benefits of, for people with
psychosis 55–69
situational reflections (SR) 29, 33, 34
6Ps 215
Slade, M. 28
Sloan, D. M. 76
Smail, D. 56–8, 65
Smith, J. 39, 44
Smith, J. A. 126
Smith, L. 170
social alienation 156
social anxiety 74, 75, 78, 82–4, 86, 101,
102, 132, 139
social avoidance 75, 140
social beliefs 133–7
social cognition 130, 133–6, 139
Social Cognition and Interaction Training
(SCIT) 139
social cognitive deficits 221
social cognitive training therapies 221
social constructionism 148, 160
social network(s) 6–8, 12–13, 15, 131,
133–6, 138, 139, 141, 180, 212;
patient's 10, 11
social participation and recovery,
enhancing, cognitive-developmental
approach to 129–44
social skills 130, 131, 133–6, 138, 141
social skills training 136
social withdrawal 9, 13, 93, 129, 150, 219,
220
Socratic questioning 35, 137
'soulfulness' 116
speech, poverty of 219
Spellman, D. 156
Spinelli, E. 112, 117
Spinhoven, K. P. 79
splitting 113, 205, 210, 213
SR: see situational reflections
STAND: see Scale To Assess Narrative
Development
Stern, S. 10
stress triggers 39
Subjective Omnipotence Scale 132
Subotnik, K. L. 38
substance abuse 94
suicidal ideation 101, 124
Sullivan, H. S. 205
Sullivan, P. R. 200

Summers, A. 205
supported discovery 101
supportive psychotherapy 200–2, 205, 206
supportive therapy, with schizophrenia 201
Sutela, M. 9
symbolism 23; higher-level 27; lower-
level 27
Systemic Family Therapy 11

tactile hallucinations 101
Tai, S. 77, 81, 86
Tait, L. 78
Talbot 39, 40
talking therapy 56
Talmon, M. 56, 66
Tarrier, N. 1, 39, 40, 190, 207
TBCT: see Team-Based Cognitive Therapy
team-based approaches 47, 192, 198, 200,
202, 208, 221, 225, 229
Team-Based Cognitive Therapy (TBCT):
care plan 189; for distress and
problematic behaviour associated with
positive symptoms 184–98; for
problematic behaviour associated with
negative symptoms 219–32
team-based therapy, Long-Term
Supportive Psychotherapy as 200–16
team debriefs 46–7
theory of mind (ToM) 132, 134, 139, 149,
221
therapeutic alliance 111, 172, 203, 205,
206; tolerating 214
therapeutic engagement 135, 161
'therapeutic hour', strict boundaries of 121
therapeutic integration, existential
approach as basis for 116
therapeutic relationship 94, 101, 106, 119,
126, 137, 140, 143, 170, 173, 178, 201,
202, 206; building of 23; longer
term 55
therapy(ies), existential 111, 112, 115, 116,
122, 123, 126
'third wave' Cognitive Behavioural
Therapy approaches 86
Thompson, M. G. 112, 114
thought disorder 30
Three Circles Model 96, 97, 102
Tidal Model 61, 67
Tillich, P. 112, 114
time-line exercise 159
ToM: see theory of mind
trandiagnostic model of therapy 181